The Greatest Criminal Cases

The Greatest Criminal Cases

Changing the Course of American Law

J. MICHAEL MARTINEZ

PRAEGER

AN IMPRINT OF ABC-CLIO, LLC

Santa Barbara, California • Denver, Colorado • Oxford, England

Library of Congress Cataloging-in-Publication Data

Martinez, J. Michael (James Michael) author.
The greatest criminal cases : changing the course of American law / J. Michael Martinez.
pages cm
Includes bibliographical references and index.
ISBN 978-1-4408-2868-3 (hardback)—ISBN 978-1-4408-2869-0 (ebook)
1. Trials—United States. 2. Criminal procedure—United States—Cases. I. Title.
KF220.M275 2014
345.73'07—dc23 2013047449

ISBN: 978-1-4408-2868-3
EISBN: 978-1-4408-2869-0

18 17 16 15 14 1 2 3 4 5

This book is also available on the World Wide Web as an eBook.
Visit www.abc-clio.com for details.

Praeger
An Imprint of ABC-CLIO, LLC

ABC-CLIO, LLC
130 Cremona Drive, P.O. Box 1911
Santa Barbara, California 93116-1911

This book is printed on acid-free paper ∞

Manufactured in the United States of America

For Skylar Renee Carter from Papa

What is my offence?
Where is the evidence that do accuse me?
What lawful quest have given their verdict up
Unto the frowning judge?

—William Shakespeare, *Richard III*,
Act I, scene iv

Contents

Introduction and Acknowledgments

"Somebody must have made a false allegation against Josef K., for he was arrested one morning without having done anything wrong."[1] Franz Kafka's classic absurdist novel, *The Trial*, opens with K., a provincial banker, arrested on his 30th birthday by two faceless, nameless law enforcement officers. They will not disclose the agency they represent or the crime with which he has been charged. Thus begins a long nightmare where an ordinary citizen vainly attempts to navigate the labyrinthine legal system. K. is summoned to court, but he is never told what time he must appear. He cannot find the correct courtroom. When he finally arrives, court is not in session. Through many plot twists and turns, K. can never pinpoint who has charged him, why he was charged, or what crime he reputedly committed. Eventually, he realizes he is guilty until proven innocent. No one is in charge of the court system. Much to his dismay, an impersonal, seemingly endless bureaucracy promulgates complex, often contradictory, rules for no discernible reason.

K. engages defense counsel, but the lawyer can only emphasize how serious the charges are, how hopeless the case is, and how well connected he, the lawyer, is. Turning away from the egotistical attorney, K. crosses paths with Titorelli, an official court painter. Titorelli has spent his time wandering the halls of the bureaucracy. Consequently, he is as well versed in the legal system as anyone. The painter patiently explains that K. can try to obtain an "innocent" verdict from a lower court, although the verdict can be reversed on a whim by a higher court. Alternatively, K. can seek to delay the lower court process indefinitely. His name will not be cleared, but at least he will not be a victim of the legal system. At the conclusion of this depressing conversation, Titorelli instructs K. to leave through a back door. As he opens the door, K. discovers an endless array of court offices.

The years pass, and the possibility of a trial for the unspecified offense never recedes. Matters come to a head on K.'s 35th birthday when two men arrive to escort him away, presumably to the courthouse. It soon becomes apparent the men intend to harm him. They lead K. to a quarry and place his head on a discarded block. One man produces a butcher knife and passes it back and forth to his companion. "At that moment," Kakfa observes, "K. was perfectly aware it was supposed to be his duty to seize the knife as it hovered from hand to hand above him and drive it into himself. But he did not do this; instead, he turned his neck, which was still free, and looked about him." He plaintively seeks a way out of his predicament. "Where was the judge he had never seen? Where was the high court he had never reached?"

The questions are not answered because no answers exist. K. is stuck in a "Kafkaesque" situation: his life is controlled by powerful, unseen forces that appear nonsensical, or at least beyond his comprehension. The legal system simply is unfathomable, a gigantic, illogical, brutal, dehumanizing, faceless bureaucracy where nothing is as it appears and justice is conspicuously absent. The tangled tale ends when the two unidentified men terminate K.'s uncertain dilemma with a measure of certitude:

> But the hands of the one gentleman were at K.'s throat while the other drove the knife into his heart and turned it there twice. With his failing sight, K. could still see the gentlemen right in front of his face, cheek pressed against cheek, as they observed the decisive moment. "Like a dog!" he said. It was as if the shame would outlive him.[2]

The Trial is a frightening existential fable because it illustrates the conundrum of postmodern man: he needs society and the institutions of government to instill order on the chaos of the natural world, yet he fears the loss of individual freedom to the Leviathan that humankind has created. When a human being willingly relinquishes a measure of freedom to live in a civil society, he places himself at the mercy of a powerful force that may control his life. To combat the possibility that the institutions of government grow too distant from his life, the individual desires a system of behavioral rules that are known and knowable beforehand. He wishes to place a limit on the powers of government through a system whereby individual freedoms are preserved, protected, and defended. The rule of law must be sacrosanct.

In the United States, the system of protecting individual freedoms from the omnipresent power of the state is found in the Bill of Rights, the first 10 amendments to the U.S. Constitution. In criminal cases, the Fourth, Fifth, Sixth, and Eighth Amendments are especially important, as is the Fourteenth Amendment, which later incorporated some of the Bill of Rights protections that apply to the federal government and applied them to the states. These provisions were designed to prevent citizens of the United States from becoming another K., the lone individual facing a powerful entity for charges he neither knows nor understands. Although the architects of the American polity did not know of Franz Kafka's work—he lived in Europe more than a century after the Constitution was written—they were all-too-familiar with the concern about too much power concentrated in too few hands. By specifying constitutionally protected civil liberties in the nation's most sacred legal document, the Founders hoped to ensure *The Trial*, or books like it, would remain a work of fiction.

In the field of American criminal procedure, the system of legal rules governing the relationship between the individual and government quickly can become complex and difficult to comprehend. The rules are not as opaque as the law appears in *The Trial*, but criminal procedure can be challenging to fathom, especially for the novice student. I have taught university-level courses for more than 18 years, including a basic course in criminal procedure for undergraduate criminal justice students. During that time, I have found that students sometimes become confused and despondent about the multitude of rules and cases. "I would not recommend my worst enemy to take this class," a student once wrote to me in a parting email. Referring to the voluminous (and occasionally convoluted and contradictory) readings and cases, he said the material "only made me feel like an idiot," which in turn made him believe he "did not deserve to be in your class."

I was alarmed by the student's experience because criminal procedure can be a fascinating topic if one can delve beneath the complex legal rules and discover the human element played out in criminal cases. Often that individual drama is part of a larger perennial debate over the freedom of the individual and the authority of government. Criminal procedure textbooks focus heavily on landmark court cases that depend on crucial factual nuances, as they should, and yet such texts typically provide only a cursory, abbreviated summary of the facts behind the court cases. It is unfortunate that the rich, evocative context of the stories is lost or neglected.

Cases and legal doctrines can be turgid and boring, especially for undergraduates, but the human drama embedded in the stories sometimes awakens a dormant interest. As an example, when my classes discuss *Powell v. Alabama* (1932), I have found that the case comes alive when I stream an *American Experience* documentary, *Scottsboro: An American Tragedy*, for students to watch. They see the faces of the defendants, hear stories about how the case became a cause célèbre, and understand the facts as well as the biases prevalent in the legal system of the Depression-era South. After watching the documentary, students have told me how much they learned in the class when we discussed the context leading up to the legal cases. "I wish all of the cases we discussed could be told as a story," I have heard many a pupil remark. "Most of the time, it's just a bunch of boring legal doctrines with Latin phrases and complicated legal tests and formulas." From these simple origins, I decided to tell the stories behind major cases in the American law of criminal procedure.

At the outset, I hoped to discuss dozens of cases and the stories behind them. It quickly became apparent that such an endeavor was hopelessly ambitious. Aside from consuming most of my natural life to explore the hundreds of cases on point, the resultant book would balloon into a 1,000+-page tome resembling a standard criminal procedure casebook and would become another hulking behemoth that remained largely inaccessible to students. Therefore, I pared it down to what I considered to be the crucial criminal cases in American criminal procedure. Most of the selections were obvious choices. *Mapp v. Ohio*, *Gideon v. Wainwright*, *Miranda v. Arizona*, and *Terry v. Ohio* are landmark cases. If a student opens any textbook on American criminal procedure published since the 1960s, each of these cases will be prominently discussed. They are the sine qua non of American constitutional criminal procedure.

I used discretion in choosing other cases. Many court cases involve the exclusionary rule, for example. Although *Silverthorne Lumber Company v. United States* contains the famous "fruit of the poisonous tree" doctrine (while the concept originated in *Silverthorne*, the metaphor was not created until 19 years later), I chose *Weeks v. United States* because it predates *Silverthorne*. Accordingly, in Chapter 2, I discuss how *Weeks* first articulated the doctrine and later cases refined it. In short, I chose what I believed to be an emblematic case that captured the essence of the issue. The purpose here is to produce a short, fast-paced, interesting supplementary text.

One last criterion was whether the facts of a case were dramatic and "teachable." I am thinking here of *Powell v. Alabama*, *Brown v. Mississippi*, and *Hamdan v. Rumsfeld.* The first two cases involve the treatment of black defendants in courtrooms of the Old South during the Great Depression, while *Hamdan* involves the war on terror and whether Osama bin Laden's chauffeur could be tried before a military tribunal in lieu of being remanded to a civilian court. Other cases cover similar issues, but I believed the facts of these cases to be suitably dramatic.

In this book, the reader will meet many unsavory characters—adulterers, gamblers, bootleggers, murderers, and terrorists, among others—as well as ordinary citizens caught up in the legal system, like K., desperately trying to comprehend the situation. It is a testament to American jurisprudence that the reader will encounter few Josef K.s, although Dollree Mapp and Clarence Earl Gideon might disagree vehemently with such an assessment.

I would be remiss if I did not thank the many kind people who helped me research and write the book. First and foremost, I appreciate the assistance I received from the kind folks at Praeger Publishers, part of ABC-CLIO, especially Beth Ptalis and Rebecca Matheson.

Many librarians and archivists assisted me in collecting information and photographs. In alphabetical order, these dedicated professionals merit special mention:

Adam Watson, State Archives of Florida; Carolyn Marr, Museum of History & Industry (MOHAI) Resource Center; Howard Giske, Museum of History & Industry (MOHAI) Resource Center; Jasminn L. Winters, the Library of Congress; Kathleen Kennedy Knies, Museum of History & Industry (MOHAI) Resource Center; Kay Menick, Permissions Department, Art Resource; Kristen Gurciullo, State Archives of Florida; Lesley Schoenfeld, Harvard Law School Library; Lily Birkhimer, the Ohio Historical Society; Silka Quintero, the Granger Collection, New York; Vern Morrison, Michael Schwartz Library, Cleveland State University; Vicki Catozza, Reference Division, Western Reserve Historical Society Research Center; and Wendi Goen, Photograph Collections, Arizona State Library, Archives and Public Records, History and Archives Division.

As always, my family and friends have been wonderful, patient, loving supporters. In alphabetical order, I extend thanks to Barbara and

Jim Wise; Bill Mellette; Bob and Peggy Youngblood; the late Charles DuBose and his wife, Glenda; Chris and Laura Mead; Chuck Redmon; Keith W. Smith; Liz Kula; Loren Mead and his late wife, Polly; Martha and Dick Pickett; Phil and Carolyn Mead; Sheila Traub; Shirley Hardrick; Wallace and Leila Jordan; Walter Mead; and Dr. William D. Richardson of the University of South Dakota.

My desire here has been to present compelling stories from the annals of American criminal procedure. If criminal procedure students find the work to be illuminating, I will consider my labors to have been worthwhile. Needless to say (but I will say it, anyway), all errors or omissions in fact or interpretation are my responsibility alone.

NOTES

1. Franz Kafka, *The Trial* (London, England: The Folio Society, 2011 [1925]), 3.
2. Ibid., 197.

CHAPTER 1

Hurtado v. California (1884) and 19th-Century Criminal Procedure

Hurtado v. California was a landmark U.S. Supreme Court case limiting the application of the U.S. Constitution's due process requirements in state criminal proceedings. When a defendant is brought before a state court facing criminal charges, he or she need not be indicted by a grand jury, the high court decided. The 7–1 opinion, with one justice taking no part, was one of many decisions establishing the parameters of due process in American courts. It originated from a seemingly run-of-the-mill domestic dispute that erupted into violence and murder.[1]

A Californian residing in Sacramento during the 1880s, Joseph Hurtado lived in a hard-drinking, male-dominated, violence-prone, frontier society. He was described as "of dark complexion, black eyes, hair and mustache, and of an Indian cast of features. He is not a bad-looking man. He has a bullet wound on both sides of his body, is slim and Hat built." Born in Sutter Creek, California, on November 13, 1853, by the time he had his most serious run-in with the law in 1882, he was 28 years old and stood five feet, four inches tall. As was the case with many men of his station, Hurtado sported a long police record for disturbing the peace and battery. Despite his propensity to use his fists, according to one newspaper account, "among the 'sporting' men, Hurtado was reckoned as cowardly."[2]

Cowardly or not, he was not reluctant to engage in the rumble-and-tumble tumult of the era, even though he was a young man of diminutive proportions. Sometime around 1870, he was involved in an altercation with a fellow named Angus Martin, although the facts were murky. Martin suffered a hip wound while Hurtado was injured, albeit not seriously. In July 1874, Hurtado "got into a difficulty" following a picnic party and "was struck in the mouth by a pistol ball," which broke several of his teeth. In May 1878, J. W. Sunderland shot Hurtado during a saloon brawl. Everyone thought Hurtado's wounds were fatal—including Hurtado himself—but he recovered. Five months later, he shot and killed John "Jack" Denny and also shot Jack's brother, Peter, seriously wounding the man, over a gambling debt. Hurtado was arrested, tried, and acquitted of the crime. In November 1881, the night before his trial, Joseph Hurtado got married.[3]

Hurtado's private life proved to be no less contentious than his public one. By all accounts, at home he was a suspicious, cruel, heavy-handed hothead—the quintessentially stern, explosively violent husband of the western frontier. His attitude was hardly surprising or unique, for Joseph Hurtado was deeply immersed in the Hispanic machismo culture of honor so prevalent during the 19th century. Hispanic men of the era enjoyed nothing better than to cast aside their burdens and step away from a hardscrabble life to frequent *pulquerias*, or saloons, imbibe prodigious quantities of liquid refreshment, gamble, and hurl epithets at each other. As the alcohol and insults flowed from a trickle to a torrent, gatherings turned violent in a flash. Fighting words could erupt at the smallest provocation, leaving a slew of injured, occasionally dead, bodies in their wake.

Of all the verbal insults, perhaps the most incendiary was a statement defaming a woman or questioning the virtue of a man's female relatives. Denouncing an acquaintance using the Mexican phrase *hijo de la borracho* (son of a violated woman) was especially insulting, even beyond the pale. Such an offensive utterance could not go unpunished. The code of honor was unscripted, but everyone understood their respective roles in the story. Men were societal leaders and family providers, while women were second-class citizens, little more than chattels, expected to act out a subservient part in caring for a husband and child.

Of course, not every woman was equal in the hierarchy. The standard machismo narrative painted a portrait of two types: a woman of virtue (a mother, sister, wife, or daughter) who must be placed on a pedestal and worshiped as a "good" person—pure of heart, noble of deed, unsullied by the vagaries of life and the failings of the human animal. The second type, a woman of easy virtue, was "bad." She devoted herself to satisfying the lascivious needs of human beings—the carnal appetites and primitive urges of rutting swine. Because she would lie, cheat, steal, and give herself to any man, she was suited to be a prostitute or mistress, but not to travel in polite society or partake of the

Joseph Hurtado lived in a male-dominated frontier society where violence was commonplace, as illustrated by this 1887 Frederic Remington drawing of a quarrel over a card game in the Old West. The illustration appeared in *Harper's Weekly* on April 23, 1887. (Library of Congress)

wholesome family life available to a virtuous wife. The culture was devoid of nuance or gradation; a woman was all one thing or all the other. Saint or sinner, noble or debased, virgin or whore—no room existed for subtlety or insight into the idiosyncrasies of the human condition.[4]

Joseph Hurtado lived in this world; he did not question its presuppositions or resist its requirements. In accordance with the code, he married a woman reputed to be a good person and apparently possessing the moral values expected of a virtuous wife. Alas, reality seldom conforms to expectations. To earn a living for himself, his wife, and the child she bore him, Hurtado engaged in several vocations—hotel runner, barge pilot, and river boatman. By 1882, he had secured a position working as a boat pilot on the Sacramento River. It was steady work, but it required his absence from home most of the time. In line with his jealous nature, Hurtado worried about his wife's activities while he was away. Sure enough, after he returned to the homestead on one occasion in February 1882, he noticed an unsettling change in the woman. Something about her demeanor was not right.[5]

Deeply suspicious of her actions, Hurtado dug around and discovered a series of letters penned by a heretofore-hidden lover. With the incriminating evidence in hand, the jealous husband confronted his wife with allegations of infidelity. Fearful of a volatile reaction, she initially denied any misconduct. Yet she could offer no reasonable explanation for the correspondence. Under relentless questioning, she admitted that she and José Antonio Estuardo (also known by the alias "Spanish Joe"), Joseph's close friend, had engaged in sexual intercourse several times. In retrospect, it was not altogether surprising. "He seemed to think the world of my wife, and often told me that 'she was too good for me,'" Hurtado recalled later. "I thought nothing of that kind of talk—only laughed at it. After a while, his actions were so peculiar that they excited my suspicions."[6]

Suspicions were one thing; evidence was another. "I found that instead of being a friend, he was the destroyer of my happiness," the infuriated husband remembered. Apoplectic, it was all Hurtado could do not to charge off, find his wife's lover, and pummel his former friend to death. If insulting a man's wife was anathema, involving her in a torrid love affair was all but unthinkable. As for his wife, she was transformed. No longer the sacred symbol of family and goodness, she was a fallen woman, a tarnished idol. Reflecting on the affair between a "close and intimate friend" and his wife, Hurtado later explained, "This broke my heart. I loved my wife, and I loved still more my child."[7]

That night, unable to settle down with vivid images of his wife and his friend locked in an amorous embrace racing through his mind, the restless husband sought out A. W. Morrison, a bookkeeper for the Western Hotel. The men were friends. Unloading his heavy burden, Joseph confessed he was inclined to seek out Spanish Joe and slay the hapless paramour.

Realizing it was a potentially volatile situation, Morrison advised his friend not to act rashly. If Hurtado killed Estuardo, the legal consequences would be dire. And what would happen with Joseph's child? They might be separated indefinitely. Although frontier courts sometimes excused retaliation by an enraged husband when he discovered incontrovertible evidence of infidelity, it was by no means a foregone conclusion that he would be acquitted of all charges. Somehow, the reasoned discussion soothed the savage beast. Trusting Morrison's advice, Joseph Hurtado even agreed to surrender his gun lest he lose control and shoot the dastardly home-wrecker. Morrison remarked that Estuardo might be induced to leave town and thereby avoid further confrontation.[8]

The following day, Hurtado confronted his nemesis. Recognizing his delicate predicament, José Estuardo could not deny the overwhelming evidence. "I am the meat and you are the knife," he supposedly said. "I have betrayed your friendship, ruined your home; do with me as you please."[9]

Estuardo was fortunate the hotheaded husband would listen to reason—for the time being. Unarmed and momentarily willing to eschew violence, Joseph Hurtado agreed to spare the poor man's life on one condition: José Estuardo must leave Sacramento and break off all contact with Hurtado's wife. A grateful Estuardo promised he would comply. Satisfied that part of the problem had been solved, Hurtado marched home and verbally accosted his wife. At the conclusion of their argument, she consented to a brief separation. She would reside with relatives so everyone could cool down.[10]

Several weeks later, Hurtado's wife, presumably chastened, returned home amid vows to reform her behavior. Joseph believed if "she could make up her mind to return with the honest intention again of being a true woman, and if I could forget the wrongs done me, that then, perhaps, we would be enabled again to live together as man and wife." Yet the jealous husband soon realized that nothing had changed. While he was returning to work, Hurtado happened upon José Estuardo. Incredibly, the unrepentant fellow was leaving Hurtado's house. As Spanish Joe ambled down the street, he spoke to Hurtado. "I see your wife has got back," he said.[11]

It was all too much. Joseph Hurtado believed he had demonstrated admirable restraint, exactly as his friend A. W. Morrison had counseled, but it had gotten him nowhere. Both his wife and her lover had reneged on their promises. Estuardo's sarcastic comment was more than he could stomach. "Every time that man spoke to me, he excited the spirit of revenge in my breast," Hurtado explained. Enraged, he ran inside, rummaged around until he found a handgun, and emerged to chase down the aggravating cuss. During the encounter, Hurtado smacked Spanish Joe in the face with the gun. He might have finished off the hateful fellow had onlookers not intervened. They separated the combatants before the matter got out of hand.[12]

A few days later, Estuardo swore out a warrant against his assailant for assault with a deadly weapon. After police arrested him, Hurtado appeared in court on February 6, 1882, to seek a continuance for the hearing. When the court granted the motion, Estuardo rose from the back of the courtroom and called out, "Judge, I want that man held on a more serious charge, that of assault to murder. He is a dangerous man to be at large." The comment, taken in conjunction with previous events, especially upset Joseph Hurtado, inflaming "the smoldering fire within my bosom." In a subsequent statement, he explained how much Estuardo's outburst exacerbated tensions. "That was the climax of the whole business. That speech sealed his doom."[13]

Despite Spanish Joe's admonition to the court, Joseph Hurtado was a free man, at least temporarily. He had faced, and beaten, serious criminal charges before, and he could do it again. Still brooding, he retired to a nearby saloon to drown his sorrows in alcohol. Three friends accompanied him.[14]

Sometime afterward, José Estuardo emerged from the police court building. One of Joseph's friends stood near the saloon door watching the street. When the alert lookout spotted Spanish Joe, he remarked, "Here comes Estuardo."

Clutching a .44-caliber self-cocking revolver, Hurtado charged from the saloon hell-bent on meting out vigilante justice for the wrongs he had suffered as a cuckold. Standing in the road directly behind a local gentleman, James L. Wyatt, Hurtado took aim and fired. His bullet pierced Estuardo's chest while inflicting a severe powder burn on Wyatt's face. Still on his feet, Estuardo staggered a few steps in a doomed attempt to escape. Hurtado gave chase and fired another shot. His victim collapsed 10 feet from the man's original position. Hovering over the prostrate body, Hurtado fired yet another bullet before pounding his gun on Spanish Joe's head. He continued until a police officer, George Rider, arrived on the scene and disarmed him. Several men lifted the victim's body from the street and carried him into the police station. The victim died within minutes.[15]

Word spread quickly throughout the community. A mob of 300 people converged on the area within half an hour. Police officers feared that matters would get out of control and a lynching might occur. Fortunately, they established control and prevented the crowd from taking matters into their own hands.[16]

Observing the scene, Joseph Hurtado was unrepentant. "The reason I pounded him over the head with the pistol after he fell was from the fact that I wanted to make sure of his death, and I was reserving that extra shot in the pistol for myself," he confessed. Officer Rider placed Hurtado under arrest before the man could take his own life. "I presume the community is down on me and condemn me for the act I know is cowardly," Hurtado observed with classic understatement. "I don't deserve any sympathy, and do not wish any. I don't expect any mercy."[17]

Police charged Hurtado with first-degree murder. He was not indicted by a grand jury, but charged by information. At the time, several states, including California, allowed prosecutors to charge a criminal defendant without relying on a grand jury. Article 1, § 8, of the California Constitution provided: "Offenses heretofore required to be prosecuted by indictment, shall be prosecuted by information, after examination and commitment by a magistrate, or by indictment, with or without such examination and commitment, as may be prescribed by law. A grand jury shall be drawn and summoned at least once a year in each county." Yet the Fifth Amendment to the U.S. Constitution reads, in part, "No person shall be held to answer for a capital, or otherwise infamous crime, unless on a presentment or indictment of a grand jury, except in cases arising in the land or naval forces, or in the militia, when in actual service in time of war or public danger."[18]

In May 1882, *The People v. Joseph Hurtado* was tried before the Superior Court of Sacramento County. Hurtado attempted to introduce evidence of his wife's affair, but the presiding judge sustained the prosecutor's objection. The evidence was not introduced into the proceedings. On May 7, a jury convicted Hurtado of first-degree murder. He was scheduled to be sentenced on May 22, but the date was changed to June 5. At the sentencing hearing, Hurtado's attorney, C. T. Jones, moved for a new trial, but the court denied the motion. When asked if he had any words to say before the court announced the sentence, Hurtado demurred."I have no remarks to make." Judge Samuel C. Denson sentenced the defendant to be hanged on July 20.[19]

The case became a cause célèbre in the local community. Although he had not tried the case, superior court judge John Aunstory set the date for the execution. Even as he performed his duties, he expressed misgivings about the harshness of the sentence considering the circumstances of the crime. The judge opined that "justice will be accomplished by commuting his sentence to imprisonment for life." Similarly, an editorial in the local newspaper pronounced Hurtado's actions "justifiable homicide." The Hispanic culture and the frontier code of honor would not allow a man to act as Estuardo had, for he "not only seduced his (i.e., Hurtado's) weak-minded wife but boasted of what he had accomplished." In the editorialist's opinion, "Hurtado killed him" and "we think he did right." The defendant had sought to introduce evidence of the deceased's actions as a mitigating factor, but the trial judge had refused to allow the jury to hear the evidence. A group of citizens petitioned for clemency, arguing that the judge's decision was a grievous error that necessitated, at a minimum, a new trial. In a letter to the governor, a Los Angeles attorney, R. F. Del Valle, contended that a defendant should not be sentenced to die "for defending his manhood, home and family."[20]

On appeal to the California Supreme Court, the question of whether Hurtado should have been allowed to introduce evidence of adultery was crucial in determining the type of homicide crime involved: murder, manslaughter, or perhaps an acquittal. California Supreme Court justice E. W. McKinstry wrote the majority opinion. The justice agreed that heat-of-passion crimes allow for a lesser sentence than first-degree murder. In this case, however, eyewitness testimony clearly indicated that Hurtado "lay in wait" for Estuardo. The defendant positioned a lookout in the saloon to raise an alarm when Estuardo exited the police court building. If Hurtado had caught the man *in flagrante delicto* with his wife and had shot Spanish Joe dead at that moment, a heat-of-passion defense would be appropriate. With the passage of time, however, the defendant had ample opportunity to calm down and consider his actions. Because he waited in the saloon for his prey to appear, Joseph Hurtado acted in a deliberative manner. Therefore, the California Supreme Court could find no errors committed by the trial court that "demands a reversal of the judgment or a new trial."[21]

Having lost the appeal, the defendant and his attorney appeared before the Superior Court of Sacramento County on July 11 to learn when, or whether, the execution would occur. During the hearing, counsel argued that Hurtado's Fifth Amendment right to be indicted by a grand jury had been violated. Because the Fifth Amendment applies to the states by incorporation through the Fourteenth Amendment, counsel argued, both amendments are necessary to ensure due process of law for criminal defendants charged with a capital offense. Specifically, the due process clause of the Fourteenth Amendment holds that no state shall "deprive any person of life, liberty, or property without due process of law." The incorporation argument was a novel constitutional interpretation for the 1880s. Consequently, the superior court did not accept this creative, unprecedented approach to criminal procedure. Instead, the presiding judge set a new execution date: August 30, 1883.[22]

After exhausting his state remedies, Hurtado appealed to the U.S. Supreme Court. In due course, the justices granted certiorari. The paramount issue, according to Justice Matthews, who wrote the majority opinion, was simple. "The proposition of law we are asked to affirm is that an indictment or presentment by a grand jury, as known to the common law of England, is essential to that 'due process of law,' when applied to prosecutions for felonies, which is secured and guaranteed by this provision of the constitution of the United States, and which accordingly it is forbidden to the states, respectively, to dispense within the administration of criminal law."[23]

The appeal involved more than merely semantics or a trek through Anglo-American history. The meaning of "due process" would affect the substantive outcome of a criminal defendant's trial. Moreover, if the U.S. Constitution could directly set procedural requirements for state court proceedings through the incorporation doctrine, the result would alter federal–state relations in myriad ways. The justices were well aware that their decision would serve as a precedent for cases far beyond a matter involving a jealous husband shooting his wife's paramour.[24]

The Supreme Court voted 7–1 (with Justice Stephen Field not taking part) that the Fourteenth Amendment did not require a grand jury indictment. Moreover, the majority decided that the Fifth Amendment was not intended to apply retroactively through the Fourteenth Amendment to state criminal trials. The justices did not believe that due process was limited by its historical uses but should be open to an evolving interpretation. As Justice Matthews observed, to require states to follow the historical preference for grand juries would freeze the concept of due process in a specific time period. Forcing state courts to comply with substantive due process requirements "would be to deny every quality of the law but its age, and to render it incapable of progress or improvement. It would be to stamp upon our jurisprudence the unchangeableness attributed to the laws of the Medes and Persians."[25] Later in the opinion, the justice continued, "It is more consonant to the true philosophy of our historical legal institutions to say that the spirit of personal liberty and individual right which they embodied was preserved and developed by a progressive growth and wise adaptation to new circumstances and situations of the forms and processes found fit to give, from time to time, new expression and greater effect to modern ideas of self-government."[26]

In a lone dissent, Justice John Marshall Harlan reviewed the long history of due process dating back to English common law. "The phrase 'due process of law' is not new in the constitutional history of this country or of England," Harlan explained. "It antedates the establishment of our institutions. Those who had been driven from the mother country by oppression and persecution brought with them, as their inheritance, which no government could rightfully impair or destroy, certain guaranties of the rights of life and liberty, and property which had long been deemed fundamental in Anglo-Saxon institutions." The inheritance must be uniform across the American republic. "'Due process of law,' within the meaning of the national Constitution, does not import one thing with reference to the powers of the States and another with reference to the powers of the general government."[27]

As for what requirements fundamentally comprise due process, Harlan's review of history and political philosophy strongly indicated that grand jury indictment was essential to Anglo-American jurisprudence. By allowing defendants to be charged on information, "in California, nothing stands between the citizen and prosecution for his life except the judgment of a justice of the peace. Had such a system prevailed in England in respect of all grades of public offences, the patriotic men who laid the foundation of our government would not have been so persistent in claiming as the inheritance of the colonists the institutions and guaranties which had been established by her fundamental laws for the protection of the rights of life, liberty and property." Harlan simply could not understand the majority's argument that requiring a grand jury indictment would limit due process and the need to adapt the Constitution to changing circumstances. Grand juries were so important to protecting individual rights that he could not envision a situation where a changing Constitution would find the grand jury system an encumbrance.[28]

Critics then and now have charged that a majority of Supreme Court justices "completed the eradication of the original understanding of 'due process of law'" in *Hurtado*. In a later era, strict constructionists would argue that the judges and justices should not read their own values into the law but should rely on precedent and the plain meaning of the words. They would also argue that federalism principles require adherence to the Founders' interpretation of constitutional provisions. Yet *Hurtado*, in rejecting the necessity of a grand jury indictment in state proceedings, was a broadly constructed opinion that changed the meaning of long-standing traditions.[29]

Although the U.S. Supreme Court later selectively incorporated Bill of Rights guarantees through the Fourteenth Amendment and applied them to the states, the grand jury provision was not included. Joseph Hurtado, his adulterous wife, and their frontier associates are long dead and gone. Yet *Hurtado v. California* lives on because it was an early case on the role of federal due process requirements in state criminal cases. The modern criminal procedure revolution did not begin until the 20th century, but the issues discussed in the *Hurtado* case set the stage for subsequent developments. The case remains good law in the U.S. criminal justice system, and it all began with an angry, frustrated, and emotional husband who sought to exact vengeance against his cheating wife's lover.[30]

Most criminal laws of the 19th century were specific to local and state jurisdictions, with very few procedural protections afforded by the federal system. Consequently, criminal defendants seldom looked to U.S. constitutional provisions to protect their rights as Americans. Over time, the criminal justice system would evolve, but its change was a long time in coming.[31]

NOTES

1. Joel Samaha, *Criminal Procedure*, 8th ed. (Belmont, Calif.: Wadsworth, 2012), 32–33.
2. The description of Joseph Hurtado's physical appearance and background comes from "San Francisco Items," *Sacramento Daily Union* 15, 86 (June 1, 1882).
3. "Murder," *Sacramento Daily Union* 14, 144 (February 7, 1882); "San Francisco Items."
4. Clare V. McKanna, Jr., *Race and Homicide in Nineteenth Century California* (Reno and Nevada: University of Nevada Press, 2002), 57–58.
5. Ibid., 57–58. See also "Murder"; Samaha, *Criminal Procedure*, 32.
6. McKanna, *Race and Homicide in Nineteenth Century California*, 57–58; "Murder"; "San Francisco Items"; "Trial of Hurtado for Murder," *Sacramento Daily Union* 15, 63 (May 5, 1882).
7. Quoted in "Murder."
8. McKanna, *Race and Homicide in Nineteenth Century California*, 57–58; "Murder."
9. Quoted in Samaha, *Criminal Procedure*, 32. See also "Murder."
10. McKanna, *Race and Homicide in Nineteenth Century California*, 57–58; "Murder"; Samaha, *Criminal Procedure*, 32.
11. Quoted in McKanna, *Race and Homicide in Nineteenth Century California*, 58.
12. McKanna, *Race and Homicide in Nineteenth Century California*, 58; "Murder"; "San Francisco Items"; "Trial of Hurtado for Murder."
13. Quoted in "Murder." See also McKanna, *Race and Homicide in Nineteenth Century California*, 58; "San Francisco Items."
14. McKanna, *Race and Homicide in Nineteenth Century California*, 58; "Murder"; Samaha, *Criminal Procedure*, 32; "San Francisco Items"; "Trial of Hurtado for Murder."

15. "The Case of Hurtado," *Sacramento Daily Union* 18, 118 (January 9, 1884), 3; McKanna, *Race and Homicide in Nineteenth Century California*, 58; "Murder"; Samaha, *Criminal Procedure*, 32; "San Francisco Items"; "Trial of Hurtado for Murder."

16. "Murder."

17. Quoted in ibid. See also McKanna, *Race and Homicide in Nineteenth Century California*, 58.

18. *Hurtado v. People of the State of California*, 110 U.S. 516 (1884) at 517. See also Samaha, *Criminal Procedure*, 32.

19. Quoted in "The Death Sentence," *Sacramento Daily Union* 15, 90 (June 6, 1882). See also 110 U.S. 516, 518.

20. "The Case of Hurtado," 3; "The Death Sentence"; "Hurtado," *Sacramento Daily Union* 54, 104 (December 21, 1885), 3; McKanna, *Race and Homicide in Nineteenth Century California*, 58–59.

21. 110 U.S. 516, 518–19. See also Samaha, *Criminal Procedure*, 32.

22. "The Case of Hurtado," 3; Samaha, *Criminal Procedure*, 32.

23. 110 U.S. 516, 520.

24. Thomas Y. Davies, "The Supreme Court Giveth and the Supreme Court Taketh Away: The Century of Fourth Amendment 'Search and Seizure' Doctrine," *The Journal of Criminal Law and Criminology* 100, 3 (Summer 2010): 947; Samaha, *Criminal Procedure*, 32–33; Donald A. Dripps, "The Fourteenth Amendment, the Bill of Rights, and the (First) Criminal Procedure Revolution," *Journal of Contemporary Legal Issues* 18, 1 (2009): 488–89.

25. 110 U.S. 516, 529.

26. 110 U.S. 516, 530.

27. 110 U.S. 516, 539.

28. 110 U.S. 516, 554.

29. Quoted in Davies, "The Supreme Court Giveth and the Supreme Court Taketh Away," 947. See also Dripps, "The Fourteenth Amendment, the Bill of Rights, and the (First) Criminal Procedure Revolution," 488–89; Samaha, *Criminal Procedure*, 32–33.

30. See, for example, Donald A. Dripps, *About Guilt and Innocence: The Origins, Development, and Future of Constitutional Criminal Procedure* (Westport, Conn.: Praeger, 2003), 1–6; Thaddeus Hoffmeister, "The Grand Jury Legal Advisor: Resurrecting the Grand Jury's Shield," *The Journal of Criminal Law and Criminology* 98, 4 (Summer 2008): 1171–1230.

31. See, for example, Barry Latzer, "Toward the Decentralization of Criminal Procedure: State Constitutional Law and Selective Disincorporation," *The Journal of Criminal Law and Criminology* 87, 1 (Autumn 1996): 63–129; Carolyn B. Ramsey, "Was the Bill of Rights Irrelevant to Nineteenth-Century State Criminal Procedure?," *Journal of Contemporary Legal Issues* 18, 1 (2009): 501–511.

CHAPTER 2

Weeks v. United States (1914) and the Origins of the Exclusionary Rule

The exclusionary rule, a key feature of modern criminal procedure that considers illegally obtained evidence to be the "fruit of the poisonous tree" and therefore inadmissible in court, has become one of the most controversial doctrines in American law. For evidence to be seized through a legal search, law enforcement officers must possess "probable cause" and procure a warrant beforehand from a duly-authorized magistrate or other competent judicial officer. A limited number of exceptions exist to the warrant requirement, but in each case law enforcement officials must be able to articulate a factual basis to satisfy the probable cause requirement. Failure to meet the requirement will result in suppression of the evidence, for the exclusionary rule dictates that "good" evidence procured through "bad" law enforcement techniques violates a fundamental precept of American law. Because the exclusionary rule is a judicial construction and cannot be found in the text of the U.S. Constitution or its amendments, some commentators contend that the doctrine is an overreaction to police mistakes. In 1926, Judge (later Justice) Benjamin Cardozo famously asked whether a "criminal is to go free because the constable has blundered."[1]

The debate over whether improperly seized evidence should be excluded from a criminal trial goes to the heart of the freedom–authority divide. According to the social contract theory of American government, citizens voluntarily surrender a measure of individual liberty in exchange for the creation of an authoritative governmental entity. The entity must protect the citizenry from internal marauders and external would-be conquerors. Upon occasion, the mechanisms of government will be employed to build roads, bridges, and other necessary construction projects. To ensure that government does not overreach and tyrannize individuals, the American Founders installed a series of checks and balances in the institutional structures of government. Ideally, the structural framework of the regime would preclude the possibility of governmental abuses. They were not merely naïve idealists, these authors of a new republic, for they recognized that no governmental design, regardless of its brilliance or prescience, could guard against every permutation and combination of malfeasance. They left it to the public officials who followed them to craft appropriate remedies for specific instances of government misconduct.[2]

The Fourth Amendment was one structural feature designed to prevent government run amok. Although the provision had not been

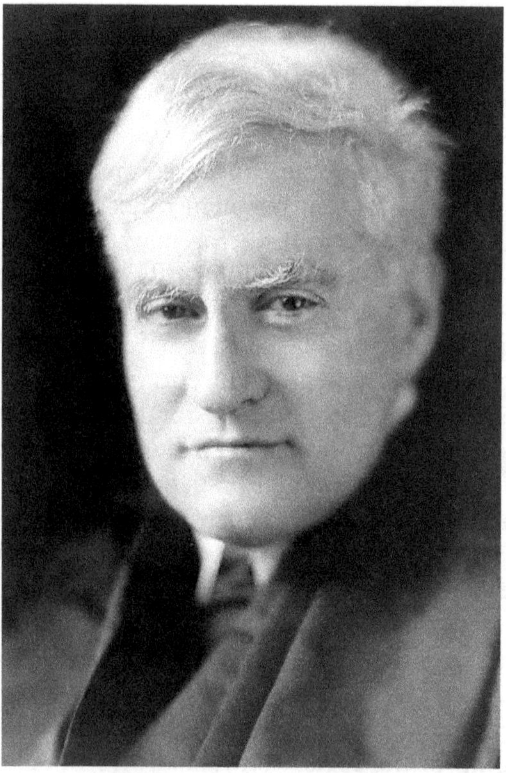

In considering the exclusionary rule, Judge (later Justice) Benjamin Cardozo famously asked whether a "criminal is to go free because the constable has blundered." (Library of Congress)

included as part of the original document, the Anti-federalists insisted on amending the Constitution to ensure that the federal government could not overreach. Colonial history was replete with episodes of overreaching by the British Crown, and the representatives of a new nation were not anxious to replicate the experience. When the states had existed as colonies of the mother country, English officers had relied on general writs of assistance to justify broad grants of authority to search for smuggled goods and stolen merchandise. James Otis Jr., the great Massachusetts lawyer, once filed a lawsuit in a colonial court against the writ on behalf of a delegation of Boston merchants. Although his challenge was unsuccessful, it served notice that the colonists were opposed to government authorities searching their books, papers, and property absent specific evidence of wrongdoing.[3]

In June 1789, James Madison set forth a series of proposals to modify the recently ratified U.S. Constitution, including a provision forbidding general warrants. In Madison's view, which was shared by many of his compatriots, individual liberty would be protected only when an officer of the law could state with particularity what evidence of criminality he expected to find before searching a suspect's property. No all-purpose "fishing expeditions" would be allowed. One of Madison's proposed amendments, reworded slightly, became the basis for the Fourth Amendment. The original proposal stated: "The rights of the people to be secure in their persons, their houses, their papers, and their other property from all unreasonable searches and seizures, shall not be violated by warrants issued without probable cause, supported by oath or affirmation, or not particularly describing the places to be searched, or the persons or things to be seized." Referred to a committee for discussion and debate, the text as it was finally adopted read: "The right of the people to be secure in their persons, houses, papers, and effects, against unreasonable searches and seizures, shall not be violated, and no Warrants shall issue, but upon probable cause, supported by Oath or affirmation, and particularly describing the place to be searched, and the persons or things to be seized."[4]

As is the case with much of the U.S. Constitution, the wording is open to competing constructions. In the "warrant preference" construction, the two clauses should be read together so that searches are deemed reasonable when a warrant is issued with sufficient particularity to protect innocent parties from unnecessary intrusion. In this reading, the act of obtaining the warrant presents a prima facie case for determining the existence of probable cause. A competing perspective, the "generalized reasonableness" interpretation, separates the two clauses. The reasonableness, or lack thereof, of the search and seizure is not a result of whether a warrant is obtained, but depends on a multiplicity of factors. In cases where a warrant is obtained, the second clause outlines the requisite procedures for its issuance. Although the former interpretation is considered the mainstream view, reading the two clauses separately gained support among some lawyers and police toward the latter half of the 20th century.[5]

For all of its importance in constitutional criminal procedure during the 20th and 21st centuries, the Fourth Amendment was seldom litigated during the first 100 years after its ratification. It was sometimes labeled a "sleeping giant." Bill of Rights protections did not apply to the states during that early era. Because most criminal trials occurred in state courts, the civil liberties protections of the Bill of Rights resided in a legal and intellectual cul-de-sac. Without judicial guidance to interpret the application of Fourth Amendment requirements, the legal effect of the provision was a great unknown.[6]

The Fourth Amendment does not specify the remedy when a search or seizure violates its strictures. The Founders never referenced an exclusionary rule, and no clear evidence suggests they ever considered it one way or the other. The Constitution and the accompanying notes on the deliberations did not delve into all the specifics necessary to operate a government across multiple centuries. The document was designed as a general framework, leaving specific matters of governance to later generations of leaders to decide. Legislative enactments or common-law developments through case-by-case adjudication would determine appropriate remedies for police errors and misconduct.[7]

The U.S. version of an exclusionary rule was not firmly established until the 20th century, but the concept stretched back to the English common law, antedating American independence. The reasoning, as Lord Chief Justice Mansfield explained in a 1769 court opinion, is that government officials who force individuals to produce their private papers, in effect, force those individuals to incriminate themselves. The Anglo-American legal system was designed to prevent self-incrimination because evidence procured through intimidation or violence is unreliable; it prejudices the resultant trial and corrupts the legal system.[8]

Across the Atlantic, criminal defendants who sought a judicial remedy for law enforcement violations prior to the 20th century were limited to filing private lawsuits against public officials. Probative evidence, regardless of how it was collected, was admissible in court. In *Boyd v. United States*, an 1886 case, the U.S. Supreme Court, relying on the Fourth and Fifth Amendments to the U.S. Constitution, held that business papers need not be produced if law enforcement officials did not possess probable cause beforehand. It was a narrowly tailored opinion and limited to private papers lawfully in a defendant's possession. The opinion did not articulate an exclusionary rule governing an impermissible search.[9] Eleven years later, in *Bram v. United States*, the high court ruled that involuntary confessions could not be introduced in court. Although these early cases suggested an affinity for excluding improperly obtained evidence, the U.S. Supreme Court stopped short of establishing a prophylactic rule.[10]

Yet the U.S. Supreme Court seemed to back away from these incremental steps toward creating an exclusionary rule in a 1904 case, *Adams v. New York*. New York police suspected Albert J. Adams of possessing gambling paraphernalia. Officers properly obtained a warrant and arrived on the premises to search for evidence. During the visit, they found personal papers with notations indicating that the defendant had known about policy slips used for gambling. Although the papers were not specified in the warrant, authorities seized them, anyway. On appeal, the defendant challenged the admissibility of the papers since they were not referenced in the search warrant. In his majority opinion for the court, Mr. Justice William R. Day wrote, "In such cases, the weight of authority as well as reason limits the inquiry to the competency of the proffered testimony, and the courts do not stop to inquire as to the means by which the evidence was obtained." The police discovered the papers while searching for evidence of criminal activity under a lawfully obtained warrant, and the defendant had not been compelled to testify against himself. These were the only relevant facts with respect to how the police gathered evidence. Beyond that, the Court would not address remedies for illegally obtained evidence because the justices refused to delve deeper into law enforcement methods.[11]

Weeks v. United States, a seminal case on the exclusionary rule, was an abrupt about-face from *Adams*, at least in federal courts. The matter began with a fortuitous event. Four days before Christmas in 1911, authorities apprehended Mrs. Olla Weeks shoplifting from a store in Kansas City, Missouri. Arrested and transported to the police station, the woman became concerned that her husband, Fremont Weeks, would be incriminated if police searched their home for additional evidence of her shoplifting booty. Anxious to send up an alarm, Mrs. Weeks scribbled a note to her husband, but police intercepted the message, read it, and decided to investigate. Based on the contents of the note, police suspected Fremont Weeks of using the U.S. mail to distribute lottery results, a clear violation of law.

The facts bore out their suspicions, for Fremont Weeks was involved in an illegal gambling business, selling "coupons" of the International Mining and Investment Company of Santo Domingo at 50 cents each. Had the officers secured a search warrant to rifle through his books and papers and invade his premises, their efforts would have withstood constitutional scrutiny. To this day, it is not altogether clear why they did not apply for a warrant. Fremont Weeks had not received his wife's note warning him of an impending search, nor was he aware of her arrest. Perhaps authorities assumed that their search for evidence of Mrs. Weeks's shoplifting was sufficient justification for a premises search, or they simply allowed their zeal for capturing a criminal to overwhelm their good judgment. In any event, two officers, William Toohey and John Owens, arrived at the Weeks's residence, a boarding house located at 1834 Penn Street in Kansas City, without a warrant. Their actions that day initiated one of the most important court cases in American history.[12]

Mr. Weeks had already left home for his job in Union Station when the officers arrived to conduct their search. In his absence, Toohey and Owens spoke to a neighbor who told them where to find the house key. Afterward, they "unlawfully and without warrant or authority so to do, broke open the door to plaintiff's said home and seized all of his books, letters, money, papers, notes, evidences of indebtedness, stock, certificates, insurance policies, deeds, abstracts, and other muniments of title, bonds, candies, clothes, and other property in said home, and this in violation of 11 and 23 to the Constitution of Missouri, and of the [Fourth] and [Fifth] Amendments to the Constitution of the United States." During the search, the officers found evidence that Weeks had, in fact, violated multiple laws against gambling. They turned over the suspect's personal papers to a local U.S. marshal, A. J. Martin.

Emboldened by their initial visit, the police officers turned up a second time with a federal postal inspector, Joseph Wolf, for a more thorough inspection of the premises. Once again, the officers did not have a search warrant and Weeks did not consent to the search. They knocked on the door and entered Weeks's room after another boarder invited them inside. Even as one group of officers searched Weeks's home, another group arrived at his place of work, the Adams Express Company, and arrested him for using the mails to transmit information about gambling and the lottery.[13]

Fremont Weeks's defense attorney, Martin J. O'Donnell, filed a pretrial motion for the property to be returned to the defendant because, among other things, the seizure violated the Fourth Amendment. U.S. District Court judge Arba S. Van Valkenburgh agreed that items unrelated to the case should be returned, but he refused to order other materials to be relinquished because, under the *Adams* precedent, they were probative evidence. After Fremont Weeks was convicted and sentenced to serve six months in the Johnson County Jail in Warrensburg, Missouri, he appealed the conviction.

In preparing a 67-page brief to the U.S. Supreme Court, O'Donnell argued that improperly obtained evidence should not be admissible in court. It was a novel legal argument, for the high court had never recognized an exclusionary rule. Assistant Attorney General Winifred T. Dennison's one-page reply cited applicable common-law precedents, including *Adams*, indicating that because courts had never prohibited the admission of competent evidence, except in limited situations that did not apply in the instant case, the conviction should be upheld.[14]

Justice Day, author of the *Adams* opinion, again wrote for the high court. He was careful to distinguish the *Adams* case. "The decision in that case rests upon incidental seizure made in the execution of a legal warrant, and in the application of the doctrine that a collateral issue will not be raised to ascertain the source from which testimony, competent in a criminal case, comes," the justice observed. In *Weeks*, however, the police officers did not obtain a search warrant. The seizure of Fremont Weeks's papers was not a "collateral issue" but was the central fact on which the outcome hinged.[15]

Gone was the Court's traditional reluctance to carve out new judicial doctrines or add constitutional requirements for law enforcement officers. Gone was the general observation that aggrieved criminal defendants could resort to civil remedies for a constable's blunders. Gone was a high court that separated the probative value of evidence from the means by which it was obtained. In a famous passage, Justice Day explained why the Supreme Court was willing to carve out an exclusionary rule where none had existed previously. "If letters and private documents can thus be seized and held and used in evidence against a citizen accused of an offense, the protection of the [Fourth] Amendment, declaring his right to be secure against such searches and seizures, is of no value, and, so far as those thus placed are concerned, might as well be stricken from the Constitution." Without providing a remedy for police misconduct, the Fourth Amendment was a "paper tiger," a seemingly ferocious, utterly toothless, provision that did not sanction violations and, therefore, could be ignored with relative impunity.[16]

The Court reversed Fremont Weeks's conviction and established a foundational principle of American criminal procedure. One of the great cases in American criminal law had arisen from an investigation into the activities of an intemperate gambler and his shoplifting wife. Following the *Weeks* opinion, the warrantless search and seizure of a suspect's papers from a private residence violated the Fourth Amendment, and such evidence could not be introduced into a court of law absent certain extenuating circumstances. Yet the *Weeks* rule was limited expressly to federal cases. However intrepid the Supreme Court seemed to be in establishing an exclusionary rule, the justices were unwilling to alter fundamental federalism principles in an era before Bill of Rights protections were applied to the states through the selective incorporation doctrine. Moreover, Mr. Weeks had requested a return of papers he legally possessed. The Court did not decide the issue of whether he would have been entitled to petition for the return of property he had illegally obtained.[17]

The Court addressed the latter issue in *Silverthorne Lumber Company v. United States*, a 1920 case that broadened the *Weeks* rule to include papers containing incriminating evidence. The case began when Frederick W. Silverthorne and his father were arrested and hauled down to the police station for questioning. While they were being detained, in the words of a subsequent court opinion, "Representatives of the Department of Justice and the United States marshal, without a shadow of authority, went to the office of their company and made a clean sweep of all the books, papers and documents found there." The officers promptly provided the materials they had collected to the district attorney.[18]

The Silverthornes filed a motion to compel government authorities to return their papers. Although the motion was granted, police officers had copied the materials, which they used to obtain a subpoena requiring the two men to surrender the original incriminating books and papers for use in a grand jury indictment. The audacity of the government officials' action was stupefying: Law enforcement personnel used illegally obtained copies of incriminating documents as the grounds for obtaining a court order requiring the defendants to surrender the original documents. After the Silverthornes refused to comply, the trial court imposed a $250 fine for contempt of court and ordered the men to be jailed.[19]

When the case came before the U.S. Supreme Court on appeal, Justice Oliver Wendell Holmes Jr. wrote the majority opinion. He admitted that police knowledge of criminal activity acquired through independent means would be admissible as probative evidence to be used against the defendants, but allowing government prosecutors to profit from an illegal search "reduces the Fourth Amendment to a form of words." If the prohibition against unreasonable searches and seizures means anything, it means that the police must acquire evidence in a lawful manner. "The essence of a provision forbidding the acquisition of evidence in a certain way is that not merely evidence so acquired shall not be used before the Court, but that it shall not be used at all," Holmes explained.[20]

Weeks and *Silverthorne* specifically applied only to private papers. Subsequent cases expanded the exclusionary rule beyond the acquisition of documents by government agencies searching through papers at a defendant's home or place of business on threat of coercion. In *Gouled v. United States* (1921), the Court concluded that an impermissible search is not necessarily limited to instances where force is used to compel production of evidence. Documents obtained through government agents' chicanery also were inadmissible.[21] *Agnello v. United States* (1925) held that contraband, such as drugs, could not be offered into evidence if police did not follow Fourth Amendment requirements in procuring the evidence.[22] In *Nardone v. United States*, Justice Felix Frankfurter introduced a memorable phrase into the lexicon when he wrote, "The trial judge must give opportunity, however closely confined, to the accused to prove that a substantial portion of the case against him was a fruit of the poisonous tree."[23]

The "fruit of the poisonous tree" doctrine and the exclusionary rule became hallmarks of 20th-century American criminal procedure. Yet even from their earliest days, these concepts were controversial. Law enforcement officers often refer to the vagaries of police work in the field, an idea akin to the "fog of war" experienced by soldiers on a battlefield. Because police officers face a multitude of fluid circumstances that change rapidly and result in unpredictable developments, excluding evidence gathered when the constable blunders, especially while acting in good faith, vastly complicates police work. In the years following the *Weeks* decision, proposals were set forth to provide exceptions to the exclusionary rule. The exceptions are discussed in subsequent chapters of this book.[24]

NOTES

1. *People v. Defore*, 242 U.S. 13, 21; 150 N.E. 585, 587 (1926). See also Yale Kamisar, "Some Reflections on Criticizing the Courts and 'Policing the Police,'" *Criminology and Police Science* 53, 4 (December 1962): 459; Mark Harold Shenfield, "Fruit-of-the-Poisonous-Tree Doctrine," *California Law Review* 60, 3 (May 1972): 870–81.

2. Akhil Reed Amar, "Fourth Amendment First Principles," *Harvard Law Review* 107, 4 (February 1994): 785–87; Lloyd L. Weinreb, "The Exclusionary Rule Redux—Again," *Fordham Urban Law Journal* 37, 3 (May 2010): 874–75.

3. Amil Reed Amar, "The Fourth Amendment, Boston, and the Writs of Assistance," *Suffolk University Law Review* 30, 1 (1996): 53–54; Joseph R. Frese, "James Otis and Writs of Assistance," *The New England Quarterly* 30, 4 (December 1957): 496–508.

4. Amar, "The Fourth Amendment, Boston, and the Writs of Assistance," 68; Thomas Y. Davies, "Recovering the Original Fourth Amendment," *Michigan Law Review* 98, 3 (December 1999): 697–706; Tracey Maclin, "The Central Meaning of the Fourth Amendment," *William and Mary Law Review* 35, 1 (1993): 208–09.

5. Amar, "The Fourth Amendment, Boston, and the Writs of Assistance," 54–55; Davies, "Recovering the Original Fourth Amendment," 557–60; David Sklansky, "The Fourth Amendment and Common Law," *Columbia Law Review* 100, 7 (November 2000): 1794–99.

6. Milton Hirsch, "Big Bill Haywood's Revenge: The Original Intent of the Exclusionary Rule," *St. Thomas Law Review* 22, 1 (October 2009): 59–61; Daniel B. Yeager, "Search, Seizure and the Positive Law: Expectations of Privacy Outside of the Fourth Amendment," *The Journal of Criminal Law & Criminology* 84, 2 (July 1993): 272–74.

7. Davies, "Recovering the Original Fourth Amendment," 550–52; Maclin, "The Central Meaning of the Fourth Amendment," 197–249; Aaron S. Wolff, editor, "The Federal Search and Seizure Exclusionary Rule: Its Origin, Development, Present Status and Trend," *Journal of Criminal Law, Criminology & Police Science* 45, 1 (May/June 1954): 51–52.

8. Sklansky, "The Fourth Amendment and Common Law," 1799–1800; Wolff, "The Federal Search and Seizure Exclusionary Rule," 51–52.

9. 116 U.S. 616 (1886).

10. 168 U.S. 532 (1897).

11. 192 U.S. 585, 594 (1904).

12. Samuel Dash, *The Intruders: Unreasonable Searches and Seizures from King John to John Ashcroft* (New Brunswick, N.J.: Rutgers University Press, 2004), 59–60; "Tickets of Santo Domingo Lottery Sold in Kansas City," *The Omaha Daily Bee*, 41, 162 (December 23, 1911), 1.

13. 232 U.S. 383, 386–87 (1914). See also Dash, *The Intruders*, 59–60; Hirsch, "Big Bill Haywood's Revenge," 61–62.

14. 232 U.S. 383, 387–88. See also Dash, *The Intruders*, 59–60.

15. 232 U.S. 383, 396.

16. 232 U.S. 383, 393.

17. Hirsch, "Big Bill Haywood's Revenge," 64–65; Yeager, "Search, Seizure and the Positive Law," 273–74.

18. 251 U.S. 385, 390 (1920).

19. 251 U.S. 385, 390–91. See also "Exclusionary Rule," *The Journal of Criminal Law & Criminology* 65, 4 (December 1974): 461; Wolff, "The Federal Search and Seizure Exclusionary Rule," 55.

20. 251 U.S. 385, 392–93.

21. 255 U.S. 298 (1921).

22. 269 U.S. 20 (1925).

23. 308 U.S. 338, 341 (1939). See also Louis L. Jaffe, "The Judicial Universe of Mr. Justice Frankfurter," *Harvard Law Review* 62, 3 (January 1949): 397.

24. For the holding on a "good faith exception" to the exclusionary rule, see *United States v. Leon*, 468 U.S. 897 (1984).

CHAPTER 3

Olmstead v. United States (1928) and Wiretapping the "Baby Lieutenant"

After the courts created the exclusionary rule, the question in subsequent cases was how far the rule should extend. Clearly, if police officers entered a private residence and seized private papers without a warrant, the rule would apply, and the evidence could not be admitted in federal court. The question was whether the exclusionary rule applied in instances where the intrusion did not appear to be as egregious or physically intrusive as entry inside of a private residence. In particular, the issue of electronic "seizures" was left unsettled until the high court considered such a situation in *Olmstead v. United States.*[1]

The case involved a colorful ex-lieutenant from the Seattle police force, Roy Olmstead, who turned to a life of crime and eventually earned the sobriquet the "King of the Puget Sound Bootleggers." During his career as a lawman, Olmstead witnessed numerous episodes involving careless, impulsive, illegal whiskey merchants, and he realized he could do much better. He also rationalized the enterprise as a victimless crime because alcohol sales and consumption were *malum prohibitum*, or prohibited by law. Engaging in bootlegging was not inherently "evil," or a *malum in se* crime such as murder or child molestation.[2]

Olmstead's early life gave no hint of his later career on both sides of the law. He was born in Beaver City, Nebraska, on September 18, 1886, to a family of farmers, John and Sarah Olmstead. In 1904, young Roy left his parents' home and moved to Seattle, Washington. He initially supported himself working in the Moran Brothers Company shipyard. On May 16, 1907, the 20-year-old joined the Seattle police force. He was described as "a large and powerful young man of keen, undisciplined intelligence and ambition." Something about the fellow stood out in a crowd. Virtually everyone who encountered the young man came away impressed with his abilities and charisma.[3]

Olmstead swiftly rose through the ranks, becoming a sergeant in 1910, acting lieutenant in 1917, and a permanent lieutenant on January 22, 1919, at the age of 32. Six days before his promotion, the Eighteenth Amendment to the U.S. Constitution prohibiting the manufacture, sale, and transportation of alcohol was certified. It went into effect on January 17, 1920. The law was to affect the young man's life in ways he could not have imagined.[4]

Washington State had implemented a statewide alcohol prohibition in 1916, well ahead of the national temperance effort. In the years that followed, Lieutenant Olmstead spent time on bootlegging raids where he observed the practice up close and personal. He saw the damage caused when competing gangs exchanged gunfire over territories and customers. Olmstead knew one man, Jack Marquette, a former policeman, from their days together working in law enforcement. Marquette hijacked liquor shipments from two brothers, Logan and Fred Billingsley. Both sides began shooting at each other instead of working together, triggering an unnecessary, internecine squabble that ensured their mutual destruction. After the police eventually caught Marquette red-handed, he agreed to inform on his competitors, thereby assisting the authorities in taking down both gangs.[5]

With the absence of the Marquette and Billingsley gangs from the Washington marketplace, a group of fragmented, marginal criminal figures emerged to fill the vacuum. At approximately the same time, the Volstead Act, the new prohibition law, authorized the use of newly empowered federal agents to pursue bootleggers aggressively. Even now, it is not altogether clear when the ambitious young police officer turned his attentions to a new avocation, but it is certain that the sideline promised lucrative financial rewards beyond the pittance paid to a man with a badge. Olmstead recognized the need for a measure of professionalism in the rum-running business, and he was exactly the man to do it. If he could clean up the rampant crime among the criminal elements struggling for ascendancy and reach an accommodation with law enforcement officials, he might earn a tidy profit and make the streets safer in the process. In his view, everyone would win.[6]

It was only a matter of time before the conflicting nature of Roy Olmstead's activities came to a head. The exact date when his career in law enforcement came undone is known with precision: March 22,

1920. On that date, federal Prohibition Bureau agents surprised a tugboat crew offloading a batch of Canadian whiskey at two o'clock in the morning on Brown's Bay beach near Meadowdale, a picturesque town situated 11 miles north of Seattle. The new federal Prohibition amendment had taken effect in January, and federal officials were anxious to demonstrate their commitment to enforcement. They had lurked in the woods, crouching behind a roadblock, for days awaiting an opportunity to apprehend the culprits. When the agents announced the raid, a confused melee ensued amid shouting, gunshots, and lights cast on the scene. Ever vigilant and quick-thinking, Roy Olmstead, one of the men unloading the alcohol, leaped into his car and raced away from the scene. Alas, several officers were acquainted with the department's shining light. They discovered his identity at once. He was arrested at his home later in the afternoon.[7]

The Brown's Bay raid was the first of its kind on the Pacific Northwest—a big, ostentatious pageant of saber-rattling and law enforcement bravado. The haul was impressive: 100 cases of liquor were confiscated and 11 bandits were rounded up. It was the largest liquor shipment ever seized in the Northwestern United States at the time.[8]

Olmstead's superiors were stunned by the contrast between their image of a young man on the move and a daring bootlegger masquerading beneath a façade of respectability. They fired the fellow immediately after his arrest. The court imposed a $500 fine even as the newspapers saddled him with the moniker of the "baby lieutenant," perhaps not an ideal pseudonym but certainly memorable. Yet any publicity, even stories about a life of crime, is a godsend for a businessman anxious to attract customers. Roy Olmstead suddenly found himself with a public reputation, and not an altogether unsympathetic one. He cut a dashing figure as a romantic outlaw who vowed never to hurt anyone physically in his quest to meet the needs of thirsty Americans.[9]

And oh, how the customers flocked to the new darling of the "wet" set. Freed from his law enforcement duties to pursue a profitable, full-time moneymaking venture, Roy threw himself into his business deals with gusto. Analyzing the market as any good businessman would, he realized he needed working capital, and he knew exactly where he could acquire it. He lined up 11 investors for $1,000 each. Afterward, he retained an attorney to handle contract negotiations, land acquisitions, and other business details. Olmstead was nothing, if not shrewd. He could withstand most forms of legal scrutiny if he established a legitimate business empire in accordance with applicable laws and regulations. He assembled a dedicated staff and set out to revolutionize the liquor market in his adopted state. Before long, his entrepreneurial skills paid off handsomely. He was raking in more than $200,000 a month and supporting a burgeoning industry of salesmen, dispatchers, drivers, bookkeepers, warehousemen, mechanics, and office workers, making him one of Puget Sound's largest employers. He chartered a fleet of automobiles and trucks and eventually bought a farm where he stored alcohol awaiting distribution. Earning more in a week than a police officer usually earned in 20 years, Roy Olmstead, Seattle's renowned "Rum King," considered himself a fortunate man.[10]

The fortunate man resolved never to descend into the morass of violent crime. Many bootleggers engaged in all manner of malfeasance and illegal activities, including gambling, prostitution, and drug-running. Roy was above all that. His delivery men were unarmed. They would not fire on law enforcement agents; they would offer inducements to secure compliance. Neither would Olmstead water down his product to increase profits at the expense of the customer. Instead, he handled only fine-quality whiskey, gin, brandy, champagne, and beer imported from Canada and Europe. He believed in an ethical code of sorts, and he prided himself on living up to his ideals. This self-made delusion was part of the man's belief that buying and selling liquor were not genuinely criminal activities, and lawmakers who enacted prohibition measures were foolish moralizers that failed to understand the vagaries of human nature.

Olmstead added local officials in the sheriff's department as well as the department's "dry squad," a group of six plainclothes Seattle police officers, to his payroll. With enough largesse to satisfy virtually everyone, for a time Olmstead seemed impervious to U.S. law. He also schooled himself on the loopholes in Canadian export requirements. The neighbor to the North had imposed a duty of $20 per case on all liquor shipments bound for the United States. Anxious to avoid unnecessary expenditures, Olmstead once again demonstrated his business acumen, if not his ethical propriety, by hiring ships originating in Vancouver, British Columbia, and bound for Mexico. The ships typically carried between 2,000 and 4,000 cases of duty-free liquor. While other bootleggers shelled out the duty when transporting shipments across the U.S.-Canadian border via truck, Olmstead's hired ship sailed away from Canadian shores, only to unload the cargo on isolated D'Arcy Island, a desolate forest area northeast of Victoria and beyond the normal shipping lanes. A dangerous nearby reef and the presence of a leprosy station ensured that few prying eyes would witness the illicit activity. Olmstead struck up a business friendship with the station keeper. The gentleman kept an eye on the product until smaller swift boats arrived to transport the cases to American ports near Puget Sound under the cover of night. Owing to frequent rain and storms, many a dark night presented less-than-ideal conditions for navigating the waters around Seattle. On these tempestuous evenings, as Coast Guard cutters and federal agents docked their boats to escape inclement weather, Olmstead's rum-runners braved the elements to take advantage of unencumbered access to convenient ports of call.[11]

By establishing an efficient delivery system and holding down costs, Roy Olmstead's bootlegging business could undercut his competitors' prices by as much as 30 percent. He eventually branched out beyond Washington State. In a 1930 article, *The New York Times* characterized the operation as "one of the most gigantic rum-running conspiracies in the country." Olmstead purchased a palatial colonial estate at 3757 Ridgeway Place in Mount Baker, a prestigious Seattle neighborhood, and ventured into ancillary business enterprises. After purchasing the American Radio Telephone Company during the summer of 1924, he established himself as the president of Seattle's first radio station, KFQX. Nothing spreads good publicity as much as a man who owns a publicity-generating company.[12]

Olmstead became a prominent man about town, flaunting his wealth and reveling in the media attention. In the words of one commentator, "Olmstead's prestige was much more than that accorded the ordinary rumrunner. His audacity touched everything he did with a cheerful sense of excitement." On several occasions, the impervious kingpin docked his ships in downtown Seattle and unloaded his bounty into trucks marked "Meat" or "Fresh Fish." It was an open secret that the self-proclaimed *bon vivant* openly defied the law because he was confident that he had virtually every local public official on his payroll.[13]

One man who learned of the shenanigans seethed with resentment. Prohibition agent William Whitney, a Seattle lawyer who had failed to win a seat in the U.S. House of Representatives, became obsessed with capturing the area's most notorious bootlegger. A person could not be allowed to violate the law continually, no matter how much contempt he felt for the underlying social policy. Without strict adherence to the letter of the law, mankind could not thrive with a working system of government. Indefatigable and ruthless, Whitney grew increasingly frustrated with his failure to apprehend the high-flying, audacious whiskey king. Whenever Whitney chartered a fast boat, Olmstead's faster boats outmaneuvered the vessel. Whenever Whitney acted on a tip, Olmstead proved to be two steps ahead and easily eluded the lawman. In a last ditch effort to trap his prey, Whitney authorized his agents, some of whom were engaged in nefarious activities themselves, to install wiretaps on Olmstead's telephones.[14]

Olmstead was aware that federal agents had him in their sights, but he blithely soldiered on, unconcerned that an arrest was in the offing. He became a family man of good standing thanks to a change in his marital status. He had married a woman earlier in his life, but they divorced in 1924. Not long thereafter, he married Elise Campbell, nicknamed "Elsie" and described as "a vivacious young woman with a taste for excitement." A rumor circulated that Elsie had been employed by the Northwest District Prohibition administrator and joined Olmstead's gang as an undercover agent. It was a widespread myth that figured in neatly with Olmstead's background in law enforcement, but the story was unfounded. The woman in question was Olmstead's first wife, who had assisted federal agents in 1922.[15]

Elsie Olmstead operated her husband's new radio station, KFQX, which featured a variety format. She was able to broadcast from a home studio installed in a spare bedroom. Beginning at 7:15 in the evening, Elsie read bedtime stories for children under the nom de plume of "Aunt Vivian." According to local legend, Aunt Vivian broadcast coded messages to her husband's bootlegging network during the nightly performances, but no evidence of this practice could be found. What was indisputable was a police raid on Olmstead's home on the evening of November 17, 1924. Federal agents entered the premises in full force, arresting Roy and Elsie Olmstead and 15 guests. In fact, Aunt Vivian was in the middle of a broadcast when she was taken off the air abruptly and escorted from the premises.[16]

On January 19, 1925, a federal grand jury indicted Roy Olmstead along with 90 other persons for conspiracy to violate the National Prohibition Act dating back to June 1923. The two counts alleged that Olmstead and his confederates had violated the law, which made it a crime "to possess, transport and import intoxicating liquors" and "to barter, sell, deliver and furnish" them to others. The defendants' actions were alleged to be offenses "against the peace and dignity of the United States of America." The resultant proceedings would be the largest trial under the Prohibition laws to date.[17]

Far from being chastened by his arrest, Roy Olmstead posted bail and immediately threw himself back into his business. In the meanwhile, his attorney, Jerry Finch, investigated the means by which the

Roy Olmstead, "King of the Puget Sound Bootleggers," is pictured here in 1925 with his wife, Elise. (The *Seattle Post-Intelligencer* Collection, Museum of History & Industry, Seattle. All Rights Reserved)

agents had collected evidence against Seattle's best known entrepreneurial liquor merchant. Olmstead had known for some time that his enemies had tapped his telephones. On some occasions, he instructed his men to removes the wiretaps. At other times, Olmstead cleverly placed calls with false information to lead agents on unproductive wild-goose chases where no one could be apprehended. Even in cases where the listening party learned anything of value, Olmstead was confident that the evidence would be inadmissible in court. Circumstances would prove him wrong.[18]

Following Olmstead's arrest, prosecutors pitted the defendants against each other in a classic prisoner's dilemma scenario (although the concept had not yet been articulated). Each defendant was assured that he would receive a lesser sentence if he cooperated with police. If he failed to cut a favorable deal, he would face stiffer penalties should one or more codefendants cooperate in his stead. The strategy yielded results. Al Hubbard, one of Olmstead's chief lieutenants, agreed to tell everything he knew in exchange for dropping the charges and, ironically, appointing him as a federal Prohibition agent. Hubbard was the mastermind behind many facets of the rum-running enterprise. He was a wizard with electronics and mechanical devices, with responsibility for keeping the organization's boats in top-operating condition. He had built the radio transmitter that Elsie used for her in-home broadcasts. Al Hubbard became the most valuable witness for the prosecution.[19]

When Jerry Finch learned that Hubbard was working for the prosecution, he burst into tears. Because he was not merely a dispassionate advocate but also complicit in the moneymaking schemes, Finch no doubt saw the handwriting on the wall: his legal career probably was over, to say nothing of his pending loss of freedom.

To all outward appearances, Roy Olmstead seemed far less concerned than Finch about the consequences. Perhaps he had accepted the situation with a resigned fatalism or his attitude may have been a public display of bravado disguising his interior fears. Whatever the case, Olmstead professed to be sanguine about the case against him.

Worse was yet to come. On Thanksgiving morning 1925, as he unloaded a supply of liquor from a boat on Woodmont Beach, Olmstead suddenly found himself surrounded by armed federal agents. Caught with the evidence at his fingertips, he had no recourse but to raise his hands and surrender to the fates. "It looks like things are going very bad for Olmstead," he was heard to muse aloud.[20]

The trial for the original offense commenced in Seattle in January 1926. Judge Jeremiah Neterer of the U.S. District Court for the Western District of Washington presided. He was a Woodrow Wilson appointee with a quarter of a century of experience on the bench, first on the Superior Court of Whatcom County, Washington, and the last dozen years on the federal court. Several co-defendants had decided to abandon Jerry Finch as their defense counsel, relying instead on a more aggressive advocate, George Vanderveer. A former prosecutor who had turned to defending the same class of defendants he once had put away, Vanderveer had earned a national reputation as a bellicose defense attorney, the "counsel for the damned." Known as a man with a taste for liquid refreshments with which to drown his sorrows following his longtime girlfriend's tragic suicide, Vanderveer specialized in bootlegging cases, having successfully defended Olmstead's nemesis Logan Billingsley, among others.[21]

Across the aisle from Finch and Vanderveer sat the quietly competent U.S. District Attorney, Thomas P. Revelle. An unsuccessful gubernatorial candidate in 1924, Revelle was personally upright and honest, having served as a Methodist minister before turning toward the law early in his career. Personally "dry," he had witnessed the corrosive effects of alcohol both on those who consumed it and on the public servants who prosecuted cases and resisted bribes from bootleggers such as Roy Olmstead. Aside from his own predilections for an aggressive prosecution, he recalled an admonition he had received from Millard T. Hartson, an aide to Republican U.S. senator Wesley Livsey Jones, a staunch proponent of Prohibition. "Colonel Hartson came to me and said I was being watched and if I did not convict Olmstead and his co-defendants, it would mean the loss of my office," he wrote after the trial.[22]

The case turned on testimonial evidence procured through Officer Whitney's wiretaps as well as the recollections of Canadian officials who had seized the defendant's ship, the *Eva B.* (Olmstead's illicit activities on Woodmont Beach two months earlier would be postponed for a separate proceeding at a future date.) A parade of witnesses told what they knew of the operation, but it was the agents who had gathered evidence on the wiretaps that sealed the case. Olmstead was said to laugh uproariously at the recorded conversations, thinking the material inadmissible and convinced he had outwitted the hapless William Whitney once again. Whitney would have the last laugh.[23]

George Vanderveer was furious because he could not hear the original recordings nor could he gain access to transcripts of the wiretapped conversations. Government witnesses frequently consulted "the book" containing the words allegedly spoken on the wiretaps as a means of refreshing faulty memories, but the transcripts were never offered into evidence. Vanderveer attacked the use of wiretaps vehemently, sometimes trading testy words with Judge Neterer. During one heated exchange, an exasperated Vanderveer complained, "I want a fair, decent white man's chance to test the truth of this," but the lack of a transcript or access to the recordings was impeding his efforts. "Just a minute," the judge instructed. "When you address the court, employ language that is fitting for the occasion." In an impolitic response, Vanderveer muttered, "I am."[24]

Recognizing the proceedings were not going well, the impassioned defense counsel objected repeatedly, although he was overruled more often than not. He cited the Washington State statute from 1909 that made anyone "who shall intercept, read or in any manner interrupt or delay the sending of a message over any telegraph or telephone line" guilty of a misdemeanor. His protests were to no avail. Although the case was going his way, Revelle also became upset and asked the judge to intervene owing to sustained hissing from defense counsel.[25]

Despite the serious nature of the charges, Roy Olmstead by all accounts smiled and laughed through much of the trial. He had long ago dismissed law enforcement and the judicial system as masquerade balls where everyone played a role, however ludicrous. Much of the evidence introduced against him consisted of the deliberately false recordings he made to throw federal agents off his trail. His own fabricated words were reproduced and used against him. Even more ironic was Olmstead's realization that some of the court personnel, witnesses, and attorneys in the courtroom were former customers. He could not help but wallow in cynicism at the ridiculous pageant unfolding in the courtroom.[26]

Ridiculous or not, the laugher ceased when the jury, after deliberating for six hours over the course of two days, found 21 of the defendants, including Olmstead, guilty as charged. Elsie Olmstead escaped conviction, but attorney Jerry Finch did not. On March 9, 1926, Judge Neterer sentenced Roy Olmstead to serve four years at hard labor in a federal penitentiary and pay an $8,000 fine. Delivering a stern lecture from the bench, the judge reflected on what might have been. "As to you, Roy Olmstead, I'll say this," he lamented. "If the same constructive force, organizing ability, which was devoted to this enterprise had been used legitimately, in harmony with the laws, the final result would have been marvelous."[27]

The trial had concluded, but the case took on a new life in the appellate court. Free on bail, Roy Olmstead sold his home, his radio station, and his household effects. He lived in limbo as he waited for his lawyers to present his case before the Ninth U.S. Circuit Court of Appeals.[28]

When the court finally announced its decision on May 9, 1927, circuit court judge William Ball Gilbert, joined by Frank Dietrich, affirmed the conviction. In Gilbert's view, the Fifth Amendment right against self-incrimination applied to government agents invading homes to seize evidence, but it did not apply beyond physical searches. Wiretapping, according to the judge, was tantamount to "evidence obtained by listening at windows and doors," which was beyond the scope of the amendment.[29]

Judge Frank H. Rudkin expressed misgivings about telephone wiretaps in a dissent that questioned the incremental, but unrelenting, encroachment on individual rights. By allowing federal agents to consult transcripts of the recordings made from the wiretaps without making the material available to the defense, the judge feared that "a better opportunity to color or fabricate testimony could not well be devised by the wit of man." Although wiretapping conversations is not a physical invasion, it is nonetheless a violation of citizens' privacy. "Must their personal, private, and confidential communications to family, friends, and business associates pass through any such scrutiny on the part of agents, in whose selection they have no choice, and for the faithful execution of whose duties they have no security?" In a rhetorical flourish, Judge Rudkin observed that "if such ills as these must be borne, our forefathers signally failed in their desire to ordain and establish a government to secure the blessings of liberty to themselves and their posterity."[30]

Having lost his appeal to the Ninth Circuit, Roy Olmstead was ordered to report to the McNeil Island Correctional Institute in unincorporated Pierce County near Steilacoom on the coast of Puget Sound to begin serving his sentence. Yet Judge Rudkin's dissent convinced Olmstead's attorneys that an appeal to the U.S. Supreme Court might be productive. The questionable legality and murky morality of wiretaps had become a pressing national issue after Attorney General Harlan F. Stone had lectured agents of the Bureau of Investigation (later rechristened the Federal Bureau of Investigation) in 1924 that wiretapping telephones comprised "unethical tactics" and should be avoided. The high court initially declined to hear the case. Owing to the salience of the issue, however, the high court agreed to weigh in on the constitutionality of the practice upon receiving a second certiorari petition. On January 9, 1928, the U.S. Supreme Court formally placed the *Olmstead* case, along with two companion cases, *Green v. United States* and *McInnis v. United States*, on the docket. Olmstead briefly won a release on bail while the final appeal went forth.[31]

Olmstead's legal contention remained the same: use of wiretapping evidence violated the Fourth and Fifth Amendments and should not have been used against him. Olmstead's case was consolidated with 72 other petitioners, but he remained the lead complainant as the case came before the U.S. Supreme Court. George Vanderveer's friend and colleague John F. Dore, a Seattle attorney once vilified as a "vicious, unscrupulous bootleg lawyer," argued the case on Olmstead's behalf. Assistant U.S. Attorney General Mabel Walker Willebrandt, the second woman appointed to that high office and renowned as the "first lady of law" for her vigorous defense of the Volstead Act from 1921 to 1929, argued the government's case. During her career, Willebrandt argued more than 40 cases before the U.S. Supreme Court, a record seldom attained by anyone. She became one of the most famous and influential women of her era.[32]

Writing the majority opinion for five members of the high court, Chief Justice William Howard Taft held that the Fourth Amendment prohibition on unreasonable searches and seizures did not apply to wiretaps. In Taft's view, "The amendment does not forbid what was done here. There was no searching. There was no seizure. The evidence was secured by the use of the sense of hearing and that only. There was no entry of the houses or offices of the defendants."[33] The chief justice was not oblivious to the dangers of unfettered police discretion, but he believed the public's interest in security outweighed an individual's interest in privacy. "A standard which would forbid the reception of evidence if obtained by other than nice ethical conduct by government officials would make society suffer and give criminals greater immunity than has been known heretofore."[34]

Justices Oliver Wendell Holmes Jr., Harlan F. Stone, and Pierce Butler filed separate dissents, but it was Justice Louis Brandeis's dissenting opinion that became famous for its eloquent defense of Fourth Amendment protections and its invocation of a privacy doctrine. "Decency, security and liberty alike demand that government officials shall be subjected to the same rules of conduct that are commands to the citizen," Brandeis argued. "In a government of laws, existence of the government will be imperiled if it fails to observe the law scrupulously. Our Government is the potent, the omnipresent teacher. For good or for ill, it teaches the whole people by its example. Crime is contagious." Justice Brandeis's logic was simple, but elegant: if the men who recorded Roy Olmstead's telephone conversations had been private citizens, they could have been prosecuted for violating the law. Wiretapping was both a state crime in Washington and a federal crime; therefore, government agents engaged in criminal behavior to collect evidence against Olmstead and the other petitioners. In Brandeis's view, government should be held to the same standard as citizens because "if the government becomes a lawbreaker, it breeds contempt for law; it invites every man to become a law unto himself; it invites anarchy. To declare that in the administration of the criminal law the end justifies the means—to declare that the government may commit crimes in order to secure the conviction of a private criminal—would bring terrible retribution. Against that pernicious doctrine this court should resolutely set its face." In addition, at the very least, the Fourth

Amendment should apply to wiretap evidence because citizens have an expectation of privacy in their telephone conversations.[35]

Alas, for all of its eloquence, Brandeis's opinion was in the minority. For the King of the Puget Sound Bootleggers, luck had run out. He had reached the end of the line. With his final appeal exhausted and his conviction upheld, Roy Olmstead reported back to the McNeil Island Correctional Institute to serve out the remainder of his sentence. He became a model prisoner and eventually won an early release for good behavior on May 12, 1931, having served 35 months of his 48-month sentence. The ever-faithful Elsie met him on the dock at Steilacoom.[36]

Justice Louis D. Brandeis wrote a famous dissent in *Olmstead v. United States*, arguing that the government should not be allowed to use wiretapping to collect evidence without a search warrant. (Library of Congress)

Although the Prohibition law had not yet been repealed, the world had changed during Olmstead's years behind bars. The Great Depression had settled over the land, money had dried up, and the good times associated with the Roaring Twenties had slipped away. One event demonstrated how much times had changed—and how much Olmstead had changed with them. On December 25, 1935, President Franklin D. Roosevelt presented Roy Olmstead with Christmas greetings by granting the former bootlegger a full presidential pardon. The action had resulted in no small measure from Elsie's tireless efforts to call attention to Roy's now-exemplary character and his impecunious circumstances by submitting letters from judges, politicians, and her minister, Dr. Mark Matthews, to the White House. The growing public unease with, and distaste for, wiretapping by federal agents may have played a part as well. It was too late to save him from serving time, but the restoration of his civil and political rights pleased Roy Olmstead immensely.[37]

Aside from changes associated with the advent of a new decade, the former bootlegger had found religion. No longer enamored of worldly things, he professed to be a new man with new ideals. Claiming to be a Christian Scientist and would-be carpenter, he set out to remake himself and his life. A skeptic could be forgiven for doubting the sincerity of the conversion, but with the passing years, Olmstead proved as good as his word. He worked with prison inmates to follow the straight and narrow upon release.

Roy's lifestyle was not the only thing that changed. Although Elise had remained loyal during his incarceration, their marriage began to deteriorate during the 1930s. She filed for divorce on May 28, 1943, alleging her husband had "deserted her without just cause." The divorce was granted on August 5, 1943. Afterward, Elsie dropped out of sight, lost to history.[38]

As for Roy, frequently he could be found preaching an anti-alcoholism agenda, an ironic development on multiple levels. He taught Sunday school and visited prisoners in the King County Jail virtually every day for years. Whenever an incredulous prisoner inquired whether the innocuous-looking fellow standing before him was the legendary "King of the Rumrunners," Olmstead's stock reply was, "no, not anymore. The old Olmstead is dead." The statement was accurate enough: the 79-year-old man who died on April 30, 1966, was unrecognizable as the arrogant, flashy, seemingly unrepentant bootlegger who had controlled the Northwest liquor trade decades earlier.[39]

As for the case and its consequences, it remained good law for almost four decades until the U.S. Supreme Court overruled *Olmstead v. United States* in a landmark decision, *Katz v. United States* (1967). The *Olmstead* case reveals the evolutionary nature of constitutional criminal procedure. During the 1920s, evidence gathering through electronic means was relatively rare. By the 1960s, such law enforcement techniques had become commonplace. As police tactics changed, so changed the courts' interpretation of the Constitution, thus ensuring the continued vitality of the founding document and its amendments.[40]

NOTES

1. 277 U.S. 438 (1928).
2. Walter F. Murphy, *Wiretapping on Trial: A Case Study in the Judicial Process* (New York: Random House, 1965), 16.
3. Quoted in Norman H. Clark, "Roy Olmstead, a Rumrunning King on Puget Sound," *The Pacific Northwest Quarterly* 54, 3 (July 1963): 89.
4. Clark, "Roy Olmstead, a Rumrunning King on Puget Sound," 89, 251–55; Richard F. Hamm, *Shaking the Eighteenth Amendment: Temperance Reform, Legal Culture, and the Polity, 1880–1920* (Chapel Hill, N.C.: University of North Carolina Press, 1995), 247–51; Philip Metcalfe, *Whispering Wires: The Tragic Tale of an American Bootlegger* (Portland, Ore.: Inkwater Press, 2007), xi.
5. Norman H. Clark, *The Dry Years: Prohibition and Social Change in Washington* (Seattle: University of Washington Press, 1965), 132.
6. Clark, "Roy Olmstead, a Rumrunning King on Puget Sound," 89–90; Hamm, *Shaking the Eighteenth Amendment*, 247–51.
7. Clark, *The Dry Years*, 56; Clark, "Roy Olmstead, a Rumrunning King on Puget Sound," 90; Metcalfe, *Whispering Wires*, 7–8.
8. Clark, "Roy Olmstead, a Rumrunning King on Puget Sound," 90–91; Metcalfe, *Whispering Wires*, 8.
9. Clark, "Roy Olmstead, a Rumrunning King on Puget Sound," 90–91; Federal Judicial Center Website, "*Olmstead v. United States:* The Constitutional Challenges of Prohibition Enforcement—Historical Background and Documents: A Short Narrative," <http://www.fjc.gov/history/home.nsf/page/tu_olmstead_narrative.html,> (Accessed February 12, 2013); Metcalfe, *Whispering Wires*, 8.
10. Clark, "Roy Olmstead, a Rumrunning King on Puget Sound," 91; Metcalfe, *Whispering Wires*, 8.
11. Clark, *The Dry Years*, 161–64; Clark, "Roy Olmstead, a Rumrunning King on Puget Sound," 91; Metcalfe, *Whispering Wires*, 15–16.

12. Quoted in "Roy Olmstead, a Rumrunning King on Puget Sound," 91. See also Federal Judicial Center Website, "*Olmstead v. United States.*"

13. Quoted in Clark, "Roy Olmstead, a Rumrunning King on Puget Sound," 92.

14. Clark, "Roy Olmstead, a Rumrunning King on Puget Sound," 93; Federal Judicial Center Website, "*Olmstead v. United States.*"; Kenneth M. Murchison, "Prohibition and the Fourth Amendment: A New Look at Some Old Cases," *The Journal of Law & Criminology* 73, 2 (Summer 1982): 485–86.

15. Quoted in Clark, "Roy Olmstead, a Rumrunning King on Puget Sound," 91. See also Federal Judicial Center Website, "*Olmstead v. United States.*"

16. Clark, *The Dry Years*, 165, 169; Murphy, *Wiretapping on Trial*, 16–20.

17. Clark, "Roy Olmstead, a Rumrunning King on Puget Sound," 94–95; Federal Judicial Center Website, "*Olmstead v. United States.*"

18. Clark, "Roy Olmstead, a Rumrunning King on Puget Sound," 94; Metcalfe, *Whispering Wires*, 119.

19. Clark, "Roy Olmstead, a Rumrunning King on Puget Sound," 96; Federal Judicial Center Website, "*Olmstead v. United States*"; Metcalfe, *Whispering Wires*, 99–101.

20. Federal Judicial Center Website, "*Olmstead v. United States*"; Metcalfe, *Whispering Wires*, 99–101.

21. Clark, "Roy Olmstead, a Rumrunning King on Puget Sound," 95; Federal Judicial Center Website, "*Olmstead v. United States*"; Metcalfe, *Whispering Wires*, 174–75.

22. Quoted in Clark, "Roy Olmstead, a Rumrunning King on Puget Sound," 96. See also Metcalfe, *Whispering Wires*, 117–18.

23. Clark, *The Dry Years*, 169; Clark, "Roy Olmstead, a Rumrunning King on Puget Sound," 95–97; Metcalfe, *Whispering Wires*, 88–91.

24. Quoted in Clark, "Roy Olmstead, a Rumrunning King on Puget Sound," 97. See also Metcalfe, *Whispering Wires*, 181–204; Murchison, "Prohibition and the Fourth Amendment," 485–86.

25. Clark, "Roy Olmstead, a Rumrunning King on Puget Sound," 97; Federal Judicial Center Website, "*Olmstead v. United States*"; Metcalfe, *Whispering Wires*, 202.

26. Clark, *The Dry Years*, 174; Clark, "Roy Olmstead, a Rumrunning King on Puget Sound," 95–97.

27. Quoted in Clark, "Roy Olmstead, a Rumrunning King on Puget Sound," 97–98. See also Clark, *The Dry Years*, 173–74; Metcalfe, *Whispering Wires*, 211.

28. Clark, *The Dry Years*, 174; Clark, "Roy Olmstead, a Rumrunning King on Puget Sound," 98; Federal Judicial Center Website, "*Olmstead v. United States.*"

29. *Olmstead v. United States*, 19 F.2d 842 (9th Cir. 1927). See also Federal Judicial Center Website, "*Olmstead v. United States.*"

30. 19 F.2d 842 at 848–50. See also Clark, *The Dry Years*, 175; Clark, "Roy Olmstead, a Rumrunning King on Puget Sound," 98; Federal Judicial Center Website, "*Olmstead v. United States.*"

31. Clark, "Roy Olmstead, a Rumrunning King on Puget Sound," 99; Federal Judicial Center Website, "*Olmstead v. United States.*"

32. Clark, *The Dry Years*, 176; Mabel Walker Willebrandt, *The Inside of Prohibition* (Indianapolis, Ind.: Bobbs-Merrill, 1929), 232–33. For more on Willebrandt, see Dorothy Marie Brown, *Mabel Walker Willebrandt: A Study of Power, Loyalty, and Law* (Knoxville: University of Tennessee Press, 1984).

33. 277 U.S. 438, 464 (1928).

34. 277 U.S. 438 at 468. See also Samuel Dash, *The Eavesdroppers* (New Brunswick, N.J.: Rutgers University Press, 1959), 28.

35. 277 U.S. 438 at 485. See also Murchison, "Prohibition and the Fourth Amendment," 487–88; Neil M. Richards, "The Puzzle of Brandeis, Privacy, and Speech," *Vanderbilt Law Review* 63, 5 (October 2010): 1336–38; Carol S. Steiker, "Brandeis in *Olmstead:* 'Our Government Is the Potent, the Omnipresent Teacher,'" *Mississippi Law Journal* 79, 1 (Fall 2009): 149–78.

36. Clark, "Roy Olmstead, a Rumrunning King on Puget Sound," 103; Federal Judicial Center Website, "*Olmstead v. United States.*"

37. Clark, *The Dry Years*, 252; Clark, "Roy Olmstead, a Rumrunning King on Puget Sound," 103; Federal Judicial Center Website, "*Olmstead v. United States.*"

38. Clark, "Roy Olmstead, a Rumrunning King on Puget Sound," 103; Federal Judicial Center Website, "*Olmstead v. United States*"; Metcalfe, *Whispering Wires*, 340–43.

39. Quoted in Clark, *The Dry Years*, 252. See also Clark, "Roy Olmstead, a Rumrunning King on Puget Sound," 103; Federal Judicial Center Website, "*Olmstead v. United States*"; Metcalfe, *Whispering Wires*, 342–43.

40. 389 U.S. 347 (1967). See also Christopher Brennan, "*Katz* Cradle: Holding on to Fourth Amendment Parity in an Age of Evolving Electronic Communication," *William & Mary Law Review* 53, 5 (April 2012): 1797–1823; Edmund W. Kitch, "*Katz v. United States:* The Limits of the Fourth Amendment," *The Supreme Court Review* 1968, 1 (1968): 133–52; Tom McInnis, "The Changing Definition of Search or Seizure," *Insights on Law and Society* 11, 2 (May 2011): 10–13, 28; Daniel T. Pesciotta, "I'm Not Dead Yet: *Katz*, *Jones*, and the Fourth Amendment in the 21st Century," *Case Western Reserve Law Review* 63, 1 (Fall 2012): 187–255.

CHAPTER 4

Powell v. Alabama (1932) and the Scottsboro Boys

When a slow-moving train departed from the Southern Railroad yards in Chattanooga, Tennessee, on March 25, 1931, no one knew that history would be made that day—albeit another chapter in the long, sad saga of bitter race relations in the South stretching back to Reconstruction and even earlier. By day's end, nine young black men stood accused of raping two white women. The case became a cause célèbre, exacerbating old wounds of race, sexuality, and due process of law, or the lack thereof. A dispassionate review of the evidence indicated that no rape had occurred, but in Alabama during the Great Depression, even-keeled analyses were few and far between. After barely escaping a lynching from an incensed mob, the "Scottsboro Boys," as the defendants were labeled, were charged with, and tried for, a capital offense. As a perfunctory gesture, local authorities assigned two inexperienced defense lawyers to counsel the defendants on their limited options. Milo Moody was a befuddled septuagenarian who had not represented clients in court for decades and Stephen Roddy was an alcoholic real estate attorney from Chattanooga, Tennessee. Moody and Roddy did their best but to no avail. The prejudices against the defendants were so overwhelming that a fair trial was all but impossible. Before they ended, the Scottsboro trials, appeals, and retrials would rewrite several chapters in the case law on American criminal procedure and illustrate the necessity of constitutional protections for unpopular defendants.[1]

The affair began at a time when almost a third of eligible Americans could not find suitable employment. The Great Depression had settled over the American landscape like a suffocating shroud, impoverishing generations of citizens, especially in the Deep South, an already impoverished region of the country. More than 200,000 Americans across the country barely eked out a living as railroad hobos, catching rides as stowaways on boxcars.[2]

After the Southern freight train left tiny Stevenson, Alabama, on March 25, 1931, a surprised stationmaster glanced up to see a group of white hobos gathered before him. One fellow was bleeding from the head as he breathlessly explained that a "bunch of Negroes" had tossed him and his traveling companions from the boxcars during a spirited ruckus. The hysterical victim insisted he would "press charges against 'em." Whether the stationmaster would have jumped to his task with such zealous alacrity had the alleged assailants been white instead of colored remains a matter for conjecture. In any case, he sprang into action with commendable efficiency. The train had already passed through nearby Scottsboro when he telephoned ahead. The stationmaster learned the freight had not yet arrived in Paint Rock, the next town on the line, so he worked the telephone to ensure the Negro ruffians would not elude the long arm of the law.[3]

When he heard the news of the melee, Jackson County Sheriff M. L. Wann called his deputy, Charlie Latham, at the Paint Rock general store and ordered him to deputize whoever he needed to so he could "capture every Negro on the train and bring them to Scottsboro." The excited deputy did as he had been instructed, assembling a posse of men at the railroad depot as a welcoming committee. The deputized squad sported pistols, rifles, and shotguns. Latham reminded his newly minted associates not to fire their guns unless they had no choice.

Immediately after the train slid to a halt, the determined band searched through all 42 boxcars. They quickly found nine black youngsters, one white man, and, to their surprise, two white women dressed in overalls. The young black men—Charley Weems, Ozie Powell, Clarence Norris, Olen Montgomery, Willie Roberson, Haywood Patterson, Andrew (Andy) Wright, Leroy (Roy) Wright, and Eugene Williams—had been riding the rails in search of a better life. Each fellow was in dire straits—impecunious, directionless, frightened, and woefully unprepared for the impending crisis. A black man accused of a crime against white men in Depression-era Alabama knew he would seldom, if ever, emerge victorious. Yet the circumstances were hardly unusual. They had tussled with the whites and tossed their competitors from the train, but it was one more row among an endless array of rows encountered in the life of a hobo. Until the posse rounded them up, the young black men had not been especially alarmed at the state of affairs.

Their attitudes quickly changed. The nine black teenagers soon learned that the March 25 brouhaha was an altogether different type of struggle. Surrounded by a growing mob of armed whites, they recognized their situation was grave. They felt some small relief when they were transported from Paint Rock to the Scottsboro jail instead of being shuffled over to the nearest tree to meet Judge Lynch. Yet exactly when the Scottsboro teens thought the circumstances were bleak but marginally improved, an accusation exacerbated their predicament.[4]

One of the two women riding on the train, Ruby Bates of Huntsville, Alabama, told Deputy Sheriff Latham that the nine young black men had gang-raped her and her friend, Victoria Price, during the journey. The idea that nine fiends would physically assault women on a slow-moving train and wait around long enough to be apprehended by law enforcement seemed preposterous at the time, and the passage of decades makes it no more plausible. Nonetheless, conventional wisdom dictated that black men were anxious to enjoy carnal relations with white women at any opportunity. Such was the prejudice of the day that the tale impressed the deputies as credible.[5]

Word filtered through a growing crowd milling about outside the jail that the nine Negro prisoners had raped two white women riding on the train. Anger erupted as the stories grew wilder. One tale recounted how the "black brutes," in their animalistic rage, had "chewed off" one of Ruby Bates' breasts. The inflamed mob chanted for vigilante justice: "Let those niggers out!" "Give 'em to us." Several voices in the crowd threatened forcible entry into the building if the alleged assailants were not released to the crowd for a taste of instant justice.[6]

Sheriff Wann hoped that after the sunset, the mob's energy would dissipate and the crowd would disperse. As the numbers dwindled along with the light of day, he was encouraged that the immediate danger had passed. Nevertheless, he recognized that he and his deputies could not hold off a large group that probably would reconvene the next morning. He instructed his men to shackle the prisoners together so they could be transported to nearby Etowah, a larger jail that would be less challenging to fortify and defend. When the deputies discovered their cars had been tampered with and the wiring for the headlamps had been cut, the sheriff finally realized the magnitude of the risk. He scrambled to a nearby telephone to call the governor for assistance.

Governor Benjamin Meeks Miller, a fiscal conservative and anti-Klan man, harbored no love for the Negro, but he saw himself as a law-and-order elected official. He would not allow a lynching to occur on his watch if he could avoid it. Recognizing the volatility of the developing situation in Scottsboro, the governor agreed to dispatch the National Guard. By 11:00 P.M., Major Joseph Starnes was on his way from Guntersville, 20 miles away, accompanied by 25 armed Guardsmen under his command. Whatever happened to the Scottsboro defendants, they would not become the victims of mob justice.[7]

Scottsboro was a sleepy little berg of 3,500 people in 1931. Unaccustomed to large crowds and political controversy, the southern hamlet was ill-prepared for the onslaught of press attention and legal wrangling that would soon engulf the town. Daylight brought plenty of both. Two local newspapers regaled readers with salacious details of the gang rape. Reporters expressed no doubt about the victims' accounts. Ruby Bates and Victoria Price had emerged from the freight car "in a terrible condition mentally and physically after their unspeakable experience at the hands of the black brutes." The unspeakable experience would be spoken of frequently in the days ahead, both orally by the townspeople and in writing throughout numerous local, state, and national publications.[8]

If the brutes would not be put to a tree, they must be put on trial. The circuit solicitor, H. G. Bailey, informed the press corps that he intended to reconvene the grand jury, which had adjourned only a week earlier. Owing to the horrific nature of the crime and the need to protect southern womanhood, the chivalrous solicitor boldly announced that he would seek the death penalty. A lesser penalty would amount to a travesty of justice.[9]

For his part, the local judge, Alfred E. Hawkins, grandiloquently told members of the press that Alabama justice would be firm, but fair. The defendants would be afforded defense counsel, presumably appointed by the bench from among the seven members of the Scottsboro Bar Association. When Judge Hawkins approached the pool of local lawyers, however, he found no one willing to step forward and risk his position as a member of the local community. One by one, each Scottsboro attorney found an excuse to refuse the judge's entreaties and recuse himself from consideration.[10]

By process of elimination, Judge Hawkins settled on Milo C. Moody, a man two months shy of his 70th birthday whose salad days, to put it charitably, were long past. He had enjoyed a modest legal career earlier in life, but by 1931 Moody was described as a "doddering, extremely unreliable, senile individual" who simply was not competent to provide adequate representation to criminal defendants in a murder trial, especially defendants as prominent and unpopular as the nine Scottsboro teens. He had enjoyed a reputation as something of an iconoclast, a champion of unpopular ideas, but in 1931 Moody's incentive for taking the case was hardly a principled stance in defense of embattled black suspects. Milo Moody needed the money.[11]

As the Scottsboro episode attracted regional and national attention, prominent black citizens feared that not only would the defendants be subjected to a kangaroo court but also their plight would set back the nascent civil rights movement for decades. Dr. P. A. Stephens, a leading black physician living in Chattanooga, took it upon himself to approach Stephen R. Roddy, a local real estate attorney. Roddy was not known for his legal acumen or his ability to stay sober for lengthy periods of time, but he was one of the few white attorneys of the era willing to represent Negro clients in court. Stephens and his associates scraped together a small retainer—$50.08—and engaged Roddy as defense counsel. The attorney agreed to handle the case for a $120 fee. He was skeptical that the Scottsboro defendants would receive a fair trial under the trying emotional circumstances prevalent in Alabama, but Roddy vowed, "It is my intention to see that the Negroes get a fair trial."[12]

When he arrived in Scottsboro, Stephen Roddy found a chaotic scene. News reporters were already in town, decrying the despicable act and lamenting the "meanest African corruption" known to man. Three National Guard officers commanded 30 enlisted men on duty outside the courthouse in a desperate effort to keep the growing crowd of Alabamians under control. Machine gun nests had been set up to guard the doors of the building. A restless, angry crowd muttered its disapproval when news circulated that the defendants' counsel had arrived. Realizing he might be afforded a hostile reception, the down-on-his-luck attorney had fortified himself with enough liquid refreshment to keep up his courage. According to one witness, Roddy was so inebriated that "he could scarcely walk straight." He was allowed to meet with his clients for only half an hour before the trial began on April 6, a mere 12 days after the assault was alleged to have occurred.[13]

With minimal assistance from Moody, Stephen Roddy fumbled through the opening phases of the trial. To no one's surprise, the defense attorneys requested a change of venue and the judge quickly denied the motion. What was surprising was the prosecution's decision to try the defendants in groups of two and three in lieu of handling the cases together in one trial. With the preliminary matters settled, first up were Clarence Norris and Charley Weems.[14]

The defense attorneys' inexperience was patently obvious. From the stand, Victoria Price spun an elaborate tale of a brutal gang rape perpetrated by vicious miscreants wielding guns and knives. Roddy sought to impeach her character by portraying her as a woman of less-than-stellar character and given to indiscriminate sexual escapades, but Judge Hawkins would have none of it. He was a southern gentleman and could not allow such an attack on southern womanhood to be introduced into evidence. Neither Roddy nor Moody questioned the flimsy medical evidence, arguably the weakest portion of the state's case. The physician who examined Victoria Price and Ruby Bates discovered "no-motile" semen, which indicated that the women had engaged in sexual intercourse but far earlier than the time of the alleged attack. Moreover, the physical examination showed no evidence of bruising and lacerations. If the brutal assault had occurred as Victoria Price testified, presumably she and Ms. Bates would have exhibited physical signs of trauma.[15]

The defense lost whatever marginal advantages it enjoyed the moment Clarence Norris took the stand. Stephen Roddy contended that a rape had never taken place. Aside from the altercation between the white and black hobos riding on the train that day, he believed Victoria Price had fabricated the story about the rape and pressured her weaker companion, Ruby Bates, to go along with the fanciful tale so that the women could escape prosecution for vagrancy. Unfortunately, his client failed to appreciate the virtues of veracity in a court of law. Clarence Norris did not believe that a judge and jury would discount a white woman's testimony about her rape at the hands of a black gang of hobos. His only hope, he believed, was to testify that a rape had occurred, but that he was not involved. It was a calamitous choice. Roddy attempted to repair the damage, but it was impossible. By admitting that a rape had taken place, Norris lent credence to the prosecution's theory of the case. His chances at exoneration had been wildly improbable when he began his testimony, but by the end a conviction was a foregone conclusion.[16]

Even as the all-white jury shuffled off to deliberate, the second trial, with Haywood Patterson tried alone, commenced inside the same courtroom. The case progressed in much the same manner as its predecessor, although Victoria Price had tidied up inconsistencies from her testimony in the earlier trial. Unlike the dress rehearsal, which had been rough around the edges, her matinee performance was close to flawless. Ruby Bates was a poor witness, but once again Roddy was unable to raise questions about the character of the accusers. Their accounts, despite inconsistencies and gaps, were admitted into evidence, essentially uncontested despite defense counsel's objections. A black man's word would never be believed over a white woman's testimony, and social mores prevented detailed questions about a white woman's sexual activities or history.[17]

As Bates left the stand, the jurors from the first trial announced they had reached a unanimous verdict. Not surprisingly, the 12 white men found Norris and Weems guilty and sentenced them to death. The crowd inside and outside the courthouse had been milling about, its bloodlust growing. As soon as they learned of the verdict, the roar of approval was deafening. In the view of most white southerners, justice had been served. During subsequent trials, eight of the nine Scottsboro defendants were convicted and sentenced to die. Twelve-year-old Roy Wright suffered a mistrial when the jury was divided over the appropriate means for punishing a child. Other than this slight deviation, everything else went according to plan. The eight defendants sentenced to death were scheduled for execution in the electric chair on July 10, 1931.[18]

The verdicts were not surprising given the tenor of the times. The issue was not whether the defendants were guilty or innocent of the crime, but whether southern society could tolerate a result that threatened the prevailing mythology about the social position of the races. One local man confessed, "We white people just couldn't afford to let these niggers off because of the effect it would have on other niggers." Alabama congressman George Huddleston, who hailed from Birmingham, reflected the view of many whites when he commented that when he learned that the defendants were "found riding on the same freight car with two white women," he did not need additional evidence to justify a conviction. "That's enough for me!"[19]

The National Association for the Advancement of Colored People (NAACP) had been monitoring the case and considering whether to intervene. The NAACP sometimes offered to represent defendants as a means of protecting Negroes from southern miscarriages of justice, but the organization was cautious in its approach. NAACP lawyers wanted to ensure the defendants were innocent before interceding. It would hamper the cause to discover halfway through a trial that the defendants were guilty as charged. With group leaders debating whether to assist in an appeal, the International Labor Defense

(ILD), the legal arm of the American Community Party, stepped into the void.

The Communist Party was a small but well-organized group in the 1930s. Its leaders were quick to recognize a propaganda opportunity and move in to exploit a situation. Recognizing the potential for gaining adherents within the Negro population, ILD lawyers contacted relatives of the Scottsboro defendants, offering to assist in overturning the verdict. NAACP lawyers finally realized that control of the case might fall under the ILD umbrella and tarnish the cause of black civil rights with a Communist affiliation. They challenged the Communists' intercession. After a bitter internecine feud among the groups, the ILD emerged victorious. It did not hurt their cause that ILD organizers provided monthly checks to the defendants' families and treated them with unflagging courtesy, while the NAACP came across as haughty and condescending. In a letter to NAACP head Walter White, Field Secretary William Pickens denounced the parents of some of the defendants as "the densest and dumbest animals it has yet been my privilege to meet." Such sentiments ensured that NAACP officials would be shunted off to one side.[20]

As outrage over the verdict spread around the world, white Alabamians were puzzled by the reaction. In contrast to years past, they had not allowed a lynch mob to string up the black rapists. If the trial was not quite a model of a restrained, deliberative judicial process, it was preferable to almost any other conceivable outcome in the justice system of the day. Even as ILD lawyers appealed to the state supreme court, the local white citizenry was confident that the verdict would be upheld owing to the fairness and decency of the process.[21]

The Alabama Supreme Court upheld the convictions by a 6–1 vote. Rather than condemn the speedy nature of the trials as overly hasty and prejudicial to the defendants' rights, the justices remarked that the dispatch with which the trial court decided the matters instilled great respect for the law and ensued that the mob would not take matters into its own hands. Similarly, the high court was not overly concerned with the tense atmosphere caused by thousands of angry people encircling the courthouse while the trials occurred. The presence of the National Guard soldiers sufficed in keeping law and order and sending a message to the community that violence would not be tolerated. Moreover, appointment of defense counsel on the morning the trial opened did not constitute a denial of the Sixth Amendment right to effective assistance of counsel. *The Montgomery Advertiser* expressed

The Scottsboro Boys are shown meeting with NAACP representatives in prison in 1936. Pictured from left to right: Ozie Powell, Olen Montgomery, Willie Roberson, Juanita Jackson Mitchell (NAACP), Charley Weems, Clarence Norris, Haywood Patterson, Laura Kellum (NAACP), Andy Wright, Eugene Williams, and Ernest W. Taggart (NAACP). Not pictured: Roy Wright, the youngest defendant. (The National Portrait Gallery, Smithsonian Institution; acquired through the generosity of Elizabeth Ann Hylton)

satisfaction with the appellate decision, observing that the quality of Alabama justice "should satisfy all reasonable persons."[22]

The Scottsboro defendants did not share the *Advertiser*'s assessment of the state supreme court's opinion. Although they were not surprised by the result, the defendants were dismayed to know they might soon face the electric chair. Even some moderate white citizens expressed concern about the mob element lurking outside the courthouse. With so many concerns expressed by critics of the case, ILD lawyers appealed to the U.S. Supreme Court. They based their appeal on three constitutional arguments. First, the constant presence of a mob outside the courthouse violated the Fourteenth Amendment due process clause. In addition, the absence of blacks from the jury pool denied the defendants the equal protection of the law and due process of law. Finally, the defendants were denied effective assistance of counsel. The U.S. Supreme Court granted certiorari and heard oral arguments on October 10, 1932.[23]

On November 7, 1932, the Court handed down its opinion. Justice Sutherland wrote for a majority of seven. After outlining the facts of the case and the nature of Stephen Roddy's legal representation, Sutherland explained why the defendants' right to competent legal counsel under the Fourteenth Amendment's due process clause had been denied. "In the light of the facts outlined in the forepart of this opinion—the ignorance and illiteracy of the defendants, their youth, the circumstances of public hostility, the imprisonment and the close surveillance of the defendants by the military forces, the fact that their friends and families were all in other states and communication with them necessarily difficult, and, above all, that they stood in deadly peril of their lives—we think the failure of the trial court to give them reasonable time and opportunity to secure counsel was a clear denial of due process," he wrote. The law requires a calm, reasoned, deliberative process. According to the Court, "In a capital case, where the defendant is unable to employ counsel and is incapable adequately of making his own defense because of ignorance, feeble mindedness, illiteracy, or the like, it is the duty of the court, whether requested or not, to assign counsel for him as a necessary requisite of due process of law, and that duty is not discharged by an assignment at such a time or under such circumstances as to preclude the giving of effective aid in the preparation and trial of the case."[24]

The Supreme Court granted the defendants a new trial consistent with the opinion in the *Powell* case. The opportunity to stand trial again was a second chance to get it right, and this time the defendants need not depend on unprepared, ill-equipped lawyers. The ILD engaged a prominent defense attorney with a national reputation, Samuel Leibowitz, second only to Clarence Darrow in public estimation as a skilled advocate. He brought to the courtroom a brilliant mind, an unrivaled tenacity, an enviable courtroom prowess, and a driving ambition to win his cases decisively.[25]

Initially, Leibowitz seemed an ideal choice to represent the Scottsboro defendants, as far removed from Stephen Roddy and Milo Moody as one could get. With the benefit of hindsight, however, he was not a desirable defense attorney to handle a case in the Deep South, despite his experience and dedication. He was a foreigner. Although he was not a Communist Party member, Leibowitz's ILD connection, Jewish surname, and "Yankee ways" made him instantly unpopular in the South. Moreover, his aggressive courtroom tactics and his apparent disdain for local customs and mores convinced jurors that the gruff outsider was attacking their way of life. The retrial became less about the guilt or innocence of the defendants than about Alabama's defense of southern traditions. The local populace viewed defense counsel as a Yankee Jew with Communist affiliations arguing on behalf of black rapists who would literally and figuratively despoil southern womanhood if freed to roam the countryside unfettered by law or tradition.[26]

The retrial of the first defendant, Haywood Patterson, commenced at the end of March 1933. Although Leibowitz exposed numerous inconsistencies in eyewitness testimony offered by the prosecution—and one alleged victim, Ruby Bates, even recanted her earlier testimony—the weight of history was inescapable. White Alabama jurors simply could not accept the word of a black man over the testimony of a white woman. The jury quickly convicted Patterson of murder and sentenced him to death. Legal experts in the North were stunned that

Samuel S. Leibowitz (center), lead attorney for the Scottsboro defendants, is pictured here in 1933 flanked by bodyguards L. M. Ouzts (left) and W. L. Snow (right). (Library of Congress)

a man could be convicted on the basis of such flimsy evidence. After he returned to New York, an embittered Leibowitz remarked, "If you ever saw those creatures, those bigots whose mouths are slits in their faces, whose eyes popped out at you like frogs, whose chins dripped tobacco juice, bewhiskered and filthy, you would not ask how they could do it." Southerners who read accounts of this interloper's derogatory remarks believed the foreign Leibowitz had exposed his true colors as an enemy of the South who would like nothing better than to denigrate her cherished traditions.[27]

If a hero was to be found in the whole sordid affair, it came in the person of Judge James Edwin Horton Jr., a genuine southern gentleman celebrated, in the words of his local newspaper, *The Limestone Democrat*, for his "unusually equable nature, great legal ability and fairness." Tapped to preside after venue was changed to the town of Decatur, he reluctantly officiated over Patterson's proceedings. It was a familiar terrain for anyone conversant with the original case, but Horton had not presided over the 1931 trials. Later confessing he believed at the outset the defendants probably were guilty, the judge gradually came to see the inconsistencies in Victoria Price's testimony, gaps in the evidence, and the improbability of a gang rape. The jury verdict convicting the defendant was hardly surprising, but the judge's decision afterward was a shocking development.[28]

Addressing a packed courtroom on June 22, 1933, Horton showed genuine moral courage or arrogant judicial activism run amok, depending on one's perspective, when he set aside the verdict and ordered a new trial. Believing the complainant had perjured herself, the judge remarked, "How can the physical condition of Price be reconciled with the gang rape she claimed to have suffered? Why did the jagged chert not bruise her back? Why did the pistol lick on her head not leave a visible wound? Why was no semen found in her pubic hair? Why was the spermatozoa in her vagina non-motile? Why was her respiration and pulse normal less than two hours after the rapes? Why was she not hysterical or crying?" In the most sympathetic interpretation, the evidence left these crucial questions unanswered. The more likely explanation, Judge Horton explained, was that the defendants had been falsely accused.

> History, sacred and profane, and the common experience of mankind teach us that women of the character shown in this case are prone for selfish reasons to make false accusations both of rape and of insult upon the slightest provocation for ulterior purposes.

> These women are shown, by the great weight of the evidence, on this very day before leaving Chattanooga, to have falsely accused two Negroes of insulting them, and of almost precipitating a fight between one of the white boys they were in company with and these two Negroes. This tendency on the part of the women shows that they are predisposed to make false accusations upon any occasion whereby their selfish ends may be gained.

Had he left his explanation at that point, Judge Horton doubtless would have been upbraided for his effrontery and castigated by many an Alabamian, but he might have continued his career as an elected official. Yet he was not quite finished.

> The Court will not pursue the evidence any further. As heretofore stated, the law declares that a defendant should not be convicted without corroboration where the testimony of the prosecutrix bears on its face indications of improbability or unreliability and particularly when it is contradicted by other evidence. The testimony of the prosecutrix in this case is not only uncorroborated, but it also bears on its face indications of improbability and is contradicted by other evidence, and in addition thereto the evidence greatly preponderates in favor of the defendant. It therefore becomes the duty of the Court under the law to grant the motion made in this case.

Accordingly, the judge had no choice but to countermand the jury's verdict, even though he probably would not be reelected as a result. "It is therefore ordered and adjudged by the Court that the motion be granted; that the verdict of the jury in this case and the judgment of the Court sentencing this defendant to death be set aside and that a new trial is hereby ordered." The judge also delayed the retrials of the other defendants.[29]

If supporters of the Scottsboro defendants thought the state might decline to retry the cases after receiving such a stinging judicial rebuke, they were sadly mistaken. The politically ambitious state attorney general, Thomas G. Knight Jr., hoped to make a name by prosecuting the case. He entertained notions of entering the governor's mansion. The judge's decision interfered with the script and infuriated the prosecutor to no end. He immediately announced his decision to hold new trials. Behind the scenes, Knight recognized the desperate need to replace Judge Horton with someone less inclined to be swayed by the evidence. As the old saying goes, a good lawyer knows the law and a great lawyer knows the judge.[30]

William Washington Callahan, a racist septuagenarian with no tolerance for black men daring to exercise the constitutional rights enjoyed by whites, fit the bill nicely. After Knight pulled strings with the Alabama Supreme Court and had Callahan installed as the judge for the next round of proceedings, the prosecution could rest easily. Callahan was so prejudiced against the defendants it was as if two prosecution teams were handling the case. Southern-style justice had nothing to fear from this new man with old ideas.[31]

When the retrials began in November 1933, the change was striking. Judge Horton had permitted black citizens to sit in on the proceedings, but no persons of color could be found inside the courtroom under a Callahan regime. A heavily armed National Guard contingent was absent as well, suggesting that the safety and security of the defendants and their ILD attorneys were not a high priority. The judge rejected a motion for change of venue and refused to allow Samuel Leibowitz to delve into Victoria Price's sexual history when he questioned her about her activities the night before the alleged rape. Not surprisingly, Haywood Patterson and Clarence Norris were convicted and once again sentenced to death.[32]

Appeals to the Alabama Supreme Court followed. After the state court upheld the convictions, the defendants appealed to the U.S. Supreme Court. In *Norris v. Alabama* and its companion case, *Patterson v. Alabama*, the high court determined that deliberate exclusion of black jurors from a black defendant's jury constituted a denial of equal protection of the laws pursuant to the Fourteenth Amendment. The most dramatic moment of the oral argument on February 15, 1935, occurred when Samuel Leibowitz asserted that someone had hastily added black voters' names to the rolls to rebut a charge that Negroes were excluded from jury service. In an impassioned, dramatic flourish, Leibowitz informed the justices that the chicanery was "not only against the defendants but against this very court itself." Astonished at the claim, Chief Justice Charles Evans Hughes challenged Leibowitz to prove the allegation. Having expected the issue to arise, Leibowitz was equipped with the evidence he needed. He promptly produced the Alabama jury rolls and a magnifying glass. The justices each took a turn hunching over the list and peering at the forged names. Whereas most of the names were arranged neatly in alphabetical order, the names of the eligible Negro voters were appended at the end of the list in the same color of ink, indicating they had been scribbled there as a deliberate act of fraud. One by one, the justices uttered indignant remarks. Leibowitz subsequently learned that the U.S. Supreme Court had never before allowed such an exhibit to be placed before the bench during an oral argument session.[33]

Six weeks later, the Court issued its opinion in *Norris v. Alabama.* Writing for the majority, the chief justice explained, "Exclusion of all negroes from a grand jury by which a negro is indicted, or from the petit jury by which he is tried for the offense, resulting from systematic and arbitrary exclusion of negroes from the jury lists solely because of their race or color, is a denial of the equal protection of the laws guaranteed to him by the Fourteenth Amendment." In reversing the defendants' convictions, the Court also made it conceptually less difficult to demonstrate racial discrimination in the makeup of jury pools. Following dicta from *Neal v. Delaware*, an old 1881 case, the Court agreed to infer intentional discrimination when blacks were conspicuously absent from jury service. It was a significant step in expanding the Supreme Court's willingness to scrutinize state court proceedings to ensure fundamental fairness in criminal proceedings.[34]

A reversal of the convictions did not free the defendants. It only required state criminal courts to conform to minimal due process standards moving forward. Despite the legal wrangling and reversals, Alabama officials remained steadfast in their commitment to retrying the defendants. On November 13, 1935, a grand jury returned a new indictment against the nine suspects. Appearing far from chastened, a feisty Judge Callahan set the new trial date for January 20, 1936.[35]

Proud, indefatigable, long-suffering defense counsel Samuel Leibowitz finally had recognized that his Yankee ways, Jewish surname, and aggressive tactics in a southern courtroom that regarded such tactics as an affront to regional mores were harming his clients' cases. He reluctantly stepped aside as Haywood Patterson's lead attorney in favor of local counsel, Clarence Watts from Huntsville. Although the change would marginally improve Patterson's chances in an Alabama courtroom, no one could forget that it was still a black man facing a legal system heavily biased against him and predisposed to judge him guilty with or without the inconvenience of a jury trial. Lest anyone should doubt the prejudices of southern justice, Judge Callahan reminded them of the central theme that blacks were considered guilty until a jury ratified the assumption. The judge was up to his usual shenanigans, clearly evincing disdain for the defendant and his attorneys while constantly intervening to utter comments sympathetic to the prosecution. He repeated a comment he had made during the previous trial that a strong legal presumption existed that a white woman, no matter how lowly she appeared, would never yield voluntarily to intercourse with a Negro. The proceedings followed the predictable track except that after he was convicted, Patterson no longer faced the death penalty. The jury sentenced him to serve 75 years in prison. It was as close to justice and mercy as an Alabama jury could come during the 1930s.[36]

Everyone was exhausted and sick of the cases, but somehow they dragged on for years. Clarence Norris was sentenced to death a third time following his inevitable conviction. Andy Wright and Charley Weems, convicted once again, drew sentences of 99 years and 75 years, respectively. Yet a major change occurred on July 25, 1937, when the prosecution concluded that insufficient evidence existed to convict the nearly blind Olen Montgomery. Willie Roberson, seriously ill with venereal disease at the time of the alleged attack, similarly won a reprieve from further prosecution. Roy Wright and Eugene Williams were juveniles in 1931 and, therefore, escaped further judicial scrutiny. The decision to release four of the nine defendants represented a significant victory for the defense, but it was hardly the exoneration sought by innocent men.[37]

The newly freed Scottsboro defendants traveled North and soon found themselves engulfed by a frenzy of media coverage. They were hailed as heroes and in high demand for public events. Yet the interest did not last. The world moves quickly and the press of intervening events and crises ensures that a major story soon becomes yesterday's news. The four freed Scottsboro Boys were shunted to one side and mostly forgotten by history.[38]

In the meantime, the problem of what to do about the remaining defendants still locked away in prison haunted Leibowitz and his defense team. Supporters were exhausted by the protracted legal maneuvering. Now that at least some of the defendants had tasted freedom, the public and media attention that had been integral in shedding light on the inequities of the Alabama legal process might be absent. Leibowitz was convinced he could keep the five young men from being executed, but languishing in an Alabama prison for decades was only a marginally preferable outcome.

In June 1938, the Alabama Supreme Court again heard Clarence Norris's appeal and again affirmed his conviction. The court also upheld convictions for Andy Wright and Charley Weems. Alabama governor Bibb Graves commuted Norris's sentence to life in prison, thereby ensuring that none of the defendants would be killed in the state's electric chair. Scottsboro defenders had hoped the governor could be persuaded to pardon the men, but he refused to do so.[39]

After the media frenzy died down and their legal appeals had been exhausted—the U.S. Supreme Court declined to review Haywood Patterson's 75-year prison sentence—the probable result seemed to be that wrongly convicted men would spend the rest of their natural lives in prison. As the years passed, however, one by one the defendants left their cells. The state quietly paroled Charley Weems on November 17, 1943. Ozie Powell won his release in 1946, but his future was anything but bright. While he was being transferred from one prison to another on January 24, 1936, a guard threatened the defendants. Powell slashed the guard's throat before another officer shot the prisoner in the face. Although Powell survived, he suffered permanent brain damage. Clarence Norris jumped parole in 1946 and headed north. In 1976, Governor George Wallace pardoned him. Three years later, Norris published his autobiography, *The Last of the Scottsboro Boys.* He died on January 23, 1989. Haywood Patterson escaped from prison in 1948. Two years later, he published his book about the episode, *The Scottsboro Boy.* When Alabama authorities discovered he was hiding in Michigan, they asked the governor there to extradite the escaped felon, but the governor declined to do so. Patterson later stabbed a man in a bar fight and was sent to prison once again. He died of cancer behind bars in 1952 after having served a year of his new sentence. Andy Wright was the last of the defendants to leave prison. He had been paroled previously, but he was forced back into custody after he violated the terms of parole. He was finally released in 1950 and moved to New York.[40]

In each of the Scottsboro cases, the lesson was that the law must be applied to defendants equally and without preconceived biases. The notion of equity—that is, treating like cases alike—absolutely requires such even-handed administration if the Constitution is to be upheld. To ensure that equity prevails, the U.S. Supreme Court interpreted the Sixth Amendment's assistance of counsel clause to mean that indigent criminal defendants have a right to appointed counsel in certain capital cases, and the right is incorporated by the Fourteenth Amendment. The U.S. Supreme Court also deemed the right to be judged by a jury of one's peers as a crucial component of a fair trial. To exclude blacks from jury service when a black defendant stood before the bar was to subvert the ends of justice and undermine constitutional criminal procedure.

NOTES

1. The most authoritative and accessible source on the case remains Dan T. Carter, *Scottsboro: A Tragedy of the American South*, Revised Edition (Baton Rouge: Louisiana State University Press, 2007). Roddy was recruited to represent the defendants although he asked not to be listed as counsel of record.

2. Much has been written on the ill effects of the Great Depression, especially among Negro workers. See, for example, Francis Butler Simkins and Charles Pierce Roland, *A History of the South*, 4th ed. (New York: Knopf, 1972), 482, 519–20.

3. Carter, *Scottsboro*, 4; Michael J. Klarman, "Scottsboro," *Marquette Law Review* 93, 2 (Winter 2009): 380.

4. *Powell v. Alabama*, 287 U.S. 45, 51 (1932). See also Carter, *Scottsboro*, 4–8; Mark Curriden, "The Saga of the Scottsboro Boys Begins—March 25, 1931," *ABA Journal* 99, 3 (March 2013): 72; James Goodman, *Stories of Scottsboro* (New York: Doubleday, 1995), 6; Klarman, "Scottsboro," 380; James A. Miller, *Remembering Scottsboro: The Legacy of an Infamous Trial* (Princeton, N.J.: Princeton University Press, 2009), 42.

5. Klarman, "Scottsboro," 381; Miller, *Remembering Scottsboro*, 10; James A. Miller, Susan D. Pennybacker, and Eve Rosenhaft, "Mother Ada Wright and the International Campaign to Free the Scottsboro Boys, 1931–1934," *The American Historical Review* 106, 2 (April 2001): 387–88.

6. Carter, *Scottsboro*, 7.

7. Ibid., 9; Goodman, *Stories of Scottsboro*, 17; Klarman, "Scottsboro," 381.

8. Carter, *Scottsboro*, 6–7, 11–13; Shanna Gildersleeve, "The Struggle for Justice: How the Media Convicted and Freed the 'Scottsboro Boys,' 1931–1937," *The Atlanta Review of Journalism History* 8, 1 (September 2009): 90–91.

9. Carter, *Scottsboro*, 16–17.

10. Ibid., 17–18; Gildersleeve, "The Struggle for Justice," 91–92; Goodman, *Stories of Scottsboro*, 13; Klarman, "Scottsboro," 381.

11. Carter, *Scottsboro*, 18; Goodman, *Stories of Scottsboro*, 41; Klarman, "Scottsboro," 383; Miller, *Remembering Scottsboro*, 42; Miller, Pennybacker, and Rosenhaft, "Mother Ada Wright and the International Campaign to Free the Scottsboro Boys," 388.

12. 287 U.S. 45, 52–53. See also Carter, *Scottsboro*, 19–20; Curriden, "The Saga of the Scottsboro Boys Begins," 72; Goodman, *Stories of Scottsboro*, 41; Klarman, "Scottsboro," 383; Miller, *Remembering Scottsboro*, 42; Miller, Pennybacker, and Rosenhaft, "Mother Ada Wright and the International Campaign to Free the Scottsboro Boys," 388; Clarence Norris and Sybil D. Washington, *The Last of the Scottsboro Boys* (New York: Putnam, 1979), 132.

13. 287 U.S. 45, 53–58. See also Carter, *Scottsboro*, 22–28; Gildersleeve, "The Struggle for Justice," 91–92; Klarman, "Scottsboro," 383.

14. Carter, *Scottsboro*, 23–24; Miller, *Remembering Scottsboro*, 10.

15. Carter, *Scottsboro*, 25–27; Gildersleeve, "The Struggle for Justice," 92; Klarman, "Scottsboro," 383–84.

16. Carter, *Scottsboro*, 32–34; Klarman, "Scottsboro," 384.

17. Carter, *Scottsboro*, 35–43; Gildersleeve, "The Struggle for Justice," 92.

18. 287 U.S. 45, 50. See also Gildersleeve, "The Struggle for Justice," 93; Klarman, "Scottsboro," 384–85.

19. Carter, *Scottsboro*, 70.

20. Ibid., 51–103; Gildersleeve, "The Struggle for Justice," 95–99; Goodman, *Stories of Scottsboro*, 101; Klarman, "Scottsboro," 385–90; Miller, *Remembering Scottsboro*, 10; Miller, Pennybacker, and Rosenhaft, "Mother Ada Wright and the International Campaign to Free the Scottsboro Boys," 390–92; Norris and Washington, *The Last of the Scottsboro Boys*, 58–59.

21. Debra Baker, "Trials of the Century," *ABA Journal* 85, 1 (January 1999): 44–45; Curriden, "The Saga of the Scottsboro Boys Begins," 72; "Scottsboro Hero," *Time* 30, 5 (August 2, 1937): 45–47.

22. 287 U.S. 45, 50. See also Carter, *Scottsboro*, 51–103; Gildersleeve, "The Struggle for Justice," 99–100; Klarman, "Scottsboro," 390–93. The *Montgomery Advertiser* quote appears on page 392 of Klarman.

23. 287 U.S. 45, 50–51. See also Klarman, "Scottsboro," 393–98.

24. 287 U.S. 45, 71.

25. Carter, *Scottsboro*, 181–83; Gildersleeve, "The Struggle for Justice," 100; Klarman, "Scottsboro," 398–400.

26. Carter, *Scottsboro*, 210, 241–42; Klarman, "Scottsboro," 400–02.

27. Leibovitz is quoted in Klarman, "Scottsboro," 402. See also Carter, *Scottsboro*, 238–42.

28. Carter, *Scottsboro*, 184, 193–239; Gildersleeve, "The Struggle for Justice," 100–101; Klarman, "Scottsboro," 399; Norris and Washington, *The Last of the Scottsboro Boys*, 64.

29. Horton is quoted in Carter, *Scottsboro*, 454–56. See also Carter, *Scottsboro*, 262–70; Gildersleeve, "The Struggle for Justice," 102; Klarman, "Scottsboro," 403–4.

30. Carter, *Scottsboro*, 270–73; Klarman, "Scottsboro," 403–404.

31. Carter, *Scottsboro*, 274–76; Goodman, *Stories of Scottsboro*, 212, 217; Gildersleeve, "The Struggle for Justice," 102; Klarman, "Scottsboro," 404.

32. Gildersleeve, "The Struggle for Justice," 103; Klarman, "Scottsboro," 405–06.

33. *Patterson v. Alabama*, 294 U.S. 600 (1935). See also Carter, *Scottsboro*, 319, 324; Klarman, "Scottsboro," 407.

34. *Norris v. Alabama*, 294 U.S. 587, 589 (1935). See also Baker, "Trials of the Century," 45; Carter, *Scottsboro*, 322–24; Curriden, "The Saga of the Scottsboro Boys Begins," 72; Gildersleeve, "The Struggle for Justice," 103; Klarman, "Scottsboro," 407–08; *Neal v. Delaware*, 103 U.S. 370, 397 (1881); Simkins and Roland, *A History of the South*, 505.

35. Carter, *Scottsboro*, 338–41; Gildersleeve, "The Struggle for Justice," 103.

36. Carter, *Scottsboro*, 342–45; Gildersleeve, "The Struggle for Justice," 103; Goodman, *Stories of Scottsboro*, 256, 303; "Scottsboro Hero," *Time* 30, 5 (August 2, 1937): 45–47.

37. Curriden, "The Saga of the Scottsboro Boys Begins," 72; "Scottsboro Hero," *Time* 30, 5 (August 2, 1937): 45–47.

38. Carter, *Scottsboro*, 375–77, 384–86; Gildersleeve, "The Struggle for Justice," 103–5.

39. Carter, *Scottsboro*, 366–67, 389–96.

40. Ibid., 411–15; Miller, *Remembering Scottsboro*, 4; Norris and Washington, *The Last of the Scottsboro Boys*, 243, 253.

CHAPTER 5

Brown v. Mississippi (1936) and Fundamental Fairness

Kemper County, Mississippi, lies 150 miles southwest of Scottsboro, Alabama, in an area virtually forgotten by modern society. Tiny DeKalb serves as the county seat. The nearest big town is Meridian, 30 miles south in Lauderdale County. In 1930, the population was 888 souls. It hardly seemed to be the time and place for examining fundamental constitutional principles, yet Kemper was the scene of a court case eerily reminiscent of the better-known Scottsboro cases.

Well into the 20th century, the county was situated in a rural area where cotton farming predominated. If cotton was king, the citizens of Kemper County were its loyal subjects. Almost everyone farmed, for they knew no other source of livelihood—not that cotton farming provided much of a livelihood. For as long as anyone could remember, citizens there had been poor, accustomed, as so many southerners were, to enduring a hardscrabble life where a victorious day meant that a fellow laid down to bed on a full stomach.

For blacks, life had always been immeasurably worse than it was for whites. A white man could imagine a day when he might pull himself up by his bootstraps and own property, vote, run for elective office, or escape to more hospitable environs. A black man was under no such illusions. Blacks laboring in rural Mississippi were only half a notch above beasts of burden. They were expected to toil at the menial, back-breaking jobs for meager wages under humiliating conditions with no relief in sight.

By the 1930s, Kemper had acquired a reputation, richly deserved, as a place where the social position of the races was firmly established and unassailable. Negroes knew their place, reminded of their lowly station by lynchings on rare occasions when black denizens crossed the color line and engaged in real or imagined transgressions. On September 10, 1930, two local blacks, "Pig" Lockett and Holly White, having sinned against the established order, were taken to a tree allegedly for robbing and menacing a white couple. Whether the defendants were guilty mattered less than the message the hangings sent throughout the community: Uppity Negroes would not be tolerated. They would be kept in line one way or another. A colored fellow who failed to know his place had no future in Kemper County. He would soon be taught a lesson on pain of death.[1]

It was an all-too-familiar scene in the southern United States during the Jim Crow era, that 80-year period in American history following the end of Reconstruction when blacks were treated as second-class citizens and expected not to rage against the dying of the light. Despite promises of equality made at the close of the Civil War, people of color were denied full citizenship across the nation. Nowhere was their plight more pronounced than south of the Mason-Dixon Line.

The origins of the term *Jim Crow* were not altogether clear, but apparently it stretched back to a popular minstrel song dating from the late 1820s. A singer-comedian named Thomas Dartmouth Rice, an itinerant entertainer who answered to "T.D." or "Daddy" Rice, performed a song called "Jump Jim Crow" (or "Jumpin' Jim Crow," in some accounts) wearing blackface beginning around 1828. The song appeared in sheet music a few years later and included these lyrics:

Come listen all you galls and boys—
I'm going to sing a little song.
My name is Jim Crow.
Weel about and turn about and do jis so.
Eb'ry time I weel about, I jump Jim Crow.

"Jump Jim Crow" was inspired by the story of a crippled African, Jim Cuff or Jim Crow, who reputedly lived in Cincinnati. Historians still dispute whether the crippled African was a real figure or a creature of a warped white imagination. In any case, "Daddy" Rice enjoyed considerable success performing his minstrel show for white audiences that howled with laughter at the shenanigans of "Daddy Jim Crow," a bumbling Negro simpleton who floundered about through one self-created mishap after another, oblivious to the depths of his stupidity. Rice was so successful in lampooning Negroes as slack-jawed cretins through his special brand of buffoonery that he spawned a legion of imitators.

By the 1830s, numerous minstrel shows toured the nation, entertaining whites with exaggerated stories constructed around the absurd antics of gullible, moronic Negro caricatures. Incapable of self-mastery or control, these inferior beings could be counted on to create all sorts of mischief as the result of foolish, impulsive, irrational, costly mistakes if left unattended by their white masters. Therein lay the source of mirth for the minstrel performer: Negroes invariably made different, presumably less-intelligent, choices than whites when it came to living and existing in the world. By inserting a simple creature into a complex situation, the performer highlighted the distinction between his white audience and the "other." Here was the standard white view of Negroes: they were simple creatures—prone to childish behavior at best and natural thieves, sexual deviants, or violent miscreants at worst. The degrading vignettes perpetuated cruel, offensive racial stereotypes that lingered for generations. Whether Rice and his competitors reflected social mores or influenced them remains a matter of conjecture and debate, although in all likelihood their performances were both the cause and effect of white disdain for black folk and their culture.[2]

The stereotypes reflected one enduring feature of 19th-century postbellum America, namely, that Negroes were not welcomed in the land of their birth. In the aftermath of emancipation, white mainstream citizens were determined not to mingle with blacks, and the law would protect them from undesired social intercourse. Beginning in the 1880s, not long after the end of Reconstruction following the Civil War, southern state legislatures enacted a series of segregation statutes to deny blacks their constitutional rights by ensuring they would be shunted off into a cultural, social, and legal cul-de-sac. Dubbed "Jim Crow" laws, these statutes, supported by numerous local, state, and federal court cases, were prevalent in the waning days of the century. Northern whites were hardly more welcoming than their southern counterparts, but the Great Migration into northern cities had not yet occurred. White Yankees could afford to be self-righteous and haughty in their racial attitudes, bemoaning the backwardness of southerners who would not provide an equal chance to their darker-hued brethren even while northerners walled themselves off from direct contact with the American Negro. It was a convenient ruse that would not survive the latter half of the 20th century.[3]

The term "Jim Crow" originated from a minstrel show popular with white audiences in the 1820s and 1830s. This infamous drawing is an illustration of "Jump Jim Crow." (Library of Congress)

In the private sector, businessmen heralding laissez-faire economic policies at the expense of radical social legislation co-opted the national Republican Party. The Party of Lincoln evolved into the Party of Commerce. Conventional wisdom at century's end dictated that Reconstruction had solved racial problems with ratification of the Thirteenth, Fourteenth, and Fifteenth amendments to the U.S. Constitution. When southern state governments were redeemed during the 1870s, racial issues no longer dominated the national political agenda. Disenfranchised Negroes were left to their own devices.[4]

A strong black middle class arose during the late 19th and early 20th centuries in northern enclaves such as Harlem, Chicago, and Detroit, but in many places, especially rural communities in the

Deep South, social relations remained unchanged from ages past. Every resident of Kemper County, Mississippi, understood that a color line existed and dire consequences would result when someone, especially a Negro, crossed that line. Woe to an uppity Negro who forgot his place. He might be hauled into a courtroom on a trumped up charge, but more likely than not, he was destined for another fate. Judge Lynch's court was not weighed down by procedure or other legal niceties. When a black person was accused of a transgression against a white citizen of the community, local citizens took matters into their own hands. Eschewing rules of evidence and ignoring any semblance of due process of law, vigilantes escorted the offender to the nearest tree of suitable size and strength and put the matter to rest without delay. From time to time, lynchings became a festive occasion—even better than attending the county fair—where local white families would gather to observe southern justice while enjoying a delicious picnic lunch and the conviviality of neighbors.[5]

If any doubt existed about the southern Negro's social position in Kemper County, Mississippi, the events that began on Friday, March 30, 1934, vividly illustrated the point. The community's orderly façade crumbled on that date after someone murdered Raymond Stewart, a prominent 60-year-old white planter in the Giles community. One or more assailants had taken an axe to the gentleman, inflicting grievous wounds before leaving him for dead. He was still alive when he was found, but he expired soon thereafter. A local newspaper breathlessly reported that "Mr. Stewart's head was beaten almost to a pulp."[6]

Investigators determined that robbery apparently was the motive. Someone had attempted to burn Stewart's house down as well. Anxious to solve the heinous crime, Sheriff J. D. Adcock brought in his faithful bloodhounds to track the dastardly culprits. Unfortunately, the trail had grown cold and the dogs lost the scent. With no physical evidence and nothing suggesting the identity of the perpetrators, law enforcement officials were at a dead end until they conveniently realized that Ed Brown, a 30-year-old Negro tenant, lived on Stewart's plantation, not far from the scene of the crime.[7]

When the sheriff and his men seized on a local Negro as the likely criminal, they quickly stumbled onto two additional Negro suspects, Arthur Ellington and Henry Shields. Ellington had drawn attention to himself when he had heard about the killings and turned up at Stewart's house to pay his respects. With Brown, Ellington, and Shields in their sights, the authorities needed to look no further. Regardless of whether they had identified the assailants, they had found three Negroes to pay for the crime. That might not be a perfect resolution to the case, but it was good enough.[8]

The officers started by visiting Ellington's home on Friday evening. Finding him there, they coerced him into accompanying them to the scene of the murder, a cottonseed storage room attached to Raymond Stewart's house. Once they arrived, a group of approximately 20 white men lying in wait surrounded the suspect and accused him of committing the crime. Ellington repeatedly denied his involvement, but everyone knew that Negroes lie. The men laid their hands on him, dragged him to a tree, attached a rope, and repeatedly lifted him up and lowered him to the ground, insisting that he confess. Despite his terror at his predicament, Ellington vehemently protested his innocence. The mob eventually tied him to a tree and whipped him incessantly. Ellington still refused to acknowledge guilt. Unable to secure a confession, the throng released the prisoner and allowed him to return home. By all accounts, a local law enforcement officer, Deputy Dial, was at the scene and wholeheartedly participated in the abuse.[9]

A day or two after the initial "interrogation," the deputy returned to Ellington's house accompanied by another police officer. They arrested the suspect and transported him to the jail. Along the way, the officers pursued a meandering course that carried them into the state of Alabama. Once outside the Mississippi borders, they abandoned all pretense of reasonableness. The deputy stopped the car and whipped Ellington again, declaring that the assault would continue until the suspect confessed. One way or the other, this aggravating Negro would own up to the crime. Unable to withstand the continued beating, Ellington eventually agreed to whatever terms the deputy imposed. "Tell me what you want me to say and I will say it," he exclaimed.[10]

Satisfied with the results of their thorough investigation, law enforcement officials rounded up Ed Brown and Henry Shields for questioning using the same proven interrogation techniques. On Sunday evening, April 1, 1934, the suspects found themselves in the jail surrounded by a group of white men, including the deputy and the jailer, who ordered them to strip off their clothes. After Brown and Shields complied, their tormentors forced the men to lie over chairs and submit to a whipping with buckled leather straps. As the U.S. Supreme Court later summarized the affairs, "The transcript reads more like pages torn from some medieval account than a record made within the confines of a modern civilization which aspires to an enlightened constitutional government." The deputy in charge informed the suspects "the whipping would be continued unless and until they confessed, and not only confessed, but confessed in every matter of detail as demanded by those present." The choice between torture and confession was not choice at all, and was calculated to produce but one result. As the Court later noted, "In this manner the defendants confessed the crime, and as the whippings progressed and were repeated, they changed or adjusted their confession in all particulars of detail so as to conform to the demands of their torturers." When the confessions were in hand, the beatings stopped, although officers warned the defendants the assaults would be repeated if the men subsequently recanted or changed their stories in any material degree.[11]

On Monday morning, April 2, two sheriffs—one from the county where the crime occurred and another from the county where the jail was located—arrived in the company of eight other men "to hear the free and voluntary confession of these miserable and abject defendants." The sheriff from the county where the crime occurred later acknowledged that he heard whippings before the defendants confessed, but he did not witness the episode. He saw one defendant limping, however, and heard the man explain that he had been lashed so severely he could not sit. Clear evidence of a rope burn was evident on another defendant's neck, visible to anyone who chose to look. Despite these signs, as the Supreme Court later observed, "The solemn farce of hearing the free and voluntary confessions was gone through with, and these two sheriffs and one other person then present were the three witnesses used in court to establish the so-called confessions, which were received by the court and admitted in evidence over the objections of the defendants."[12]

Although the three men were afforded defense counsel, their convictions were a foregone conclusion in light of their race and the existence of the defendants' confessions. They pleaded not guilty, were tried and convicted, and sentenced to death. John C. Stennis, the district attorney, later enjoyed a storied career as a U.S. senator from Mississippi known for his spirited defense of state rights and segregation. Stennis faced four defense attorneys, but he was unconcerned. He enjoyed the advantages that accrue to a prosecutor who need not wrestle with the concept of reasonable doubt. Three black men on trial for the murder of a white man in Mississippi of the 1930s stood virtually no chance of an acquittal. Even if the jurors had been unbiased, three of the four defense attorneys admitted they were convinced

Black citizens were well aware of the dangers of the lash, a practice extending back to hundreds of years of American history. (Library of Congress)

of their client's guilt. The fourth, John A. Clark, was not sure his client was guilty, but he was influenced by the mob mentality surrounding the affair. Clark realized he must not present a vigorous defense if he hoped to practice law in Mississippi after the case concluded. He later admitted he "was simply going through the motions of a trial." The other defense counsel apparently agreed with Clark's assessment since no one on the team even bothered to file perfunctory motions for separate trials, a change of venue, or a special venire from which to select unbiased jurors.[13]

The entire matter was resolved with lightning speed. The confessions were obtained on April 2, the court ordered the grand jury to convene on April 3, the grand jury returned an indictment on April 4, the trial began on April 5, and the defendants were convicted on April 6. A dispassionate observer would question the fairness of a patently shoddy stab at due process of law, but the local newspaper, *The Meridian Star*, was of a different opinion. By hastening to try and convict the offending Negroes, quick-thinking law enforcement personnel had forestalled extrajudicial actions stemming from a community "mobocracy." Judge Lynch need not step in because the courts had done their job in delivering a timely guilty verdict. "Group action is unneeded when courts are 'on the job,'" an editorial opined. "A few more examples of swift and certain retribution—and 'rabble' illegality will disappear throughout the South."[14]

The brazenness of the law enforcement officers was astonishing. When questioned about the method used to obtain the confessions, the deputy sheriff unabashedly admitted the defendants had been tortured. Asked if he had whipped the defendant Ellington, the deputy said that he had but "not too much for a Negro; not as much as I would have done if it were left to me." Despite this obvious travesty, an all-white jury did not hesitate to convict the defendants and sentence them to die, citing the confessions as the crucial piece of evidence. The Mississippi Supreme Court, not surprisingly, affirmed the convictions.[15]

On certiorari, the U.S. Supreme Court overruled the Mississippi courts, holding that a defendant's involuntary confession extracted by police violence cannot be entered as evidence and violates the due process clause of the Fourteenth Amendment. Writing for a unanimous court, Chief Justice Charles Evan Hughes could barely contain his incredulity as he reviewed the facts. "The State is free to regulate the procedure of its courts in accordance with its own conceptions of policy unless, in so doing, it 'offends some principle of justice so rooted in the traditions and conscience of our people as to be ranked as fundamental,'" the chief justice remarked, careful not to usurp state authority within the U.S. system of federalism. "But the freedom of the State in establishing its policy is the freedom of constitutional government, and is limited by the requirement of due process of law. Because a State may dispense with a jury trial, it does not follow that it may substitute trial by ordeal. The rack and torture chamber may not be substituted for the witness stand. The State may not permit an accused to be hurried to conviction under mob domination—where the whole proceeding is but a mask—without supplying corrective process."[16]

After reversing the convictions, the Court ordered a new trial. At this point, however, Brown, Shields, and Ellington faced the facts that every Negro understood in the Jim Crow South. Regardless of the constitutional niceties articulated by the U.S. Supreme Court, these men lived in Mississippi. They would not be acquitted in a state court on criminal charges filed by whites. On remand, the defendants pleaded nolo contendere to manslaughter instead of risking another jury verdict.[17]

Brown v. Mississippi came to stand for the proposition that due process of law requires fundamental fairness. It was not the first case where the high court decided that a mob-dominated trial was tantamount to a denial of due process of law—as early as 1923 the Court had ruled on the issue in *Moore v. Dempsey*—but it was among the first decisions holding that a court of law must ensure the circumstances surrounding the trial afford a criminal defendant a reasonable opportunity to be heard absent coercion.[18] Until the selective incorporation doctrine replaced the fundamental fairness doctrine, the latter required several factors for a criminal case to be deemed "fundamentally fair." Defendants had to be informed of the charges against them and a hearing based on the facts of the case had to be held before punishment could be administered. These factors remain important components of the American criminal justice system to this day.[19]

NOTES

1. Richard C. Cortner, *A "Scottsboro" Case in Mississippi: The Supreme Court and Brown v. Mississippi* (Jackson: University of Mississippi Press, 1986), 4–5.

2. Eric Foner, *Forever Free: The Story of Emancipation and Reconstruction*, illustrations edited with a commentary by Joshua Brown (New York: Knopf, 2005), 37–38, 208; C. Vann Woodward, *Origins of the New South, 1877–1913* (Baton Rouge: Louisiana State University Press, 1951), 211–12, 353–54; C. Vann Woodward, *The Strange Career of Jim Crow*, 2nd. ed. (Oxford and New York: Oxford University Press, 1966), 7–8.

3. See, for example, Leon F. Litwack, *Trouble in Mind: Black Southerners in the Age of Jim Crow* (New York: Vintage, 1998) and Douglas A. Blackmon, *Slavery by Another Name: The Re-Enslavement of Black Americans from the Civil War to World War II* (New York: Doubleday, 2008). On the Great Migration, see, for example, Nicholas Lemann, *The Promised Land: The Great Migration*

and How It Changed America (New York: Vintage, 1992) and Isabel Wilkerson, *The Warmth of Other Suns: The Epic Story of America's Great Migration* (New York: Random House, 2010).

4. Foner, *Forever Free*, 207–11; Eric Foner, *Reconstruction: America's Unfinished Revolution: 1863–1877* (New York: Francis Parkman Prize Edition, History Book Club, 2005 [1988]), 602–12; Michael J. Klarman, *From Jim Crow to Civil Rights: The Supreme Court and the Struggle for Equality* (New York and Oxford: Oxford University Press, 2004), 10–14; Jackson Lears, *Rebirth of a Nation: The Making of Modern America, 1877–1920* (New York: HarperCollins, 2009), 22–23; Rayford W. Logan, *The Betrayal of the Negro: From Rutherford B. Hayes to Woodrow Wilson* (Cambridge, Mass.: Da Capo Press, 1997 [1965]), 12–13, 83; Richard M. Valelly, *The Two Reconstructions: The Struggle for Black Enfranchisement* (Chicago and London: The University of Chicago Press, 2004), 117–18.

5. See, for example, Philip Dray, *At the Hands of Persons Unknown: The Lynching of Black America* (New York: New American Library, 2002), 176–79.

6. Quoted in Cortner, *A "Scottsboro" Case in Mississippi*, 6. See also Neil R. McMillen, *Dark Journey: Black Mississippians in the Age of Jim Crow* (Champaign: University of Illinois Press, 1990), 197.

7. *Brown v. Mississippi*, 297 U.S. 278, 282 (1936). See also Cortner, *A "Scottsboro" Case in Mississippi*, 6.

8. 297 U.S. 278, 281–82. See also Cortner, *A "Scottsboro" Case in Mississippi*, 5–6; McMillen, *Dark Journey*, 197–98.

9. 297 U.S. 278, 281. See also M. Katherine B. Darmer, "Reliability, Waterboarded Confessions and Reclaiming the Lessons of *Brown v. Mississippi* in the Terrorism Cases," *Guild Practitioner* 66, 1 (Spring 2009): 20; McMillen, *Dark Journey*, 197.

10. 297 U.S.278, 281–82. See also Cortner, *A "Scottsboro" Case in Mississippi*, 6–7; McMillen, *Dark Journey*, 198.

11. 297 U.S. 278, 282. See also Cortner, *A "Scottsboro" Case in Mississippi*, 6–7; McMillen, *Dark Journey*, 198.

12. 297 U.S. 278, 283. See also Michael J. Klarman, "The Racial Origins of Modern Criminal Procedure," *Michigan Law Review* 99, 1 (October 2000): 68; Anne Elizabeth Link, "Fifth Amendment—The Constitutionality of Custodial Confessions," *The Journal of Criminal Law & Criminology* 82, 4 (Winter 1992): 879.

13. Quoted in McMillen, *Dark Journey*, 198. See also Klarman, "The Racial Origins of Modern Criminal Procedure," 68–69.

14. Quoted in McMillen, *Dark Journey*, 199. See also 297 U.S. 278, 283–84.

15. 297 U.S. 278, 284. See also Klarman, "The Racial Origins of Modern Criminal Procedure," 68; McMillen, *Dark Journey*, 199–200.

16. 297 U.S. 278, 285–86. See also Dray, *At the Hands of Persons Unknown*, 316–17; Klarman, "The Racial Origins of Modern Criminal Procedure," 68;

Link, "Fifth Amendment—The Constitutionality of Custodial Confessions," 879.

17. Dray, *At the Hands of Persons Unknown*, 317.

18. *Moore v. Dempsey, et al.*, 261 U.S. 86 (1923).

19. Dray, *At the Hands of Persons Unknown*, 317; Klarman, "The Racial Origins of Modern Criminal Procedure," 48–50; Link, "Fifth Amendment—The Constitutionality of Custodial Confessions," 879.

CHAPTER 6

Mapp v. Ohio (1961) and the Exclusionary Rule Redux

On May 20, 1957, Donald "the Kid" King was 25 years old. By all accounts, he was a rough character in his hometown of Cleveland, Ohio. The Kid had attended Kent State University for a spell, but eventually he grew bored with the academic life and turned his attention to the numbers racket, making a name as a "clearinghouse operator." He had already been in trouble with the law for shooting a man who had attempted to rob his gambling operation, although the charge was changed to justifiable homicide. In 1966, King would beat a man to death over an unpaid debt and serve four years in prison for manslaughter. During the 1970s, he would become world famous as a boxing promoter renowned for his sharp business practices, gift of gab, effervescent personality, and a distinctive hairstyle where the locks appeared to stand up vertically.[1]

The Kid's notorious career as a promoter and trendsetting hair stylist was far in the future when someone detonated a bomb under the porch of his home in the wee morning hours of May 20. As a young man new to the Cleveland gambling business, King was convinced that one of his many enemies, a Cleveland gangster named Alex (Shondor) Birns, was behind the crime because King had refused to pay Birns money. Physically, King was unscathed by the attack, but the experience left him fretful of what was yet to come. To forestall a second assault, he telephoned the Cleveland Police Department and spoke to Sergeant Carl I. Delau of the Bureau of Special Investigation. Delau agreed to investigate the matter along with his eight-man team.[2]

At the time, Delau was a 38-year-old veteran of World War II and a seasoned police officer with more than 10 years of service under his belt. In November 1949, he was selected to join the Bureau of Special Investigation, a prestigious posting. The Bureau was assigned to vice duty. It was plain to everyone that Carl Delau took to his new duties with relish. Impressing his superiors with his skill and professional dedication, he quickly won promotion to sergeant.[3]

After receiving King's call, the Bureau of Special Investigation rounded up the usual suspects for questioning. Birns initially seemed to be a promising person of interest. Everyone believed, in the words of an article from the *Cleveland Press*, that the bombing was "a new offensive by Shondor Birns to control Cleveland's numbers racket." Sometimes feuding gamblers exacted vengeance for real or perceived

Donald King, pictured here at the age of 25, later gained fame as a boxing promoter. When his home was bombed on May 20, 1957, he operated an illegal gambling business. (Special Collections Department, Michael Schwartz Library, Cleveland State University)

transgressions outside of the law, but the Kid, for a change, chose to play by the rules. He telephoned the police and told them of Birns's threats. He also said that if Birns did not look good for the crime, he could think of four other possible suspects.[4]

Delau and his officers set to work on the case. Because so few interviewees were willing to talk, however, the investigation stalled until Delau received an anonymous tip that a suspect named Virgil Ogletree—"one of the five pistols who bombed me," King had told a newspaper reporter—was hiding out in a house on Milverton Road in the Shaker Heights section of Cleveland. The tipster further intimated that the officers would discover evidence of the gambling operation at the house as well.[5]

The officer recognized the address at once: Dollree Mapp lived there. Delau later claimed to know of Dollree Mapp's reputation as a numbers runner who had had her share of run-ins with the law prior to 1957. He realized this "foxy girl" displayed a "swagger" stemming from street smarts she had developed over years of living among Cleveland's gambling crowd. Unlike many Negroes of that era, Mapp was anything but a cowering second-class citizen. She presented a tough-as-nail exterior façade that appeared impenetrable to even the most threatening lawman or street tough. Taking on such a strong, combative personality would not be easy.[6]

Dollree was a tough lady, all right. She had been born in Austin, Texas, on Halloween in 1924 to a mixed race couple in an era when such couplings were rare and controversial. When she was 10 years old, Dollree ran away from home to live with an aunt in Cleveland. She became pregnant as an adolescent and gave birth to her only child, a daughter. Cleveland was an exciting place in those days, and the young woman ran with a dangerous crowd of boxers and gamblers. She eventually married a world-class slugger, Jimmy Bivins. Unfortunately for his bride, the boxer brought the same manner of ferocity home that he exhibited in the ring. After she and Bivins divorced, Dollree became engaged to another champion, Archie Moore. When Moore broke off the engagement, his jilted lover sued for $750,000. No one could say Dollree Mapp was a victim or a person prone to go gentle into that good night. She knew the world was a tough place and she was determined to take what was hers.[7]

Officer Delau arrived at 14705 Milverton Road, Mapp's residence, around 1:30 on that soon-to-be famous afternoon of May 23, the day he received the tip. Officers Thomas J. Dever and Michael J. Haney accompanied him. They believed the information was reliable when they noticed Virgil Ogletree's car parked outside the house. The men reconnoitered the building "for a long time." Eventually, they grew frustrated with the inactivity and agreed to knock on the door and announce themselves. As the three lawmen approached the residence that day, they wore no uniforms. They strolled up to the door in street clothes.[8]

When the police rang the bell, Dollree Mapp was upstairs. She opened the window and leaned out to ask what the men wanted. Officer Delau was forthright. He said they wanted to "come in and take a look around." Mapp was no quivering simpleton. She refused to allow the officers inside until she had consulted with her attorney. Even as she dialed the telephone number to consult her legal counsel, A. L. Kearns, the officers repeatedly rang the doorbell and demanded immediate entry. Kearns was unavailable, but a young lawyer in Kearns's office, Walter L. Greene, instructed the client to ask for a copy of the search warrant.[9]

Based on this advice, Mapp leaned out the upstairs window again and asked if the officers had secured a search warrant. Delau reluctantly admitted they had not. When she heard this admission, Mapp refused to allow them inside because the officers lacked sufficient probable cause.[10]

Delau was aggravated. He had conducted numerous warrantless searches and believed that niceties such as a search warrant were not required under Ohio law. He was mistaken. A search warrant was required in approximately half of all American states at the time, and Ohio was one of the states. Nonetheless, the exclusionary rule was the province of the federal courts. Police officers were unaccustomed to probative evidence being excluded from court even if the evidence was obtained illegally. In light of the lack of consequences for conducting a warrantless search, many police officers ignored the requirement. Officer Delau later recalled how much Mapp's intransigence upset him at the time. "You have to have had contact with her to understand her," he remarked. "She was a cunning, daring, and audacious person."[11]

The verbal exchange ended after Mapp told Officer Delau to have his boss, Lieutenant Thomas Cooley, contact her personally if the police still desired entry into her home. Delau and his colleagues returned to the car, drove a block away, and called Cooley. Afterward, Cooley telephoned Mapp to explain the urgency of a police search. She remained defiant.[12]

When Mapp hung up the telephone and looked out the window, she was startled to see the officers. They had returned and were watching her house intently. Her tough exterior began to crumble. Worried about what might happen next, Mapp called Walter Greene again and told him of her plight. He agreed to come over to her house to provide assistance on the assumption that the police would continue demanding entry and the situation would escalate.

And escalate it did. Greene recalled arriving at the Mapp residence around 4:30 P.M. The scene was reminiscent of a movie or television show. Between 10 and 15 officers, some in uniform and other wearing street clothes, gathered around the house. Police cars lined the street. Even the paddy wagon had made an appearance in case it was necessary to whisk suspects away with all deliberate speed. Neighbors cautiously craned their necks from adjoining houses and yards in a vain attempt to understand what was happening in their community.

Greene approached Officer Delau and his associates and asked if they had procured a search warrant. At the time Greene confronted the policemen, they were attempting to force entry into the house. Greene told them that if they had a warrant, forcible entry was unnecessary. "Just show it to Ms. Mapp," he recalled telling them. The problem, as Greene later explained, was that although the officers claimed to have a warrant, "they refused to show it to anybody. I never did see a warrant." Throughout the ordeal that followed, Greene protested that he should be allowed to see his client, but to no avail. He possessed a small camera and attempted to snap photographs, to the officers' consternation, but the pictures never developed properly.[13]

Suddenly, amid all the commotion, the officers pried open the screen door with a tool, perhaps a crowbar, and broke a pane of glass to gain entry. When Greene sought to enter as well, the officers refused to allow him inside to confer with his client. As the break-in occurred, Dollree Mapp rushed down the stairs demanding to see the warrant.

Lieutenant Thomas White from the Central Police Station brandished a piece of paper that he claimed was a warrant. "Here is the search warrant," he assured her. "You can't see it." His action was not as unreasonable as it initially appears. In an era before photocopies were widespread, a search warrant was a precious piece of paper. The police officer serving the warrant was expected to "endorse" the warrant and return it to the judicial officer who had issued it along with an inventory of the items searched and seized. A lost or destroyed warrant would present police officers with a difficult problem. The concern explains at least some of White's reluctance to allow the suspect to take hold of the paper.[14]

Dollree Mapp did not view matters the way the police did. When White waved the paper in front of her, she snatched it from the lieutenant's hand and slipped it into the front of her dress. The officer would have a difficult time returning the warrant to the issuing judge now.

The police manuals did not provide guidance on the proper reaction under these circumstances. "What are we going to do now?" someone asked.

Officer Delau spoke up. "I'm going down after it."

"No, you're not," Mapp told him.

Despite Mapp's objections, Delau reached into the woman's dress to fish out the warrant. The officer later dismissed the hysterical woman as "quite belligerent," but he retrieved the paper. His successful assault only infuriated Dollree Mapp further. Delau explained that she was abusive and "real nasty." In his words, "I think she took a swing at one of the uniformed men if I'm not mistaken." To prevent further difficulties, the officers handcuffed her as they went about their search. Someone led her upstairs and a uniformed officer hovered over her as the others searched the premises.[15]

Mapp had rented a downstairs apartment to a tenant, Minerva Fitzpatrick Lockheart. Virgil Ogletree, the bombing suspect, lurked inside Lockheart's apartment, and it was there the police found the man they sought. Still, even after Ogletree had been led away in handcuffs, the search continued. The officers were determined to find damning evidence linking Ogletree to the Donald King bombing. Whether they also were searching for evidence of illegal gambling—"policy paraphernalia"—would become controversial.

Delau and his associates resolved to leave no stone unturned. They opened every bureau drawer and every closet they could find. Dollree Mapp recalled that the officer watching over her eventually handcuffed her to the stairwell banister so he could assist in the search.[16]

Although they never uncovered evidence of a bomber, law enforcement officials discovered a trunk filled with sexually explicit materials inside Mapp's bedroom. Four books—*London Stage Affairs*, *Affairs of a Troubadour*, *Memoirs of a Hotel Man*, and *Little Darlings*—caught the officers' eye. Dollree Mapp remembered the officers leering at the books. In her view, "they seemed to enjoy them immensely." Believing the materials met the legal definition of obscenity, the officers arrested Mapp despite her protests that the trunk belonged to a previous tenant in the house. Apart from Virgil Ogletree hiding in the downstairs apartment, they had not found physical evidence tying

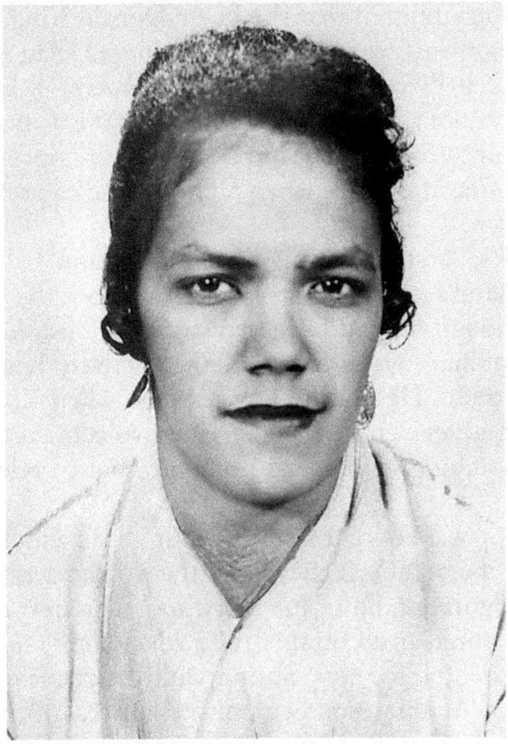

Dollree Mapp was arrested for possessing obscene materials in 1957 in a case involving race and aggressive police tactics. (Special Collections Department, Michael Schwartz Library, Cleveland State University)

Mapp to the bombing, but they had found enough evidence to serve as a pretext for arrest.[17]

After transporting the prisoner to the Cleveland municipal police station, Delau was determined to have another crack at the recalcitrant defendant. Mapp was convinced that the all-white police force had singled her out for harassment on racial grounds, but Sergeant Delau saw the matter a different way. Because he knew the suspect was a person of sordid character, at least by reputation, he believed she knew more about the bombing than she was willing to admit. He was determined to penetrate her gruff façade and get at the truth—even if he had to use rough police tactics to accomplish the goal.[18]

Dollree Mapp admitted that she knew Donald King, but she vehemently denied any involvement in the bombing. Delau remained skeptical. He found her "very evasive in her answers," which compelled him to be ever more aggressive in questioning the woman. Eventually, the police resolved to detain Mapp overnight in hopes that her resistance would soften after she spent a night in a jail cell reflecting on her predicament.[19]

Questioned separately, Virgil Ogletree explained that he had arrived at the Mapp residence a few minutes before the police initially appeared. Although he had been arrested previously on a "clearinghouse," or gambling, violation, he denied actively being engaged in the gambling trade. He said he was at home when King's house was bombed. With no evidence of Ogletree's involvement in illegal gambling or the bombing, police had no choice but to release him from custody.[20]

Dollree Mapp was another story. Even if Delau and his squad could not link her to the bombing, they knew the woman was up to no good. The press had gotten hold of the story, too. The next day's *Cleveland Plain Dealer* featured an account of the raid and provided a level of detail that suggested police cooperation with the reporter. One way or another, Dollree Mapp would be punished for real or imagined transgressions. Whether racial animus was a factor in the zealousness with which the police prosecuted this proud, angry black woman remains a source of controversy to this day.[21]

A. L. Kearns, the attorney Mapp originally attempted to contact when the police arrived at her home, represented her during her appearance before the Cleveland Municipal Court the morning after her detention. A skilled, seasoned advocate, Kearns convinced the court to drop the original charges because, despite her reputation, Dollree Mapp could not be tied to the bombing or illegal gambling.[22]

For all intents and purposes, the matter should have ended there, but it did not. On September 19, 1957, a grand jury indicted Mapp for "possession of obscene pictures and books." She pleaded not guilty the following day, posted bail, and headed home. As she awaited her fate before the courts, Mapp's anger only increased. She was convinced the affair contained a racial component. Not only was the Bureau of Special Investigation a lawless, out-of-control organization, but its officers were power-hungry and unconcerned about a black citizen's civil liberties. "They were very prejudiced," she recalled. "Hitlers. They would target certain people in the community."[23]

Although his client repeatedly protested her innocence and remained defiant, Kearns had four decades of experience in the criminal courts. He knew that juries are unpredictable and even a winnable case has a way of unexpectedly collapsing. During the interregnum between indictment and trial, he approached the prosecution to discuss a plea bargain. In July 1958, Kearns appeared before Judge Joseph A. Artl in the Court of Common Pleas and tried to cut a deal whereby his client would plead guilty in exchange for a fine with no prison time. When the prosecution refused to accede to the plea bargain, the deal fell apart.[24]

With a plea bargain out of the question, Dollree Mapp renewed her "not guilty" plea on August 1. Her trial for "Possession of Obscene Literature," Case No. 68326, began on September 3, 1958, before Judge Donald F. Lybarger. Kearns and Walter Greene appeared as defense counsel. Cuyahoga County assistant prosecuting attorney Gertrude Bauer Mahon, a lawyer with 16 years of experience and one of the few female members of the Ohio bar, represented the people.[25]

The first order of business was to consider a defense motion to suppress the evidence. Kearns argued that although the police claimed to have a valid search warrant when they entered Ms. Mapp's home, no one representing the defendant had seen the paper. "Now, we say that the State of Ohio did not have a search warrant setting forth the items that are mentioned in this indictment, which the State of Ohio intends to use in this case against this defendant," he said. Accordingly, "for that reason we are asking that particular evidence be suppressed."[26]

Kearns recognized that he faced a difficult hurdle. The *Weeks* case held that illegally obtained evidence was inadmissible in court, but that case involved the application of the Fourth Amendment in a federal court matter. A 1936 Ohio Supreme Court case, *State v. Lindway*, had decided that illegally obtained evidence was admissible in an Ohio court because the Fourth Amendment only applied to federal courts.[27] As if that were not enough, the U.S. Supreme Court supported the Ohio remedy in a 1949 case, *Wolf v. Colorado. Wolf* incorporated Fourth Amendment protections to the states through the Fourteenth Amendment, but the high court limited the exclusionary rule to the federal courts.[28] The Ohio Constitution allowed a suit for trespass against an officer acting on an illegal warrant, or no warrant at all, but a civil remedy appeared to be the only redress available to Dollree Mapp when she stood trial in Cuyahoga County in 1958.[29]

The question of the search warrant was problematic. In some instances, Kearns seemed to argue that a warrant existed but that it was deficient because it did not set forth "the items that are mentioned in this indictment." At other times the question of whether a search warrant existed was at issue. Judge Lybarger sought clarity on the point. He turned to the assistant prosecuting attorney and asked her directly. "Yes, your honor," Mahon assured him. "A search warrant was issued." Kearns's rejoinder was that even if a warrant existed, it did not satisfy the particularity requirement of the law, but the judge overruled him based on the *Lindway* precedent. The evidence would be allowed at trial. It was the crucial issue. Without the admission of the obscene materials, the prosecution would not have been able to satisfy its burden of proving Dollree Mapp's guilt beyond a reasonable doubt.[30]

As soon as the court ruled on the motion, the trial commenced. Each side predictably painted a different picture of the May 23rd events. Mahon described a lawful police search that yielded valuable probative evidence and clearly indicated the defendant's guilt. Kearns argued that police officers had forced their way inside the house and ransacked the place in search of illegal activity while violating Dollree Mapp's constitutional rights against unreasonable search and seizure.[31]

The prosecution offered two witnesses—Patrolman Michael Haney and Sergeant Carl Delau. Both men described the search in terms favorable to the state. Haney explained that Mapp had agreed to allow the police into her house voluntarily. Afterward, the officers found obscene materials in her bedroom, not in the basement, as the defendant contended. Delau corroborated Haney's testimony with one crucial distinction. Unlike Haney, Delau admitted that the officers forced the screen door open to gain entry. Both men were adamant that Lieutenant White arrived with what they believed to be a valid search warrant, although neither man examined the contents. They took White's word that he had secured a valid search warrant and thought no more about it. Because neither side called the lieutenant to the stand, he did not testify to the validity, or lack thereof, of the search warrant. In fact, no one who testified at trial could say definitively what was in the warrant or whether, in fact, it ever existed.[32]

Defense counsel attacked the search warrant by allowing Walter Greene to testify that he had never been shown a copy despite repeated requests. Next, Mapp's friend Dolores Clark testified that she had assisted in boxing up the belongings of a previous tenant, Morris Jones. Mr. Jones's personal property included the obscene materials in question. Mapp herself explained that the books were not hers. Asked why she had snatched the warrant from Lieutenant White, she explained that her attorney, Walter Greene, had told her that she should read the warrant before allowing the police to enter the premises. Since they refused to show it to her, she decided to take the warrant.[33]

The attorneys presented closing arguments the next day. After deliberately only 20 minutes, the jury found Dollree Mapp guilty as charged. The judge later sentenced her to between one and seven years in the Ohio Reformatory for Women and imposed a fine of between $200 and $2,000. The guilty verdict and the lengthy prison sentence struck Mapp and her defense team as unusually harsh in light of the crime.[34]

A. L. Kearns filed a motion for a new trial, but Judge Lybarger, not surprisingly, denied the motion. The next step in the judicial process was to prepare an appeal. The attorney focused on three arguments. First, he contended that the trial court erred in finding that Dollree Mapp maintained control over the obscene materials. The second point was related to the first. The jury instruction that "one who deposits articles in a place of concealment may still be deemed to have them in his possession" prejudiced the jurors and all but required them to convict. Finally, Kearns argued that the harsh sentence violated the state constitution because the drafters could not have intended to punish a defendant so severely for failing "to destroy the articles of a roomer."[35]

The Eighth District Court of Appeals, which handled appeals from Cuyahoga County, handled down its decision on March 28, 1959, in a short statement unencumbered by extraneous (or explanatory) comments. The presiding judge, Joy Seth Hurd, came straight to the point: "Upon review of the entire case, we find no error prejudicial to the rights of the defendant." Kearns and his team were disappointed by the opinion, but not shocked. They immediately prepared an appeal to the Ohio Supreme Court.[36]

At this stage, the defense team emphasized two constitutional arguments that had been absent from the trial and initial appeal. First, the lawyers contended that the Ohio anti-obscenity statute was so vague and imprecise it violated the defendant's free speech rights under the First and Fourteenth amendments to the U.S. Constitution. The second claim was that the trial court's decision to allow illegally seized materials to be admitted into evidence violated Mapp's due process rights. According to Kearns, "the alleged 'warrant' was never presented in evidence or shown to exist," and therefore, "the conclusion was that the paper was a ruse."

When the state filed the standard motion to dismiss the appellant's case, prosecutors learned that the matter had assumed higher visibility. The Ohio Civil Liberties Union (OCLU), the state chapter of the American Civil Liberties Union (ACLU), asked for permission to submit an amicus curiae (friend of the court) brief on behalf of the appellant. The ACLU was especially interested in challenging the constitutionality of the Ohio anti-obscenity statute and this case appeared to be a suitable vehicle for doing so.[37]

By the time the Ohio Supreme Court announced its opinion on March 23, 1960, almost three years had elapsed since the officers had arrived at Dollree Mapp's house to search for evidence of illegal activity. Four of the seven justices voted to reverse the conviction because the statute unconstitutionally burdened free speech rights, but a simple majority was not sufficient. Under the state constitution, "No law shall be held unconstitutional and void by the Ohio Supreme Court without the concurrence of at least all but one of the judges." The question of whether a warrant existed did not affect the court's decision. Citing *State v. Lindway*, which allowed illegally seized material to be admitted into evidence in a state court, and the U.S. Supreme Court opinion in *Wolf v. Colorado*, which allowed states to determine their own law on whether to exclude illegally obtained evidence, the state supreme court did not dwell on the Fourth Amendment issues.[38]

The outcome in the Ohio Supreme Court case was quixotic. All seven justices agreed that the search was illegal, but some members of the court felt constrained by precedent from ruling the evidence inadmissible. Four found the anti-obscenity statute to be unconstitutional. Yet for all of the justices' doubts and lamentations, the conviction stood. All hope was not lost, however. Because the state court upheld a state statute that had been challenged on U.S. constitutional grounds, Dollree Mapp's legal team had a strong basis for an appeal to the U.S. Supreme Court.[39]

Walter Greene took the lead in writing the petition for certiorari. He raised a multitude of interrelated issues. First, echoing the challenge before the Ohio Supreme Court, he contended that the Ohio anti-obscenity statute violated the Fourth, Fifth, and Fourteenth amendments. He also challenged the harsh sentence on the grounds that it constituted cruel and unusual punishment in contravention of the Eighth Amendment to the U.S. Constitution. As a third argument, the petition charged that police conduct in the case violated the Fourth, Fifth, and Fourteenth amendments. Greene criticized the Ohio courts' decision not to review Mapp's sentence and the improper jury instructions because they violated the defendant's Sixth Amendment right to a fair trial.[40]

The odds against the high court accepting the case for review were long. In 1960, the justices received approximately 2,000 petitions for certiorari and considered 250, with only 140 cases receiving a thorough review through oral argument and written opinions. Despite the odds, all but one justice, Felix Frankfurter, agreed to review what initially appeared to be an obscenity case. Dollree Mapp would have one more day in court.[41]

Although the justices' conference sessions are famously private, what little is known about their deliberations in *Mapp v. Ohio* suggests that their initial discussions focused on the constitutionality, or lack thereof, of the Ohio anti-obscenity statute. Walter Greene, who prepared the first draft of the certiorari petition, and A. L. Kearns, who appeared for the oral argument, had advanced a theory of the case relying on the statute's privacy rights violations under the Fourth and Fourteenth amendments, but the justices seized on a concern about over the breadth of the state law. The statute was so poorly worded that it was difficult for the average citizen to understand exactly what type of material was prohibited by the law. Such imprecision could create a chilling effect on First Amendment freedoms.[42]

Associate Justice William O. Douglas apparently was the first member of the court to raise the question of whether *Mapp* was an appropriate vehicle for revisiting the court's well-known opinion in *Wolf v. Colorado.* In that landmark 1949 case, the Supreme Court specifically had declined to extend the exclusionary rule to the states even as it incorporated Fourth Amendment protections to state court proceedings. Justice Frankfurter, known for his belief in judicial restraint, had authored the *Wolf* opinion. He saw the need for extending Fourth Amendment due process requirements to the states, but he stopped short of extending the exclusionary rule because he viewed such a judicially created doctrine as an affront to federalism principles. States should decide the manner in which they penalized Fourth Amendment violations. Consequently, in the years since *Wolf* had been decided, state courts had crafted their own Fourth Amendment jurisprudence, with a minority of jurisdictions adopting an exclusionary rule but most rejecting it. It was difficult to imagine the court significantly altering *Wolf* only a dozen years after it had been written.[43]

Chief Justice Earl Warren assigned the majority opinion to Justice Tom Clark. It was clear at the outset that Mapp's conviction would be overturned owing to concerns about the Ohio statute's First Amendment violations. Yet something happened between the time the justices met in the initial conference and the time Justice Clark produced his opinion. Some critics have viewed the result as a perversion of the original intent of the Fourth Amendment, while other commentators have welcomed the approach as the inevitable give-and-take of judicial politics. In any case, Justice Clark changed his mind about the reasons for overturning Mapp's conviction between the time the brethren met in the initial conference and the time he penned the majority opinion. "Wouldn't this be a good case to apply the exclusionary rule and do what *Wolf* didn't do?" Clark asked two fellow justices, William Brennan and Hugo Black, as the three men shuffled into the court elevator. From the comment, it sounded as though Clark had planted himself firmly in Douglas's camp.[44] Justice Potter Stewart later wrote in a law review article, "What transpired in the month following our conference on the case is really a matter of speculation on my part, but I have always suspected that the members of the soon-to-be *Mapp* majority had met in what I affectionately call a 'rump caucus' to discuss a different basis for their decision." It might be labeled "elevator jurisprudence."[45]

If Clark chose to modify the *Wolf* ruling, he could count Douglas, Brennan, and Chief Justice Warren on his side. He needed at least one additional justice to join him. Hugo Black, the crusty old civil libertarian from Alabama, propounded an idiosyncratic view of American jurisprudence. On one hand, he was viewed as a staunch supporter of politically liberal policies such as an expansive application of the First Amendment. When the Framers wrote that "Congress shall make no law" abridging free speech, they meant exactly that. "No law" did not mean "no unreasonable law." Black also believed that all Bill of Rights protections should apply to the states; that is, he wanted to incorporate civil liberties protections through the Fourteenth Amendment. A majority of the court had selectively incorporated Bill of Rights protections in accordance with a famous 1937 case, *Palko v. Connecticut*, in which Justice Louis Brandeis wrote that only those Bill of Rights protections that constituted "the very essence of a scheme of ordered liberty" would apply in state criminal proceedings. A new member of the high court at the time, Black had joined the majority opinion in *Palko* but, unlike a majority of the justices in 1937 and in 1961, he believed selective incorporation did not go far enough.[46]

Yet despite Black's willingness to support unusual, creative constitutional construction, he had little patience for judicially created tests and standards that changed the original meaning of the most sacred of the country's legal documents. This strict interpretation also meant that Black was not predisposed to support opinions that he might personally agree with but which enjoyed no constitutional support in the language or history of the Constitution. He had concurred in the *Wolf* case, arguing that the exclusionary rule was "not a command of the Fourth Amendment" but a "judicially created rule of evidence." It simply appeared unfathomable before 1961 that Black could be induced to move beyond his own special brand of constitutional construction to join an opinion that proposed to extend the exclusionary rule to the states since that rule was a judge-made doctrine not supported by the text of the Constitution.[47]

Justice Clark initiated a dialogue with his colleague through a series of memoranda to determine whether Black's views had changed over time; they had. To his astonishment, Clark realized that Justice Black not only was willing to incorporate the Fourth Amendment and the exclusionary rule to the states, but the old man believed *Mapp* was a case that called for incorporation of the Fifth Amendment as well. No one else was willing to follow Justice Black onto this terrain. As a result, Black would join in the court opinion and add a concurrence of his own.[48]

The Supreme Court announced its opinion in *Mapp v. Ohio* on June 19, 1961—the final "Decision Monday" of the 1960 term of court. Writing for the majority, Clark began with a statement of the facts and the dubious authenticity of the search warrant. "At the trial," he noted, "no search warrant was produced by the prosecution, nor was the failure to produce one explained or accounted for." Quoting the conclusion of the Ohio Supreme Court, he observed, "At best, 'there is, in the record, considerable doubt as to whether there ever was any warrant for the search of defendant's home.'"[49]

Next, Clark reviewed the turbulent history of Fourth Amendment jurisprudence as well as the application of the exclusionary rule beginning with *Weeks v. United States* and *Olmstead v. United States*. He also noted that before *Wolf v. Colorado* was handed down in 1949, "almost two-thirds of the States were opposed to the use of the exclusionary rule; now, despite the *Wolf* case, more than half of those since passing upon it, by their own legislative or judicial decision, have wholly or partly adopted or adhered to the *Weeks* rule." In short, it was time to revisit *Wolf* in light of the changing nature of constitutional criminal procedure and the realization by states that excluding illegally seized evidence was a necessary component of a fair trial.[50]

Clark explained the court's reasoning unequivocally:

> Today we once again examine *Wolf's* constitutional documentation of the right to privacy free from unreasonable state intrusion, and, after its dozen years on our books, are led by it to close

> the only courtroom door remaining open to evidence secured by official lawlessness in flagrant abuse of that basic right, reserved to all persons as a specific guarantee against that very same unlawful conduct. We hold that all evidence obtained by searches and seizures in violation of the Constitution is, by that same authority, inadmissible in a state court.[51]

Without the exclusionary rule as a check on the egregious behavior of police conducting a search, the Fourth Amendment would be less effective. "Just as without the *Weeks* rule the assurance against unreasonable federal searches and seizures would be 'a form of words,' valueless and undeserving of mention in a perpetual charter of inestimable human liberties, so too, without that rule, the freedom from state invasions of privacy would be so ephemeral and so neatly severed from its conceptual nexus with the freedom from all brutish means of coercing evidence as not to merit this Court's high regard as a freedom 'implicit in the concept of ordered liberty.'"[52]

Clark questioned whether it would be reasonable to apply one set of rules to federal court proceedings and another to state trials. "Moreover, our holding that the exclusionary rule is an essential part of both the Fourth and Fourteenth Amendments is not only the logical dictate of prior cases, but it also makes very good sense," he wrote. "There is no war between the Constitution and common sense."[53] For the inevitable critics who would ask, as Judge (later Justice) Cardozo did, whether the "criminal is to go free because the constable has blundered," Clark explained that the "criminal goes free, if he must, but it is the law that sets him free. Nothing can destroy a government more quickly than its failure to observe its own laws, or worse, its disregard of the charter of its own existence." He quoted Justice Brandeis's famous dissent in *Olmstead v. United States:* "If the Government becomes a lawbreaker, it breeds contempt for law; it invites every man to become a law unto himself; it invites anarchy."[54] He concluded the opinion with stirring words: "Our decision, founded on reason and truth, gives to the individual no more than that which the Constitution guarantees him, to the police officer no less than that to which honest law enforcement is entitled, and, to the courts, that judicial integrity so necessary in the true administration of justice."[55]

In his concurrence, Justice Black stuck to his opinion that the Fourth and Fifth amendments must be considered in tandem. He argued that "when the Fourth Amendment's ban against unreasonable searches and seizures is considered together with the Fifth Amendment's ban against compelled self-incrimination, a constitutional basis emerges which not only justifies, but actually requires, the exclusionary rule."[56] He was disturbed by judicial doctrines created from the mind and imagination of judicial activists, but Justice Black believed something else was going on in *Mapp* and similar cases. "As I understand the Court's opinion in this case, we again reject the confusing 'shock the conscience' standard of the *Wolf* and *Rochin* cases and, instead, set aside this state conviction in reliance upon the precise, intelligible and more predictable constitutional doctrine enunciated in the *Boyd* case." Aside from *Wolf*, Black was referring to *Rochin v. California*, a 1952 case that held police conduct that "shocked the conscience" was unconstitutional and the evidence seized as a result could be excluded from trial.[57] *Boyd v. United States*, an 1886 opinion, concluded that private papers incriminating someone cannot be used if those papers were illegally seized because they violate the Fifth Amendment's protection against self-incrimination.[58] Black's point was that the exclusionary rule does not require case-by-case adjudication to determine the circumstances when police actions do or do not shock the conscience. Such piecemeal jurisprudence fails to provide adequate judicial guidance on the proper legal standards and creates an atmosphere of uncertainty. "The courts of the country are entitled to know with as much certainty as possible what scope they cover. The Court's opinion, in my judgment, dissipates the doubt and uncertainty in this field of constitutional law, and I am persuaded, for this and other reasons stated, to depart from my prior views, to accept the *Boyd* doctrine as controlling in this state case, and to join the Court's judgment and opinion, which are in accordance with that constitutional doctrine."[59]

Justice Douglas joined the majority opinion, but he could not refrain from adding his perspective on the "lawless search and seizure" in a separate concurrence. After reviewing the facts, he explained that the court's decision in *Mapp* was necessary to reinvigorate the Fourth Amendment. "When we allowed States to give constitutional sanction to the 'shabby business' of unlawful entry into a home (to use an expression of Mr. Justice Murphy, *Wolf v. Colorado*, at 338 U.S. 46), we did indeed rob the Fourth Amendment of much meaningful force." Authorizing police departments to penalize rogue officers who violate a suspect's Fourth Amendment rights is unworkable, Douglas wrote, again quoting Justice Murphy from *Wolf v. Colorado:* "Self-scrutiny is a lofty ideal, but its exaltation reaches new heights if we expect a District Attorney to prosecute himself or his associates for well meaning violations of the search and seizure clause during a raid the District Attorney or his associates have ordered." As for allowing suspects to file civil suits for trespass, Douglas observed that "Mr. Justice Murphy showed how onerous and difficult it would be for the citizen to maintain that action, and how meager the relief even if the citizen prevails. The truth is that trespass actions against officers who make unlawful searches and seizures are mainly illusory remedies." If the Fourth Amendment is to be enforced rigorously, Douglas concluded, the exclusionary rule is required.[60]

Justice John Marshall Harlan II, a strong advocate of judicial restraint, was alarmed by the majority opinion. "In overruling the *Wolf* case, the Court, in my opinion, has forgotten the sense of judicial restraint which, with due regard for stare decisis, is one element that should enter into deciding whether a past decision of this Court should be overruled," he complained in a dissent joined by Justices Felix Frankfurter and Charles Evans Whittaker. "Apart from that, I also believe that the *Wolf* rule represents sounder Constitutional doctrine than the new rule which now replaces it."[61]

Harlan observed that the majority had seized on the exclusionary rule as a crucial decision point, but he reminded his brethren that the central issue was "whether § 2905.34 of the Ohio Revised Code, making criminal the *mere* knowing possession or control of obscene material, and under which appellant has been convicted, is consistent with the rights of free thought and expression assured against state action by the Fourteenth Amendment." In drafting a broadly tailored opinion, "I think it fair to say that five members of this Court have simply 'reached out' to overrule *Wolf*."[62] The majority's overreaching meant that *Wolf*, a relatively recent case, was discarded without thoroughly debating the repercussions of such a decision. A judicial restraintist such as Justice Harlan seeks to decide cases on narrow grounds, whenever possible, because he is always cognizant that federal judges and justices are unelected and, therefore, not directly accountable to the people. If a judge or justice earnestly desires to change the law, he or she can stand for elective office.

After explaining his objections to the process by which the court majority arrived at its decision, Harlan turned to the logic of the opinion:

> At the heart of the majority's opinion in this case is the following syllogism: (1) the rule excluding in federal criminal trials evidence which is the product of an illegal search and seizure is "part and parcel" of the Fourth Amendment; (2) *Wolf* held that the "privacy" assured against federal action by the Fourth Amendment is also protected against state action by the Fourteenth Amendment, and (3) it is therefore "logically and constitutionally necessary" that the *Weeks* exclusionary rule should also be enforced against the States.[63]

Harlan argued that the majority was making an inferential leap not supported by the facts of the case. In doing so, it was undermining well-established federalism principles by unnecessarily imposing federal rules of procedure—many of which were highly contested—onto states with little or no regard for the consequences for state sovereignty. Referring to the exclusionary rule, Harlan wrote, "I would not impose upon the States this federal exclusionary remedy. The reasons given by the majority for now suddenly turning its back on *Wolf* seem to me notably unconvincing." His concern was not whether the search and seizure in the *Mapp* case was egregious but "whether the States are constitutionally free to follow it or not as they may themselves determine."[64]

Harlan concluded his opinion with an oft-stated concern about the long-range effect a U.S. Supreme Court opinion involving broad public policy changes would have on respect for the U.S. Constitution. "I regret that I find so unwise in principle and so inexpedient in policy a decision motivated by the high purpose of increasing respect for constitutional rights," he mused. "But, in the last analysis, I think this Court can increase respect for the Constitution only if it rigidly respects the limitations which the Constitution places upon it, and respects as well the principles inherent in its own processes. In the present case, I think we exceed both, and that our voice becomes only a voice of power, not of reason."[65]

Mapp v. Ohio became one of the signature decisions of the Warren Court, an opinion loved and hated in almost equal measure. In the ensuing decades, the state and federal courts grappled with what became known as the "due process revolution" of the Warren tenure. Some parts of the story of the exclusionary rule, already discussed in previous chapters of this book, will inform later chapters as well, especially Chapter 12, which discusses *United States v. Leon*, the case that carved out a "good faith exception" to the rule.[66]

Dollree Mapp was both pleased and enervated by the high court's ruling. "Of course I was relieved that I didn't have to go to jail," she later confessed. "But I felt empty. I didn't feel anything special." Her reaction initially sounds counterintuitive, but it is consistent with the feelings expressed by many persons who endure a period of stress and heightened tension only to find the resolution of the problem strangely anticlimactic. Veterans sometimes speak of missing the heat of battle. Survivors of terrible trauma explain that resuming a "normal" life is boring and unfulfilling. Perhaps the commonality in the responses stems from feeling that life at the center of a highly visible tumult has meaning and purpose. Afterward, the participant discovers only historical obscurity.[67]

Mapp slipped into obscurity for a time, but she endured another brief taste of notoriety at the end of the 1960s. No longer facing a lengthy prison sentence in the wake of the Supreme Court decision, she lived in Cleveland until 1968, when she moved to New York. She later explained she was bored and "wanted a different environment." A different environment she got, but it did not change her life markedly. She continued to live on the fringes of society, purchasing a furniture store but always keeping company with marginal characters. In October 1969, a confidential informant told the police that Mapp and her associate, Alan Lyons, were selling narcotics. For several weeks, law enforcement personnel observed the pair. When they had obtained sufficient evidence to obtain a valid search warrant, officers descended on a Queens apartment Mapp had rented and discovered more than a pound of heroin, which possessed a street value of $1 million at the time. She was arrested. Police searched her house and found nothing. Several months after Mapp was released on bond, police received another tip. This time, she was reputed to be receiving stolen property. Police again obtained a search warrant and rifled through her home. Unlike the first occasion, this time they found $150,000 worth of heroin and $100,000 in stolen property, including television sets, portable radios, and antiques. She was arrested and bound over for trial.

On April 23, 1971, Mapp and Lyons were convicted in the Queens County Supreme Court (the state of New York's general jurisdiction trial court) for narcotics possession and sentenced to the mandatory sentence of 20 years to life. Predictably, Mapp appealed the conviction. On June 26, 1972, the New York Appellate Division overturned her conviction owing to errors attributed to the trial judge. Unfortunately for Mapp, she was retried, convicted again, and resentenced to

20 years to life. She was transported to the State Correctional Institution for Women in Bedford Hills, New York, to serve out her time. New York governor Hugh Carey later commuted the sentence and Mapp left prison in 1981.

Dollree Mapp eventually worked for a New York nonprofit organization, Voluntary Attorney Service Team (VAST), a group dedicated to providing legal assistance for inmates. By that time, of course, she had already made a name for herself in the annals of American criminal law. Forever after, she would be known as the feisty, proud black woman who had helped extend Fourth Amendment protections via the exclusionary rule to state court proceedings.[68]

NOTES

1. John S. Dempsey and Linda S. Forst, *An Introduction to Policing*, 6th ed. (Clifton Park, N.Y.: Delmar Cengage Learning, 2011), 384; Jack Newfield, *The Life and Crimes of Don King: The Shame of Boxing in America* (Sag Harbor, N.Y.: Harbor Electronic Publishing, 2003), 15–28; Priscilla H. Machado Zotti, *Injustice for All: Mapp v. Ohio and the Fourth Amendment* (New York: Peter Lang, 2005), 8–10.

2. Peter Blauner, "King on the Ropes: Boxing's Gabby Promoter Fights for His Professional Life," *New York Magazine* 24, 11 (March 18, 1991): 43; Leon Scully, "Civil Wrongs," *National Review* 44, 10 (May 25, 1992): 23.

3. Carolyn N. Long, *Mapp v. Ohio: Guarding against Unreasonable Searches and Seizures* (Lawrence: University Press of Kansas, 2006), 9–10; Zotti, *Injustice for All*, 32–39.

4. Quoted in Scully, "Civil Wrongs," 23. See also Long, *Mapp v. Ohio*, 5.

5. Dempsey and Forst, *An Introduction to Policing*, 384; Scully, "Civil Wrongs," 23; Zotti, *Injustice for All*, 40.

6. Quoted in Long, *Mapp v. Ohio*, 6.

7. R. Marc Kantrowitz, "Good Golly, Miss Dolly," *Rhode Island Lawyers Weekly* (April 28, 2011), Available at http://rilawyersweekly.com/blog/2011/04/28/good-golly-miss-dolly/ (Accessed April 14, 2013); Long, *Mapp v. Ohio*, 1–2; Zotti, *Injustice for All*, 13–14.

8. Long, *Mapp v. Ohio*, 6; Scully, "Civil Wrongs," 23.

9. Long, *Mapp v. Ohio*, 6; Zotti, *Injustice for All*, 18–19.

10. Long, *Mapp v. Ohio*, 6–7; Thomas McInnis, *The Evolution of the Fourth Amendment* (Lanham, Md.: Lexington Books, 2009), 37.

11. Quoted in Long, *Mapp v. Ohio*, 7. See also McInnis, *The Evolution of the Fourth Amendment*, 37; Scully, "Civil Wrongs," 23.

12. Long, *Mapp v. Ohio*, 7; Scully, "Civil Wrongs," 23.

13. Quoted in Long, *Mapp v. Ohio*, 7.

14. Long, *Mapp v. Ohio*, 7–8; Scully, "Civil Wrongs," 23–24.

15. Quoted in Long, *Mapp v. Ohio*, 8. See also *Mapp v. Ohio*, 367 U.S. 643, 644 (1961); Dempsey and Forst, *An Introduction to Policing*, 384; Lewis R. Katz, "*Mapp* after Forty Years: Its Impact on Race in America," *Case Western Reserve Law Review* 52, 2 (Winter 2001): 471–72; Polly J. Price, "*Mapp v. Ohio* Revisited: A law Clerk's Diary," *Journal of Supreme Court History* 35, 1 (2010): 60.

16. 367 U.S. 643, 644–45; Dempsey and Forst, *An Introduction to Policing*, 384; Long, *Mapp v. Ohio*, 8–9; Scully, "Civil Wrongs," 24.

17. 367 U.S. 643, 645; Katz, "*Mapp* after Forty Years," 471; McInnis, *The Evolution of the Fourth Amendment*, 37; Price, "*Mapp v. Ohio* Revisited," 60.

18. Long, *Mapp v. Ohio*, 11–12; Katz, "*Mapp* after Forty Years," 471–73.

19. Long, *Mapp v. Ohio*, 12.

20. Long, *Mapp v. Ohio*, 12; Scully, "Civil Wrongs," 24.

21. Katz, "*Mapp* after Forty Years," 473–75; Long, *Mapp v. Ohio*, 12.

22. Kantrowitz, "Good Golly, Miss Dolly"; Long, *Mapp v. Ohio*, 13.

23. Quoted in Long, *Mapp v. Ohio*, 14. See also Kantrowitz, "Good Golly, Miss Dolly"; Scully, "Civil Wrongs," 24.

24. Long, *Mapp v. Ohio*, 15; Scully, "Civil Wrongs," 24.

25. Kantrowitz, "Good Golly, Miss Dolly"; Long, *Mapp v. Ohio*, 15–18; Scully, "Civil Wrongs," 24, 26.

26. Quoted in Scully, "Civil Wrongs," 24, 26. See also Kantrowitz, "Good Golly, Miss Dolly"; Katz, "*Mapp* after Forty Years," 471.

27. *State v. Lindway*, 131 Ohio St. 166 (1936).

28. *Wolf v. Colorado*, 338 U.S. 25 (1949).

29. Long, *Mapp v. Ohio*, 17.

30. Ibid., 17; Scully, "Civil Wrongs," 26.

31. Kantrowitz, "Good Golly, Miss Dolly"; Katz, "*Mapp* after Forty Years," 473; Long, *Mapp v. Ohio*, 17–18; Scully, "Civil Wrongs," 26.

32. Long, *Mapp v. Ohio*, 18–20.

33. 367 U.S. 643, 644. See also Kantrowitz, "Good Golly, Miss Dolly"; Long, *Mapp v. Ohio*, 20–21.

34. Kantrowitz, "Good Golly, Miss Dolly"; Long, *Mapp v. Ohio*, 21–22.

35. Long, *Mapp v. Ohio*, 22–24; Scully, "Civil Wrongs," 26.

36. Quoted in Long, *Mapp v. Ohio*, 24. See also Zotti, *Injustice for All*, 86.

37. Long, *Mapp v. Ohio*, 24–28; Price, "*Mapp v. Ohio* Revisited," 60–61; Zotti, *Injustice for All*, 68.

38. 367 U.S. 643, 645. See also Long, *Mapp v. Ohio*, 28–32; Zotti, *Injustice for All*, 98.

39. 367 U.S. 643, 645. See also Long, *Mapp v. Ohio*, 28–32; Scully, "Civil Wrongs," 26.

40. 367 U.S. 643, 645–46. See also Long, *Mapp v. Ohio*, 58–60.

41. Long, *Mapp v. Ohio*, 62.

42. McInnis, *The Evolution of the Fourth Amendment*, 38; Scully, "Civil Wrongs," 26.

43. Long, *Mapp v. Ohio*, 72–74, 82; McInnis, *The Evolution of the Fourth Amendment*, 378; Roger J. Traynor, "*Mapp v. Ohio* at Large in the Fifty States," *Duke Law Journal* 1962, 3 (Summer 1962): 323–28.

44. Quoted in Long, *Mapp v. Ohio*, 84. See also Dennis D. Dorin, "Marshalling *Mapp:* Justice Tom Clark's Role in *Mapp v. Ohio*'s Extension of the Exclusionary Rule to State Searches and Seizures," *Case Western Reserve Law Review* 52, 2 (Winter 2001): 401–40; Price, "*Mapp v. Ohio* Revisited," 61–68; Leon F. Scully, Jr., *Bombers, Bolsheviks and Bootleggers: A Study in Constitutional Subversion* (Charlottesville, Va.: Publius Press, 2001).

45. Potter Stewart, "The Road to *Mapp v. Ohio* and Beyond: The Origins, Development and Future of the Exclusionary Rule in Search-and-Seizure Cases," *Columbia Law Review* 83, 6 (October 1983): 1368.

46. *Palko v. Connecticut*, 302 U.S. 319, 325 (1937). See also Loren P. Beth, "Mr. Justice Black and the First Amendment: Comments on the Dilemma of Constitutional Interpretation," *Journal of Politics* 41, 4 (November 1979): 1114–15.

47. Long, *Mapp v. Ohio*, 84; Price, "*Mapp v. Ohio* Revisited," 62–64.

48. 367 U.S. 643, 661. See also Long, *Mapp v. Ohio*, 82–96, 100–103; Price, "*Mapp v. Ohio* Revisited," 64.

49. 367 U.S. 643, 645. See also Long, *Mapp v. Ohio*, 105.

50. 367 U.S. 643. 651.

51. 367 U.S. 643, 654–55.

52. 367 U.S. 643, 655.

53. 367 U.S. 643, 657.

54. 367 U.S. 643, 659.

55. 367 U.S. 643, 660.

56. 367 U.S. 643, 662.

57. *Rochin v. California*, 342 U.S. 165 (1952).

58. *Boyd v. United States*, 116 U.S. 616 (1886).

59. 367 U.S. 643, 666.

60. 367 U.S. 643, 670.

61. 367 U.S. 643, 672.

62. 367 U.S. 643, 673, 674.

63. 367 U.S. 643, 678.

64. 367 U.S. 643, 680.

65. 367 U.S. 643, 686.

66. The literature on whether the Warren Court initiated a due process revolution and, if so, the nature and extent of that revolution is voluminous. See, for example, Justin Driver, "The Constitutional Conservatism of the Warren Court," *California Law Review* 100, 5 (October 2012): 1101–67; Fred P. Graham, *The Due Process Revolution: The Warren Court's Impact on Criminal*

Law (New York: Hayden Book Company, 1970); Eric J. Miller, "The Warren Court's Regulatory Revolution in Criminal Procedure," *Connecticut Law Review* 43, 1 (November 2010): 1–82. *United States v. Leon* is found at 468 U.S. 897 (1984).

67. Quoted in Long, *Mapp v. Ohio*, 105.

68. Information on Dollree Mapp's life after the Supreme Court case that bore her name can be found in Kantrowitz, "Good Golly, Miss Dolly"; Long, *Mapp v. Ohio*, 196–200.

CHAPTER 7
Gideon v. Wainwright (1963) and the Right to Counsel

On June 3, 1961, a burglar broke into the Bay Harbor poolroom in Panama City, Florida, vandalized the jukebox and cigarette machine, and apparently absconded with a small amount of money, wine, and beer. As they investigated the matter, police interrogated Clarence Earl Gideon, a local drifter and ex-convict. Because he had a pocketful of coins, a long arrest record, and a witness claimed to have spotted him inside the poolroom, Gideon was the prime suspect. He faced a formal charge that he "did unlawfully and feloniously break and enter a building of another, to-wit, the Bay Harbor Poolroom, property of Ira Strickland, Jr., lessee, with intent to commit a misdemeanor within said building, to-wit, petit larceny." It was unquestionably a petty crime with nothing to suggest that the run-of-the-mill circumstances would give rise to a landmark criminal procedure case.

The evidence amassed against Gideon was compelling but not overwhelming. Henry Cook of Panama City testified that he had been standing outside of the poolroom around 5:30 A.M. on June 3 when Gideon came out of the establishment with a pint of wine. According to Cook, Gideon used a nearby pay phone to make a call. A few minutes later, a taxicab arrived and Gideon slipped inside the vehicle to depart from the scene. Cook testified that when he looked at the poolroom after Gideon had left, he "saw it had been broken into." At no time during the direct examination did Cook explain why he had been loitering about the poolroom at 5:30 A.M. or why he did not summon the police when he discovered evidence of the crime.[1]

Gideon professed his innocence during his first encounter with law enforcement in June 1961. He also asked that defense counsel be appointed to represent him because he did not have the funds to hire his own attorney. The trial judge, Robert L. McCrary Jr., told him that indigent criminal defendants were entitled to court-appointed counsel only in capital cases. Under controlling precedents at the time, expressed by the U.S. Supreme Court in a landmark 1942 case, *Betts v. Brady*, the trial judge was correct in his application of the law.[2]

Judge McCrary was hardly an ogre. He was sympathetic to Gideon's plight. Recognizing the defendant was unschooled in courtroom procedures, at trial he instructed the man to "just walk right around there where you can see" the jurors "and tell them what you expect the evidence to show in your favor. Talk loud enough for them to hear you, now." Court reporters in Florida courts did not always record opening statements in that era, so it is difficult to say definitively what Gideon told the six gentlemen on the petit jury apart from proclaiming his innocence. His cross-examination of Henry Cook, however, was captured by a court reporter for posterity.

Gideon commenced his examination, astutely enough, by asking Cook why the young man had been hanging out in front of the poolroom so early in the morning. Cook explained that he had "just come from a dance, down in Apalachicola—stayed out all night." An experienced defense attorney no doubt would have probed this promising line of questioning, but Gideon was hardly a skilled advocate. He dropped the subject. When Gideon asked whether Cook had ever been arrested, the prosecution objected and the judge sustained the objection. Gideon tried a new tact. Had Cook ever been convicted of a felony, he inquired. Cook swore he had not. The rest of Gideon's rambling cross-examination revealed no new information helpful to either side of the case.

Clarence Earl Gideon was not a well-educated man, but neither was he mentally challenged or lacking in faculties. He conducted a cross-examination as well as most men of his station could be expected to do without legal training. Nonetheless, his questioning left much to be desired. As subsequent events would reveal, his inability to delve into Henry Cook's whereabouts and motives on June 3 severely undermined the defendant's case and did much to ensure his conviction.

The second, and last, prosecution witness, Ira Strickland Jr., operated the Bay Harbor poolroom. He described his actions the night before the break-in. He said that he had locked the doors and windows and departed around midnight on June 2. When he arrived at 8:00 the following morning, he met the deputy sheriff, who was already on the scene, and found the jukebox and cigarette machine had been burglarized. Strickland was unable to provide a complete inventory of the money or merchandize that was missing apart from concluding that "a small amount of beer and some wine" were gone. Gideon attempted to cross-examine the witness but, once again, he elicited little useful information.

Gideon called eight witnesses for the defense. The first, Officer Henry Berryhill, had stumbled onto the scene in the course of a routine patrol. As he described the situation, Officer Berryhill admitted he had encountered Henry Cook in front of the poolroom. Recalling the conversation, the officer testified that Cook "said he saw you [Gideon] leave the building." Gideon did not pursue this testimony. By failing to follow up on the Cook–Berryhill exchange, Gideon missed a prime opportunity to impeach Cook's credibility. In fact, when Berryhill stepped down from the witness stand, his recollection of the conversation with Henry Cook only reinforced the strength of the prosecution's case. Sheriff Duell Pitts Jr. next took the stand and testified in the same manner as his deputy. He recalled Cook telling him that Cook had seen Clarence Earl Gideon inside the poolroom after hours.

Preston Bray, the cabdriver who had arrived to pick up Gideon that morning, agreed that as far as he could tell, his fare had not been drunk. This tidbit was not helpful to Gideon. Although the lack of intoxication might have served as an indirect character reference—"at least Gideon isn't a drunkard"—in reality the information harmed his case more than it helped. Owing to his inexperience serving as defense counsel, Gideon did not realize that intoxication was a possible defense to burglary under Florida law. In establishing that he was not visibly inebriated at the time of the break-in, Gideon had undermined his position. A defendant acting *pro se* (on one's own behalf) would not be expected to comprehend the vagaries of the state criminal law, but a competent, experienced defense attorney would have known this fact.

Gideon failed to explore other salient points. Irene Rhodes, a local resident testifying on the defendant's behalf, recalled seeing Gideon near the poolroom that morning—hardly a point supporting the defense—but she observed that he was often in the vicinity because "he helps out in there occasionally." Preston Bray had mentioned this same fact. Gideon would have been wise to explore these issues; they were strong facts for the defense. If Clarence Earl Gideon helped out in the poolroom from time to time, he would have had a plausible excuse for being on the premises even after the building was closed. Moreover, a man who enjoyed regular access to the building could credibly argue that he need not break into areas where he could gain access lawfully.

The next three defense witnesses did nothing to bolster Gideon's case. He called the owner of the building and two poolroom employees, but they had no direct evidence to present. Gideon's landlady, Velva Estelle Morris, also testified. She owned the Bay Harbor Hotel located across the street from the poolroom. She told the jurors her tenant often crossed the road to use the outdoor pay telephone adjacent to the poolroom. Again, Gideon used a witness to establish that he was not habitually drunk when he asked Morris whether she had ever seen him intoxicated, but the information did not strengthen his defense.

The defendant's closing argument, which required 11 minutes, was not transcribed, although the court reporter noted that Gideon repeatedly emphasized his innocence. The prosecution required nine minutes. The judge charged the jury that the defendant could be found guilty if the six gentlemen agreed that Gideon committed the crime in Bay County within the past two years. The judge did not advise the jurors of the elements of the crime or the language of the appropriate Florida law. Gideon could have requested such instructions had he been aware of the law or his right to request a particular jury charge.

Predictably, Gideon's defense did not succeed. The jury returned a guilty verdict. Judge McCrary delayed sentencing until August 25 so he could review Gideon's past criminal record. Based on the defendant's prior arrests, the judge eventually sentenced Gideon to serve five years in prison, the maximum time allowed by law.

No one is as self-righteous as an innocent man wrongly convicted. Gideon repeatedly insisted he should have been represented by counsel. As he remarked during the initial trial, "The United States Supreme Court says I am entitled to be represented by counsel." Judge McCrary attempted to disabuse the defendant of this notion. "Under the laws of the State of Florida," the judge correctly told him, "the only time the court can appoint counsel to represent a Defendant is when that person is charged with a capital offense. I am sorry, but I will have to deny your request to appoint counsel in this case."[3]

If Gideon was not entitled to counsel, he reasoned, he *ought* to have been entitled. Consequently, still full of resentment at his unjust conviction, he filed a habeas corpus petition, a civil action challenging the validity of his detention. When the Florida Supreme Court denied his

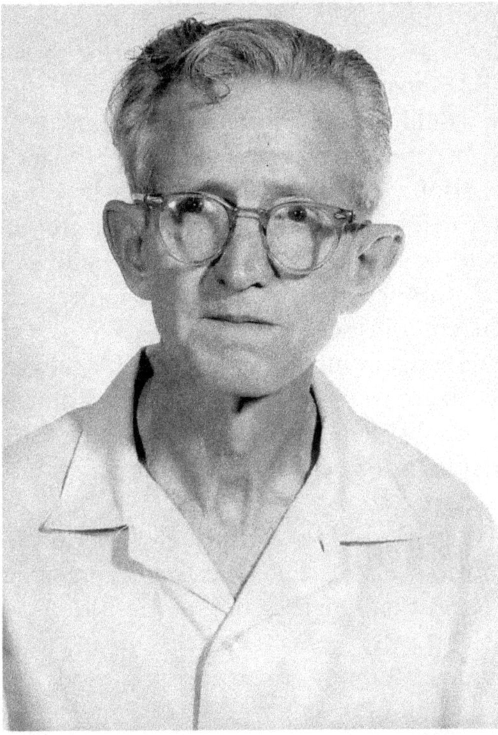

Clarence Earl Gideon petitioned the U.S. Supreme Court arguing that he should have been afforded an attorney after he was arrested for allegedly vandalizing a pool hall in 1961. (State Archives of Florida, Florida Memory, http://floridamemory.com/items/show/35169, Woody Wisner, photographer)

request, Gideon filed a petition for certiorari in forma pauperis with the U.S. Supreme Court alleging that his Sixth Amendment right to assistance of counsel, as applied to the states through the Fourteenth Amendment, had been denied.[4]

Each year thousands of disaffected litigants file appeals with the high court. The justices grant the petition in less than 1 percent of the cases. Even among that small number, most "pauper's petitions" do not fare as well as a traditional appeal. Justice William O. Douglas, a jurist sympathetic to the rights of criminal defendants, admitted that prisoner appeals, which frequently are filed in forma pauperis, "are often fantastic, surpassing credulity. They are for the most part frivolous." When Gideon sent his appeal to the justices, it was extremely unlikely that he would receive another day in court.[5]

Gideon's handwritten petition was held for 30 days while the head of the Florida prison system, H. G. Cochran Jr., was provided with an opportunity to respond. Because states typically did not respond to prisoners' petitions during that era, the deadline passed with no reply. Afterward, the petition wound up in Chief Justice Earl Warren's queue. The chief justice's law clerks typically read through petitions and provide written memoranda on the legal issues raised by a case, paying special attention to in forma pauperis appeals to ensure no legitimate appellant is denied a review. In sifting through the petitions, the clerks look for questions involving federal laws, treaties, or constitutional interpretation.

When Earl Warren's clerks read through Gideon's appeal, they recognized a meritorious claim. The court had been struggling with the rule in *Betts v. Brady* that defense counsel must be appointed for indigents only in capital cases. Several justices had expressed reservations about the continued validity of the rule—if, indeed, it was a valid rule in the first place. The Gideon appeal seemed to be well suited for a reconsideration of the issue. Warren agreed with his clerks and instructed them to contact the office of the Florida attorney general, Richard W. Ervin, asking for a response to the prisoner's petition.[6]

The state attorney general submitted a reply on April 9, 1962. Signed by Ervin and his assistant, Bruce R. Jacob, the brief followed the expected line of reasoning. Because *Betts v. Brady* only required the appointment of state-financed counsel in noncapital cases where "special circumstances" exist and the record did not indicate that such circumstances were present in Gideon's case, the defendant's petition for certiorari should be denied. Clarence Earl Gideon had received a fair trial under the applicable legal standards of the day. "Petitioner Gideon has made no affirmative showing of any exceptional circumstances which would entitle him to counsel under the Fourteenth Amendment," the respondents explained. "Petitioner merely alleges that he was without funds, that he pleaded not guilty and that he requested court-appointed counsel, while being tried on a non-capital charge." As far as the state of Florida was concerned, under current law, Gideon's "petition is notable for its lack of material allegations as to exceptional circumstances."[7]

Gideon was provided with an opportunity to reply to the attorney general's brief. In a simple, surprisingly eloquent statement, he reiterated his claim that he had been unduly prejudiced by the inability to afford defense counsel. In his view, "a citizen of the state of Florida cannot get a just and fair trial without the aid of counsel." As for special circumstances, Gideon did not understand their relevance. "It makes no difference how old I am or what color I am or what church I belong too [*sic*] if any."[8]

During the justices' conference deliberations on June 1, 1962, the court agreed to hear Gideon's case. They transferred the matter to the appellate docket, as is customary when a petition for certiorari is granted, and directed the parties to submit briefs and prepare for oral argument on one crucial issue: "Should this Court's holding in *Betts v. Brady*, 316 U.S. 455, be reconsidered?"[9]

Although Clarence Earl Gideon had been forced to serve as his own attorney in the trial court, the U.S. Supreme Court appointed counsel upon request. To ensure that Gideon made such a request in a timely manner, the chief deputy clerk of the court, Edmund P. Cullinan, sent the prisoner a note telling him that he must request counsel. Gideon replied quickly, stating, "I do desire the Court to appoint a competent attorney to represent me in this Court."

Appointment to represent a litigant before the U.S. Supreme Court during oral argument is a high honor, often capping a distinguished legal career. The justices do not follow hard-and-fast rules on the appointment process, but they usually seek out eminent members of the bar. Because the high court decides cases that hold enormous public policy implications, they consider lofty, fundamental legal principles and jurisprudential concepts in their deliberations. They expect a high quality of argument and seek to ensure well-prepared, professional advocates appear in the courtroom. For that reason, they appoint well-known, skilled attorneys who will present the best possible legal and philosophical arguments during the proceedings.[10]

The court appointed Abe Fortas to represent Gideon before the bar. At the time of his appointment, Fortas was a renowned 52-year-old lawyer known for his liberal views and New Deal background. A principal in the law firm of Arnold, Fortas and Porter, he had attended Yale Law School, where he was editor of the school's venerable law journal. After graduation, he worked for famous New Deal proponents such as William O. Douglas, Fortas's former professor, as well as Jerome Frank and Harold Ickes. When he entered the private practice of law,

Fortas quickly acquired a richly deserved reputation as an exceptional oral advocate. He also became an important counselor to the rich and powerful, spending time advising corporate officers and elected officials on the means for staying abreast of complex legal requirements. He became one of Lyndon B. Johnson's closest political and legal advisers. Johnson later appointed Fortas to the U.S. Supreme Court.[11]

When he received word that he would represent Gideon before the high court, Fortas assembled the trial record and other documents related to the case to determine whether he could reverse the conviction without asking the court to overrule *Betts v. Brady*. Although several justices had hinted at their displeasure with the state of the law, Fortas understood that courts generally adhere to the principle of stare decisis. They prefer not to overrule previous decisions absent a clear and compelling reason to do so. Although Fortas had no love for *Betts v. Brady*, his foremost duty was to his client. He would search for any and all legal means by which he could persuade the court to overturn

Renowned appellate attorney Abe Fortas, shown here, represented Clarence Earl Gideon in the U.S. Supreme Court. (Library of Congress)

Gideon's conviction. He would argue for wholesale rejection of the *Betts* rule, but he was obligated to look for less intrusive means of assisting his client as well.[12]

The Sixth Amendment to the U.S. Constitution guarantees a criminal defendant the right "to have the Assistance of Counsel for his defence." Much of the Constitution is written in vague language and is open to multiple interpretations. The amendment does not suggest that government is obliged to provide counsel for the accused if he or she is indigent. Moreover, the Bill of Rights applies to the federal government, not the states. Even if the Sixth Amendment can be broadly construed to require appointment of government-financed counsel, the question of whether the requirement can be extended to state court proceedings via selective incorporation through the Fourteenth Amendment's due process clause requires a separate analysis. In fact, the holding in a 1938 case, *Johnson v. Zerbst*, indicated that the requirement would be different for state and federal courts. In *Johnson*, the Court had limited the right to counsel to federal cases.[13] In the normal course of events, asking the Supreme Court to change the *Betts* and *Johnson* holdings would be exceedingly difficult because courts do not reverse their precedents without grave reservations and serious reflection.[14]

The institutions of government, often deeply tied to the past, are slow to respond to societal changes. The Supreme Court is no exception to the phenomenon of institutional inertia. Yet Clarence Earl Gideon filed his case at a fortuitous moment in history. The 1960s were a time of social unrest. The much-ballyhooed "due process revolution" of the Warren Court may have been exaggerated in the historical record, but by 1963 a majority of the justices was willing to consider a more expansive interpretation of constitutional provisions involving criminal procedure than it had been willing to accept in previous epochs.[15]

Gideon also was fortunate in another regard. In a typical criminal case, the state enjoys the advantages of enormous financial resources and the almost limitless investigatory techniques of the police. When Gideon's case came before the U.S. Supreme Court, the tables were turned. The indigent defendant was represented by one of the ablest lawyers ever to practice before the Supreme Court bar. Fortas was a man of gravitas with the intellectual prowess and vast experience necessary to present his client's case in the best possible light. His venerable law firm was staffed by skilled associates, who were able to devote numerous hours to exploring the penumbra of every legal doctrine on point.

The state of Florida, by contrast, depended on the work of an inexperienced, young assistant attorney general, Bruce Jacob. Just 27 years old, Jacob was new to Supreme Court practice. He could not call upon an army of assistants to chase down every legal tidbit or sift through turgid law review articles in search of a nuanced position. He called upon his fellow assistant attorneys general for advice on their procedures for appointing counsel to indigent defendants, but the heaviest burden for preparing the legal brief and practicing his oral argument fell on Jacob's shoulders.[16]

By all accounts, Abe Fortas acquitted himself well during the oral argument. Anything less than a stellar performance would have been surprising, but he met all expectations. Deftly handling questions from the justices sitting on the bench, Fortas attacked *Betts v. Brady* as administratively unworkable. Determining when special circumstances exist before the trial begins—the stage at which a trial judge most likely would appoint counsel for an indigent defendant—is problematic and can result in gross inequities. Recognizing that the Court was not required to answer the question as to when the right to counsel would attach, Fortas nonetheless ventured an opinion. A lawyer should be provided at least at the first arraignment before a court, he said. Later, during his rebuttal, the master advocate summarized the position succinctly. "I think *Betts and Brady* was wrong when it was decided," he said. "I think time has made that clear. And I think time has now made it possible for the correct rule, the civilized rule, the rule of American constitutionalism, the rule of due process to be stated by this Court with limited disturbance to the states."[17]

Former U.S. solicitor general J. Lee Rankin then spoke on behalf of the American Civil Liberties Union (ACLU) as a friend of the court supporting Gideon, and George D. Mentz, assistant attorney general of Alabama, later spoke on Florida's behalf. Bruce Jacob, the young assistant attorney general who represented the state of Florida, generated the most contentious discussion when he attempted to defend the *Betts* rule. Jacob went on to enjoy a distinguished career as a legal advocate and law professor, but when he appeared before the justices on the morning of January 15, 1963, he was a novice standing on the wrong side of history.

Whereas Fortas had emphasized lofty constitutional principles, the assistant attorney general worried about the burdens placed on the states if they had to provide and pay for counsel in potentially thousands upon thousands of criminal cases. He also feared the damage such a prophylactic rule might occasion for principles of federalism.

"By imposing an inflexible rule," he mused, "we feel this Court would be intruding into an area reserved to the states. It would stifle state experimentation. For example, a state might eliminate prosecutors as well as defense counsel and leave the whole trial to a judge." Justice John Marshall Harlan admonished the young man not to go too far with his argument. Other justices peppered him with questions, most of which seemed to cause him great consternation. At one point, Jacob conceded he had misspoken when he lamented, "I'm sorry, your honor, that was a stupid answer." It was not a calamitous argument in light of Jacob's youth and inexperience, but he must have known that Fortas had gotten the better of him. In light of the majority's disdain for the *Betts* rule, however, Bruce Jacob probably would not have changed the outcome no matter what he said that day.[18]

On March 18, 1963, a little more than two months after hearing oral argument, the Supreme Court announced its decision in *Gideon v. Wainwright*. (The respondent's name had changed because H. G. Cochran Jr. had retired and Louie L. Wainwright had succeeded him as director of corrections for the state of Florida.) Justice Hugo Black wrote the majority opinion. Although the case contained three concurring opinions, none of the justices filed a dissent. Whatever the reasoning, it was clear that the Supreme Court was prepared to recognize that *Betts v. Brady* should no longer serve as controlling precedent.[19]

Justice Black began by outlining the facts and noting the similarities between the *Gideon* and *Betts* cases. "Since the facts and circumstances of the two cases are so nearly indistinguishable, we think the *Betts v. Brady* holding, if left standing, would require us to reject Gideon's claim that the Constitution guarantees him the assistance of counsel," Black reasoned. "Upon full reconsideration, we conclude that *Betts v. Brady* should be overruled."[20]

Noting that the Court's opinion in the Scottsboro case, *Powell v. Alabama*, required defense counsel to be appointed for indigent defendants in capital cases as a major component of due process of law, Justice Black discussed the difficulties experienced by impecunious criminal defendants even in noncapital cases. Although the *Betts v. Brady* opinion had required court-appointed counsel in noncapital cases when special circumstances such as the illiteracy or stupidity of the defendants existed, as a practical matter it was extremely difficult to determine beforehand what constituted a "special circumstance." Owing to the difficulty in applying the "special circumstances" doctrine, the *Gideon* court concluded that *Betts* could not stand. Aside from the administrative burden in determining what constitutes a special circumstance, Black argued that effective assistance of counsel is a fundamental right and essential for a fair trial.[21]

Unlike the justices who thought the *Betts* case had been valid when it was decided, Justice Black believed it was irremediably flawed, and he was not a jurist to mince words. He agreed with Abe Fortas that while *Betts* had quite rightly concluded that fundamental rights necessary for a fair trial apply to all U.S. courts, the case should have characterized the right to counsel as fundamental. "We accept *Betts v. Brady*'s assumption, based as it was on our prior cases, that a provision of the Bill of Rights which is 'fundamental and essential to a fair trial' is made obligatory upon the States by the Fourteenth Amendment," he conceded. "We think the Court in *Betts* was wrong, however, in concluding that the Sixth Amendment's guarantee of counsel is not one of these fundamental rights." Referring to the case of the Scottsboro boys, he remarked, "Ten years before *Betts v. Brady*, this Court, after full consideration of all the historical data examined in *Betts*, had unequivocally declared that 'the right to the aid of counsel is of this fundamental character.'"[22]

Black stated a principle that Gideon had erroneously assumed to be axiomatic, namely, that "reason and reflection" in criminal trials "require us to recognize that, in our adversary system of criminal justice, any person haled into court, who is too poor to hire a lawyer, cannot be assured a fair trial unless counsel is provided for him. This seems to us to be an obvious truth." The right to enjoy a day in court is meaningless if the layperson does not have the means to make his or her voice heard. The Founders, in their wisdom, realized the awesome might of the state arrayed against the individual and sought to ensure that the citizenry would not be oppressed by the heavy hand of the law. "From the very beginning," Black observed, "our state and national constitutions and laws have laid great emphasis on procedural and substantive safeguards designed to assure fair trials before impartial tribunals in which every defendant stands equal before the law. This noble ideal cannot be realized if the poor man charged with crime has to face his accusers without a lawyer to assist him." Noting that 22 states had filed amicus curiae briefs arguing "that *Betts* was 'an anachronism when handed down,' and that it should now be overruled," Black concluded his opinion by reversing Gideon's conviction and remanding the case to the Supreme Court of Florida "or further action not inconsistent with this opinion.[23]

The opinion was a triumph for the proposition that adequate procedural safeguards are necessary for due process of law to prevail. From 1963 onward, anyone charged with a crime in a state or federal court in the United States would be afforded an opportunity to seek assistance from a qualified, competent defense attorney regardless of whether the defendant could pay for legal representation.[24]

Justice Douglas joined the Court's opinion but filed a separate concurrence to argue for total incorporation of the Bill of Rights protections to the states via the due process clause of the Fourteenth Amendment. Douglas lamented the fact that the justices had been unwilling to accept this doctrine. "Yet, happily, all constitutional questions are always open," he concluded in a hopeful vein. "And what we do today does not foreclose the matter."[25]

In his concurring opinion, Justice Tom Clark remarked that the Supreme Court previously had construed the law to require an absolute right to counsel in capital cases. Yet Clark could see no logical reason for distinguishing between capital and noncapital cases. "The Fourteenth Amendment requires due process of law for the deprival of 'liberty,' just as for deprival of 'life,' and there cannot constitutionally be a difference in the quality of the process based merely upon a supposed difference in the sanction involved," he contended. "How can the Fourteenth Amendment tolerate a procedure which it condemns in capital cases on the ground that deprival of liberty may be less onerous than deprival of life—a value judgment not universally accepted—or that only the latter deprival is irrevocable? I can find no acceptable rationalization for such a result, and I therefore concur in the judgment of the Court."[26]

Justice John Marshall Harlan II also filed a concurrence. "I agree that *Betts v. Brady* should be overruled, but consider it entitled to a more respectful burial than has been accorded, at least on the part of those of us who were not on the Court when that case was decided."[27] Harlan believed that Justice Black had been too emphatic in denouncing the *Betts* rule. According to Harlan, *Betts* had expanded the right to counsel when it was announced in 1942 by indicating that the right extended beyond capital cases when special circumstances existed. *Betts* was an attempt to respect federalism principles by not forcing burdensome criminal procedure requirements on the states. Over time, however, the *Betts* rule had eroded. "The special circumstances rule has been formally abandoned in capital cases, and the time has now come when it should be similarly abandoned in noncapital cases, at least as to offenses which, as the one involved here, carry the possibility of a substantial prison sentence," he stated. "(Whether the rule should extend to all criminal cases need not now be decided.) This indeed does no more than to make explicit something that has long since been foreshadowed in our decisions."[28]

Gideon v. Wainwright portended tremendous changes for American constitutional law. States reviewed, and sometimes revamped, their public defender laws in the aftermath of the decision. In some instances, courts appointed local attorneys to handle criminal cases on behalf of indigents and compensated appointed counsel at an established (and usually reduced) rate. Other states created a public defender office employing part-time or full-time lawyers to handle indigent defense using tax dollars as the primary source of revenue. Occasionally, a local legal aid society would provide attorneys to indigent clients. Several states provided legal services on a sliding scale, requiring criminal defendants to pay part of the costs of representation depending on their income.[29]

As for Clarence Earl Gideon, he faced a retrial for the break-in at the Bay Harbor poolroom. He was, of course, delighted to learn that Abe Fortas had so ably represented his interests before the Supreme Court bar, but Gideon was convinced that a retrial would constitute double jeopardy, clearly a violation of the U.S. Constitution. Several times he was told that a new trial afforded to a criminal defendant on his own motion would not constitute double jeopardy, but he was unwilling or unable to understand the subtleties of the issue.[30]

Fortas wrote to the Florida Civil Liberties Union to secure a defense attorney for Gideon's new trial. Tobias Simon of Miami had filed an amicus curiae brief in the *Gideon* case on behalf of the ACLU. He seemed an ideal choice to handle the trial defense. In response to Fortas's letter, Simon took up the case. When he appeared in Panama City with his co-counsel, Irwin J. Block, formerly a chief prosecutor in Miami, Simon found Gideon in a state of high anxiety. Aside from his double jeopardy concerns, he was adamant that he would never receive a fair, impartial trial in Panama City. The next morning, standing before Judge McCrary, the original trial judge, in chambers, Gideon made his displeasure known in no uncertain terms. When informed that Simon had signed papers identifying himself as counsel of record, Gideon objected. "I didn't authorize Mr. Simon to sign anything for me," he said. "I'll do my own signing. I do not want him to represent me."

It was mystifying. Gideon had fought so long and hard to be represented by counsel. Now, with a new trial in the offing, the irascible old fellow seemed strangely obdurate. When the judge asked whether Gideon wanted someone other than Simon and Block to represent him, he said no. He also said he wasn't ready for trial. In frustration, McCrary asked, "What do you want, then?"

Gideon complained that a trial in the same venue with the same judge would not lead to justice. He even argued that he should be permitted to handle his own defense. Judge McCrary knew better than to allow Gideon, the man now famous for requesting a lawyer in a criminal trial, to handle his own case. After a round of verbal sparring, Gideon mentioned that a local attorney, W. Fred Turner, would be a suitable choice. The judge agreed, telling the court clerk to record that "I am going to appoint Mr. Fred Turner to represent this defendant, Clarence Earl Gideon."[31]

Fred Turner was an experienced trial attorney from Panama City. Told he had been appointed to represent Gideon, he immediately went to work. When Henry Cook took the stand at the retrial in August 1963, he faced a far more difficult line of questioning than he had faced during the initial proceedings. Turner had spent time in Bay Harbor investigating the facts. On cross-examination, he asked why Cook had been hanging around the pool hall. He observed that advertising boards in front of the pool hall would have made it difficult for Cook to look through the window and see inside. Finally, Turner suggested that Cook, who had returned from Apalachicola earlier that morning, had served as the lookout while his friends looted the establishment. Of course, Henry Cook was not on trial, and he vehemently denied the allegations. The point was made, however. Fred Turner knew he did not have to prove that the witness was guilty of the crime. All he had to do was raise the specter of reasonable doubt. Turner succeeded in doing exactly that when he showed that Cook's claim at the first trial never to have been convicted of a felony—Cook had pleaded guilty before a jury verdict could be rendered—had been false and misleading. Other witnesses followed, but Gideon's guilt was suddenly not so clear.

Fred Turner's representation unequivocally illustrated the importance of retaining competent defense counsel. The Panama City advocate knew how to investigate a case, examine a witness, object to evidence, pick a jury, and bargain for an appropriate jury charge. Clarence Earl Gideon's insight that a criminal defendant required court-appointed counsel to ensure a fair trial proved to be prescient. The jury acquitted the defendant on retrial.[32]

Gideon v. Wainwright became part of a line of cases announced by the Warren Court during the 1960s that led to a "due process revolution" in U.S. criminal procedure. As U.S. Attorney General Robert F. Kennedy stated:

> If an obscure Florida convict named Clarence Earl Gideon had not sat down in prison with a pencil and paper to write a letter to the Supreme Court; and if the Supreme Court had not taken the trouble to look at the merits in that one crude petition among all the bundles of mail it must receive every day, the vast machinery of American law would have gone on functioning undisturbed. But Gideon did write that letter; the court did look into his case; he was re-tried with the help of competent defense counsel; found not guilty and released from prison after two years of punishment for a crime he did not commit. And the whole course of legal history has been changed.[33]

NOTES

1. Douglas L. Colbert, "Connecting Theory and Reality: Teaching *Gideon* and Indigent Defendants' Non-Right to Counsel at Bail," *Ohio State Journal of Criminal Law* 4, 1 (Fall 2006): 172–73; Colin Evans, "Clarence Earl Gideon Trials: 1961 & 1963," in *Great American Trials: From Salem Witchcraft to Rodney King*, Edward W. Knappman, editor (Detroit, Mich.: Visible Ink Press, a Division of Gale Research, Inc., 1994), 494; Bruce R. Jacob, "50 Years Later: Memories of *Gideon v. Wainwright*," *Florida Bar Journal* 87, 3 (March 2013): 11; Bruce R. Jacob, "Memories of and Reflections about *Gideon v. Wainwright*," *Stetson Law Review* 33, 1 (Fall 2003): 184–85; Yale Kamisar, "*Gideon v. Wainwright:* A Quarter-Century Later," *Pace Law Review* 10, 2 (Spring 2010): 344; Anthony Lewis, *Gideon's Trumpet* (Birmingham, Ala.: The Notable Trials Library, 1991 [1964]), 57–59; David A. Simon, "Equal before the Law: Toward a Restoration of *Gideon*'s Promise," *Harvard Civil Rights-Civil Liberties Law Review* 43, 2 (Summer 2008): 581; Randal Yakey, "Panama City Case Changed Legal History 50 Years Ago," *New Herald* (Panama City, Florida, 17 March 2013).

2. *Betts v. Brady*, 316 U.S. 455 (1942). See also Colbert, "Connecting Theory and Reality," 172–74; Jacob, "Memories of and Reflections about *Gideon v. Wainwright*," 200–203; Lewis, *Gideon's Trumpet*, 9–10.

3. The trial transcript is summarized in Lewis, *Gideon's Trumpet*, 57–62. See also Evans, "Clarence Earl Gideon Trials," 494–95; Jacob,

"50 Years Later," 11; Jacob, "Memories of and Reflections about *Gideon v. Wainwright*," 205–212; Yakey, "Panama City Case Changed Legal History 50 Years Ago."

4. *Gideon v. Wainwright*, 372 U.S. 335, 336–37 (1963). See also Evans, "Clarence Earl Gideon Trials," 495.

5. Quoted in Lewis, *Gideon's Trumpet*, 34. See also Laurence Baum, *The Supreme Court*, 3rd ed. (Washington, DC: CQ Press, 1989), 104–6; David M. O'Brien, *Storm Center: The Supreme Court in American Politics* (New York: Norton, 1986), 161, 163.

6. Jacob, "50 Years Later," 11–12; Lewis, *Gideon's Trumpet*, 34–36; Mark Walsh, "Living Up to the *Gideon* Ideal," *ABA Journal* 99, 3 (March 2013): 45–46.

7. Jacob, "50 Years Later," 11–12; Jacob, "Memories of and Reflections about *Gideon v. Wainwright*," 217–20; Lewis, *Gideon's Trumpet*, 36–37.

8. Lewis, *Gideon's Trumpet*, 37–38.

9. 372 U.S. 335, 338–39.

10. Lewis, *Gideon's Trumpet*, 44–48.

11. Baum, *The Supreme Court*, 79; Jacob, "Memories of and Reflections about *Gideon v. Wainwright*," 221–22; Kamisar, "*Gideon v. Wainwright*," 345; Lewis, *Gideon's Trumpet*, 48–53.

12. Baum, *The Supreme Court*, 124–27; Lewis, *Gideon's Trumpet*, 117–28; Ellen S. Podgor, "*Gideon* at 40: Facing the Crisis, Fulfilling the Promise," *The American Criminal Law Review* 41, 1 (Winter 2004): 138–40.

13. *Johnson v. Zerbst*, 304 U.S. 458 (1938).

14. See, for example, O'Brien, *Storm Center*, 158; "Rethinking the Boundaries of the Sixth Amendment Right to Choice of Counsel," *Harvard Law Review* 124, 6 (April 2011): 1550–71.

15. See, for example, Corinna Barrett Lain, "Countermajoritarian Hero or Zero? Rethinking the Warren Court's Role in the Criminal Procedure Revolution," *University of Pennsylvania Law Review* 152, 4 (April 2004): 1361–1452.

16. Jacob, "Memories of and Reflections about *Gideon v. Wainwright*," 217–18; Lewis, *Gideon's Trumpet*, 137–41.

17. Quoted in Lewis, *Gideon's Trumpet*, 180. See also Baum, *The Supreme Court*, 132; Jacob, "Memories of and Reflections about *Gideon v. Wainwright*," 241–43; Lewis, *Gideon's Trumpet*, 169–74.

18. Jacob, "Memories of and Reflections about *Gideon v. Wainwright*," 243–49; Lewis, *Gideon's Trumpet*, 176–79.

19. 372 U.S. 335. See also Evans, "Clarence Earl Gideon Trials," 496; Jacob, "50 Years Later," 16; Kamisar, "*Gideon v. Wainwright*," 347–48; Lewis, *Gideon's Trumpet*, 184–86; Podgor, "*Gideon* at 40," 139–40.

20. 372 U.S. 335, 339.

21. Baum, *The Supreme Court*, 120; Tracey L. Meares, "What's Wrong with *Gideon*?," *The University of Chicago Law Review* 70, 1 (Winter 2003): 222–23; O'Brien, *Storm Center*, 159; Podgor, "*Gideon* at 40," 140.

22. 372 U.S. 335, 342.

23. 372 U.S. 335, 344. See also Kamisar, "*Gideon v. Wainwright*," 345; Lewis, *Gideon's Trumpet*, 141–50.

24. The Supreme Court would modify the terms and conditions for legal representation in the years after Earl Warren left the bench, but the general principle had been established. Meares, "What's Wrong with *Gideon?*," 215–31; "Rethinking the Boundaries of the Sixth Amendment Right to Choice of Counsel," 1550–71; Simon, "Equal before the Law," 581–94; Allan D. Sobel, "Fulfilling the Promise of *Gideon*," *Judicature* 88, 1 (July/August 2004): 5, 37; Walsh, "Living Up to the *Gideon* Ideal," 45–49.

25. 372 U.S. 335, 346.

26. 372 U.S. 335, 349.

27. 372 U.S. 335, 349.

28. 372 U.S. 335, 351.

29. See, for example, Allison D. Kuhns, "If You Cannot Afford an Attorney, Will One Be Appointed for You? How (Some) States Force Criminal Defendants to Choose between Posting Bond and Getting a Court-Appointed Attorney," *Iowa Law Review* 97, 5 (July 2012): 1787–1810; Ronald F. Wright, "Anatomy of a Public Defender System: Public Defender Elections and Popular Control Over Criminal Justice," *Missouri Law Review* 75, 3 (Summer 2010): 803–29.

30. Jacob, "Memories of and Reflections about *Gideon v. Wainwright*," 257–59; Lewis, *Gideon's Trumpet*, 223–24.

31. Jacob, "50 Years Later," 16; Lewis, *Gideon's Trumpet*, 223–28.

32. Evans, "Clarence Earl Gideon Trials," 496; Jacob, "50 Years Later," 16; Lewis, *Gideon's Trumpet*, 226, 228–37.

33. Quoted in Yakey, "Panama City Case Changed Legal History 50 Years Ago." See also Sobel, "Fulfilling the Promise of *Gideon*," 5.

CHAPTER 8

Miranda v. Arizona (1966) and the Right to Remain Silent

Ernesto Arturo Miranda, by all accounts, was a disturbed young man. Born in Mesa, Arizona, on March 9, 1941, he was in and out of trouble throughout his life. He first crossed paths with law enforcement when he was in the eighth grade. The next year, he was convicted of burglary and sent to the Arizona State Industrial School for Boys. Released after a year, he immediately fell back into his old ways and returned to the reformatory.[1]

Miranda could never find his place in society, probably because he was emotionally unstable and intellectually challenged. He drifted around the Southwest as a young man, doing time in California and Texas jails before serving a sentence in the federal prison system after he stole a car and transported it across state lines. By the time he was in his early twenties, he was back in Phoenix working on and off as a day laborer. He eventually met and started living with Twila Hoffman, a woman six years his senior. She had two children—a boy and a girl—by another man, but Ernesto Miranda seemed unfazed by the unusual arrangement.[2]

Around the same time Hoffman and Miranda began living together late in 1962, Phoenix police noticed a disturbing pattern of crimes. On November 27, a young female bank teller, identified in court records as "Barbara Doe," remained downtown after work to attend a night-time training class. As she walked to her car after class, a man lunged from the shadows and grabbed her. It was difficult to see his face, but she later described her assailant as a short, slender Hispanic man in his twenties. He forced his way into her car and drove to a nearby alley. The man brandished a knife but said that he would not hurt Barbara if she stayed quiet. After fumbling with her blouse for a few minutes in an apparent rape attempt, he lost his nerve. Frustrated and fearful of discovery, he stole $8 from the hysterical victim and fled the scene.[3]

Three months later, on February 22, 1963, an 18-year-old telephone dispatcher, pseudonymously known as "Sylvia Doe," was unlocking her car after working a late-night shift when, suddenly, seemingly out of nowhere, a slender Hispanic man approached her. He displayed a knife and demanded that she surrender the automobile and whatever money she had in her purse. As he pawed at her clothes, the woman screamed. The man grew alarmed and fled.[4]

On March 2, 1963, a little more than a week after the attack on Sylvia Doe, an 18-year-old employee of the downtown Paramount Theatre, "Patricia Doe," caught a bus home at 11:45 P.M., as was her custom. The bus dropped her three blocks from the apartment she shared with her parents in central Phoenix. During the short walk home, Patricia noticed nothing unusual until she was a block from her front door. It was just after midnight. In a swift, surprising maneuver, an older-model four-door sedan pulled up to the curb beside her. Without a word, the driver jumped from the car and held something sharp, probably a knife, against her throat. Pushing the frightened woman inside his car, the kidnapper drove her to the end of a dirt road on the outskirts of the city. Patricia, hysterical and crying, protested vehemently, but to no avail. No one was around to hear her screams. The man raped her. After committing the crime, the assailant drove her back toward her apartment before releasing her onto the street around 2:00 A.M.[5]

The distraught woman reported the rape to the Phoenix Police Department. The next day, Sgt. Seymour Nealis assigned the case to Detective Carroll Cooley. Cooley had served on the force for five years and was thoroughly familiar with criminal investigations involving assault, kidnapping, and rape. After reviewing the facts, he knew the case would be difficult to solve. The victim was understandably confused and imprecise about many details, hardly unusual when persons have suffered through a traumatic episode. Patricia described the rapist as a Mexican man in his twenties wearing glasses. His car was a 1950s Ford or Chevrolet, but she could not be certain. Nealis and Cooley discussed the case and recognized that it fit into a pattern with the assaults on young women in downtown Phoenix beginning the previous November. Witness descriptions of the assailant and his behavior were too similar to be a coincidence, although in the last case, his behavior had escalated to rape.[6]

Cooley promised to pursue all leads aggressively, but the problem was a paucity of usable information. Fortunately, a break in the case came a week later. To alleviate Patricia's fears, a male cousin who lived at her house began meeting her when her bus arrived each evening. As he waited for the bus one evening, the cousin spotted a slow-moving sedan cruising across the street. He could not see the driver's face from where he waited, but something about the way the car drove past the scene convinced him the man behind the wheel might be the attacker. He remained hypervigilant. When the vehicle disappeared down the block only to reappear a few minutes later, the cousin was convinced the rapist was on the prowl. The driver apparently realized he was being scrutinized because he sped away when the cousin tried to write down the license plate number. Fortunately, the cousin captured a partial number—DFL-312—and recognized the make of the sedan as a Packard.[7]

When the cousin reported what he had seen to Detective Cooley, the information provided investigators with their first major lead in the case. Cooley and Patricia's cousin visited local automobile dealerships to ensure they had identified the correct model of the car—a 1953 Packard sedan. When he was satisfied the information was accurate, Cooley traced the partial license plate number and located the registered owner of a vehicle matching the cousin's description. The owner's name was Twila Hoffman, and she lived with a man who physically resembled the attacker. He was 23-year-old Ernesto Arturo Miranda.[8]

Detective Cooley and his partner, Detective Wilfred Young, visited the Hoffman home and knocked on the door. A woman with a baby on her hip answered. Yes, she owned that car, she said, but her boyfriend sometimes borrowed it. She told the detectives her boyfriend was at home, but he was sleeping. When she offered to wake him, they asked her to do so.

The sleepy-eyed man who ambled over to talk with the officers certainly matched the witnesses' descriptions. Ernesto Miranda was a slender Hispanic man in his twenties, and he wore glasses. The officers were convinced they had their man until they questioned him. Instead of appearing frightened or guilty, Miranda freely answered questions and did not seem especially worried about talking with police officers. When they asked if he would accompany them to the police station, he readily agreed.[9]

The three men rode together for almost 30 minutes to the police station. Detective Cooley later admitted the case against Miranda was circumstantial and slim. The evidence probably would not have held up in court. Miranda had a lengthy arrest record and he physically resembled the man who had attacked the three women, but the details about the car were far from conclusive. The police had no forensic evidence and only a generic eyewitness description of the suspect. They had no way to link the suspect to the scene of the crime. Miranda's demeanor also seemed relaxed, hardly what one would expect from a guilty man.

When they arrived at the police station, Cooley and Young escorted the young man into an interrogation room and peppered him with questions about Patricia Doe's rape as well as the November 27 attack on Barbara Doe. Miranda swore he was innocent of both crimes. When the interrogation failed to rattle the suspect, Cooley asked Miranda to stand in a lineup. Cooley said he would be free to leave after the eyewitnesses cleared him of wrongdoing. Miranda agreed to participate.[10]

Ernesto Miranda (wearing the number 1) is shown in the lineup that preceded his arrest for rape in 1963. (Arizona State Library, Archives and Public Records, History and Archives Division, Phoenix, #97-9306)

Observing the lineup behind a two-way mirror, Barbara and Patricia said the man holding the number "1" in the lineup (Miranda) appeared to be the attacker, but neither woman was certain. Their lack of certainty was especially vexing because witness descriptions had indicated the attacker wore eyeglasses. Miranda was the only person wearing glasses in the lineup. The tentative identification was not the definitive conclusion Cooley needed to close a weak case. "I was somewhat dejected and frustrated," he later admitted. If Miranda continued proclaiming his innocence, the detective was afraid he would not have sufficient evidence to arrest, much less charge or convict, the suspect.[11]

The authorities were stymied and almost ready to release Miranda when an inspired improvisation changed the nature of the case. A worried Detective Cooley returned to the interrogation room, perturbed because he was reasonably certain he had his man but could not prove it. When Ernesto Miranda saw the expression on the detective's face, however, he misinterpreted its meaning.

The suspect nervously asked, "How did I do?"

Cooley paused. The previously unflappable young man suddenly seemed alarmed and shaken. Police officers routinely trick suspects, and the officer decided on the spur of the moment to take advantage of Miranda's changed demeanor. In response to the suspect's query, Cooley muttered, "Not too good, Ernie."

The response upset Miranda even more. "They identified me then?"

"Yes, Ernie, they did," Cooley told him. If it was not quite a lie, the detective's comment did not convey the tentative nature of the witness identifications.

Miranda appeared to resign himself to his predicament. "I guess I'd better tell you about it then."[12]

In this way, Detective Cooley gained a confession from his man. Surprised that Miranda had broken so easily and fearful he might change his mind if afforded time for reflection, the officer scrambled to nail down the confession. Cooley retrieved a written form that contained standard boilerplate language: "I do hereby swear that I make this statement voluntarily and of my own free will, with no threats, coercion, or promises of immunity, and with full knowledge of my legal rights, understanding any statement I make may be used against me." The next sentence contained blanks for the suspect to fill in before providing details of the crimes. The detective slid the papers across the table to the young man and instructed him to fill in the spaces. When completed, the form read, "I, Ernesto Miranda, am 23 years of age and have completed the eighth grade in school." Below that, in a space reserved for the confessor's summary of events, in his halting prose and poor grammar, Miranda wrote:

> Seen a girl walking up street stopped a little ahead of her got out of car walked towards her grabbed her by the arm and asked to get in car. Got in car without force tied hands and ankles. Drove away for a few mile. Stopped asked to take clothes off. Did not, asked me to take her back home. I started to take clothes off without any force and with cooperation. Asked her to lay down and she did. Could not get penis into vagina got about 1/2 (half) inch in. Told her to get clothes back on. Drove her home. I couldn't say I was sorry for what I had done but asked her to pray for me.

Miranda signed the confession above a preprinted statement: "I have read and understand the foregoing statement and hereby swear to its truthfulness." Detectives Cooley and Young also signed the confession as witnesses.[13]

After producing a written confession in the rape case, Miranda verbally admitted he had robbed Barbara Doe in November and had attempted to rob Sylvia in February. The detectives considered directing Miranda to prepare a written confession for all the crimes he had committed in 1962 and 1963, but ultimately they rejected the idea. They were concerned that the rape confession might be particularly vulnerable to attack if the statement referred to multiple crimes. "You threw in every crime you could think of, real or imagined," defense counsel might argue. If evidence for one crime was lacking or questionable, the judge could exclude the entire confession from evidence or direct the jury to discount its value. Because the rape was the most serious charge, the officers wanted to ensure that Miranda would be held responsible for that offense. The lesser crimes were secondary concerns.

Despite the presence of a written confession, the detectives took one final step to close the cases. They wanted an unequivocal identification of the perpetrator. To accomplish that objective, they ushered Patricia Doe into the interrogation room and asked Miranda to state his name. He complied with the request. He even said that he recognized the victim: "She's the one I was talking about." Afterward, Barbara Doe also came into the room and heard Miranda say he recognized her. The process went far better than the detectives had anticipated. Not surprisingly, the two women said that they were certain the police had identified the culprit after the other suspects in the lineup had been eliminated. Miranda's identification of the victims was an unexpected benefit.

Detectives Cooley and Young were satisfied they had prepared a case that could withstand judicial scrutiny and lead to the defendant's conviction. They had secured a written confession and two positive eyewitness identifications from the crime victims. Accordingly, following the identifications, Cooley and Young formally arrested Ernesto Miranda. The officers never informed him of his constitutional right to remain silent or request representation by a defense attorney during the interrogation. At the time, police officers were not required to advise a criminal defendant that such rights existed. For detectives anxious to solve a rape case, telling a suspect he could remain silent and advising him to ask for a lawyer before the interrogation began seemed counterintuitive and an unnecessary impediment to an ongoing police investigation.[14]

The court scheduled Miranda's robbery trial for the November 27 encounter with Barbara Doe as the first order of business. Trial commenced on June 26, 1963. Laurence "Larry" Turoff, a young lawyer who had handled numerous property crime offenses, prosecuted the case. Presiding judge Yale McFate appointed 73-year-old Alvin Moore, a skilled civil attorney with little experience in criminal matters, to represent the indigent defendant. With a confession in hand, witness identifications on file, and an unsympathetic defendant, Turoff considered the matter routine. It was as close to an open-and-shut case as a prosecutor could desire. As expected, the jury convicted the defendant by day's end. The only remarkable exchange occurred when Moore cross-examined Detective Cooley and asked whether the officer had informed Miranda that anything he said would be used against him in court or that he had the right to an attorney.

Cooley answered that he had not informed the defendant of those rights. Moore's inexperience in defending criminal cases had been painfully apparent throughout the day, but in this instance he seized on what he viewed as a major weakness in the state's case. Turning to address the judge, Moore sought to exclude Miranda's confession from evidence because it was coerced. "We object," he said, "not voluntarily given." If he could have the confession excluded from evidence, his chances of winning an acquittal would increase significantly.

"I don't believe that is necessary," Turoff replied. Judge McFate agreed, overruling the defense objection. In time, the issue of whether the defendant was advised of his constitutional rights would prove to be the crucial point in Ernesto Miranda's appeal of his subsequent rape conviction.

After the jury found the defendant guilty of robbery, the judge deferred sentencing until after the rape trial, which was scheduled to begin the following day. Although a new jury would be selected for the rape case, the same lawyers, witnesses, and courtroom would be involved. In some ways, the robbery trial was a dress rehearsal for what was yet to come.[15]

The rape trial opened on the morning of June 27. Patricia Doe took the stand and narrated the details of her ordeal. According to observers, she was a credible, sympathetic witness, and her tale was gripping and heart-wrenching. Patricia's sister followed with testimony explaining the horrific after-effects of the rape on the poor woman's state of mind. Detective Cooley was up next. He skillfully led the jurors through the steps of his investigation.

Although he was not an experienced criminal defense attorney, Alvin Moore realized his only reasonable defense was to attack the circumstances under which Miranda had signed his confession. He asked Cooley whether an attorney had been present when Miranda had been interrogated or when he had written his confession. In a departure from his testimony at the robbery trial, Cooley admitted that no lawyer had been present, but he said he had informed Miranda of his rights. Curiously, Moore did not challenge the detective for providing a prior inconsistent statement.

Cooley's partner, Wilfred Young, agreed that no attorney had been present during the interrogation, but he did not remember offering the defendant the opportunity to secure counsel. The admission that Miranda had not been informed of his rights before being interrogated was exactly the opening Moore needed. He objected that a confession obtained without defense counsel present could not be considered voluntary. As in the robbery trial, Judge McFate overruled the objection. The confession was entered into evidence.[16]

The jury only required a matter of minutes to convict Ernesto Miranda of rape and kidnapping. Seven days later, the judge sentenced the defendant to serve 20 to 30 years in prison on each of the two counts, rape and kidnapping, in the indictment. He also passed sentence on the $8 robbery conviction. Miranda was required to serve 25 years for robbery, with the sentence to run concurrently with the rape and kidnapping sentences.[17]

Facing a lengthy prison term, Miranda gave notice of intent to appeal the convictions. On appeal, the Arizona Supreme Court affirmed, explaining that Miranda had not requested an attorney at any time during the interrogation. The court's decision begged the question of whether the suspect should have been told that he had the right to request an attorney.[18] In the law-and-order atmosphere of Arizona during the 1960s, a serial offender's complaint that he had not been afforded his constitutional rights fell on deaf ears.[19]

In one final attempt to overturn his conviction, Miranda filed an in forma pauperis appeal to the U.S. Supreme Court in June 1965. He filed his petition at a propitious time in the history of American criminal justice. By the 1960s, the U.S. Supreme Court had begun to clarify the rights of criminal defendants in landmark cases such as *Mapp v. Ohio* and *Gideon v. Wainwright*, discussed in previous chapters of this book. Encouraged by the Warren Court's willingness to confront long-simmering criminal procedure issues, civil libertarians were debating the need for greater constitutional protections in interrogation cases. Miranda's petition caught the attention of representatives from the American Civil Liberties Union (ACLU), a nonprofit lobbying organization devoted to protecting individual liberties from encroachment by government authority. Recognizing that Miranda's trial attorney, Alvin Moore, was suffering from major health problems and was inexperienced in criminal appeals, ACLU attorney Robert J. Corcoran asked a seasoned criminal defense attorney, John J. Flynn, and his partner, John P. Frank, to represent Miranda on the appeal. They agreed to do so along with another attorney, Peter D. Baird of Lewis & Roca, a Phoenix law firm. The attorneys submitted a 2,500-word petition supporting Miranda's handwritten petition to the high court.[20]

In November 1965, the U.S. Supreme Court granted certiorari to consider *Miranda v. Arizona.* The high court consolidated three other cases along with *Miranda.* In each instance, the legal question was whether a suspect had provided a voluntary confession. In the first of the three consolidated cases, *Westover v. United States*, Carl Calvin Westover was arrested in Kansas City, Missouri, on March 20, 1963, and charged with two robberies. While the suspect was in custody, authorities discovered he was wanted on a felony warrant in California. When agents from the Federal Bureau of Investigation (FBI) learned that Westover had been apprehended, they contacted Kansas City police and asked that he be detained long enough for Bureau agents to question him. After enduring lengthy questioning from local authorities in the morning, Westover sat through a second round of questioning as FBI investigators interrogated him during the afternoon. At the conclusion of their session, the agents persuaded the suspect to write a detailed confession in longhand describing two robberies he had committed in Sacramento, California. With the confession in hand, federal officials whisked Westover back to Sacramento to stand trial for his crimes in that jurisdiction.

After Westover was convicted, he appealed to the Ninth Circuit, which affirmed the conviction. The Ninth Circuit judges concluded that in the original trial, Westover had never challenged the confession or his lack of counsel during his interrogation; therefore, the issue was not open to challenge in a higher court. On appeal to the U.S. Supreme Court, Westover argued that he had never been informed that the confession would be used against him in court or that he had the right to an attorney. The fact that he had not raised the issue previously should not bar him from raising the question on appeal. In fact, the entire case stemmed from his lack of knowledge about his rights and the authorities' failure to explain them to him.

The second case, *Vignera v. State of New York*, involved a defendant, Michael Vignera, who robbed a Brooklyn, New York, dress shop on October 11, 1960. Three days later, police stopped a man who attempted to use the dress shop owner's credit card. When he was questioned, the man claimed to have received the stolen credit card from Michael Vignera. Police picked up Vignera and drove him to the dress shop. The owner immediately identified him. After placing the suspect under arrest, officers transported the man to the police station and interrogated him. Vignera confessed his involvement in the crime to the detective asking the questions. Later, he repeated his story to an assistant district attorney with a stenographer on hand to produce a written version of the confession. Both the oral and written confessions were admitted at trial. Following his conviction, Vignera challenged the admission of the confession into evidence because he had not been advised of his right to remain silent or his right to obtain defense counsel.

The third case, *State of California v. Stewart*, concerned Roy Allen Stewart, a defendant accused of robbing five women, one of whom he murdered, in Los Angeles between December 21, 1962, and January 30, 1963. As police officers investigated the serial crimes, they learned Stewart had cashed checks stolen during the spree. Based on this evidence, police appeared at Stewart's home on January 31, arrested him and four other men on the premises, and uncovered evidence of the robberies during a search of the home. Stewart initially denied any involvement in the crimes, but after being placed in a cell from January 31 until February 5 and questioned at length on nine separate occasions, he eventually broke down and confessed to robbing the murder victim. Police tape-recorded two of the confessions. The tapes were admitted at trial and helped convict Stewart of the robbery and the murder. He received the death penalty. On appeal to the California Supreme Court, he alleged he had not been provided with defense counsel after his arrest. California state law recognized a more expansive view of the Sixth Amendment right to counsel than many other states at the time. As a result, the California Supreme Court reversed Stewart's conviction because he had not been advised of his right to remain silent or his right to counsel.[21]

The U.S. Supreme Court often grants certiorari to hear a case when the lower federal courts or the state courts are silent or ambiguous on a point of law. After percolating through the state and federal court systems for years, the issue of whether a defendant must be notified of his or her constitutional rights under the Fifth and Sixth amendments appeared ripe for judicial review in the highest court of the land. Owing to precedents extending back for decades, at least since *Powell v. Alabama* in 1932 (see Chapter 4) and the more recent *Gideon v. Wainwright* (1963) (see Chapter 7), no one doubted that criminal defendants had the right to an attorney under the Sixth Amendment as well as the right not to be compelled to testify against oneself under the Fifth Amendment. The question for *Miranda v. Arizona* and its companion cases was whether the police were required to notify a suspect of those rights.

In each of the four cases on appeal in *Miranda*, the authorities had taken advantage of a defendant's lack of knowledge about his Fifth and Sixth Amendment rights. Chicanery had been a police tactic for as long as anyone could remember. Provided that a confession obtained by police was not coerced through physical torture and was factually accurate, the means by which police tricked or cajoled a suspect into admitting criminal liability was immaterial in many jurisdictions. The U.S. Supreme Court would confront this issue head-on in *Miranda v. Arizona:* Does the Constitution allow police to take advantage of a suspect who is ignorant of his or her constitutional rights? If not, must authorities inform the suspect of those rights before interrogating him or her?[22]

Ernesto Miranda's lead attorneys, John Flynn and John P. Frank, submitted their brief to the Supreme Court in January 1966. They argued that by questioning Miranda without defense counsel present, the Phoenix Police Department had violated the defendant's Sixth Amendment rights. During oral argument, the attorneys added a Fifth Amendment claim, contending that the police should have informed Miranda that he had the right to remain silent and thereby not testify against himself.[23]

Assistant Attorney General Gary K. Nelson appeared on behalf of Arizona. He challenged Miranda's attorneys by suggesting their claim was not a Fifth Amendment issue but merely a means for expanding the court's Sixth Amendment ruling in *Escobedo v. Illinois.* That 1964 case followed *Gideon v. Wainwright* (see Chapter 7). *Gideon* held that indigent defendants have the right to a state-financed attorney at the time they go to trial. Building on that case, *Escobedo* expanded the rule by holding that a suspect has the right to an attorney before trial, specifically when he or she is interrogated by police. Five justices in *Escobedo* decided that the right to counsel begins when an individual becomes the primary suspect in a criminal case. Nelson's argument in *Miranda* was that the defendant's attorneys sought to expand the right to counsel beyond *Escobedo.* Nelson admitted that a clarification of when the right to counsel attaches would be helpful, but he worried the Supreme Court might extend the *Escobedo* rule too far and impede law enforcement efforts to investigate crimes.[24]

Nelson expressed a concern that many attorneys and law enforcement officers felt about the evolving nature of criminal procedure and the relationship between suspects and law enforcement. At various times, the Supreme Court has subscribed to competing, sometimes overlapping, theories: the due process approach, the right-to-counsel approach, and the self-incrimination approach. The due process approach is rooted in the Fourteenth Amendment due process clause, which provides that no state can "deprive any person of life, liberty, or property without due process of law." The right-to-counsel approach refers to the Sixth Amendment requirement that "In all criminal prosecutions, the accused shall enjoy the right . . . to have the assistance of counsel for his defense." The self-incrimination approach relies on the Fifth Amendment admonition that "no person . . . shall be compelled in any criminal case to be a witness against himself." As a majority of the justices would make clear in *Miranda*, the Court was prepared to champion the self-incrimination approach over the competing theories.[25]

U.S. solicitor general Thurgood Marshall appeared on the federal government's behalf. Eschewing deep philosophical arguments, Marshall expressed the Johnson administration's concerns that informing a suspect of his or her rights probably would decrease the number of confessions and increase the number of court-appointed defense attorneys in criminal cases. Requiring government to provide more attorneys for indigent defendants would burden an already-overburdened criminal justice system. Following the *Gideon* decision, states developed a public defender system for indigents bound over for trial, but extending the requirement to primary suspects undergoing custodial interrogation would present enormous practical difficulties.[26]

The justices were mindful of the repercussions of the decision, but for a majority of the court, a jurisprudential principle was at stake. Chief Justice Earl Warren assigned himself the majority opinion so that he could explain the Court's new thinking on how criminal defendants should be treated while they are detained in police custody. Writing for a 5–4 majority of the Court, he overturned Miranda's conviction. "The cases before us raise questions which go to the roots of our concepts of American criminal jurisprudence: the restraints society must observe consistent with the Federal Constitution in prosecuting individuals for crime," he began. "More specifically, we deal with the admissibility of statements obtained from an individual who is subjected to custodial police interrogation and the necessity for procedures which assure that the individual is accorded his privilege under the Fifth Amendment to the Constitution not to be compelled to incriminate himself."[27]

The chief justice recognized that the *Escobedo* decision had been fiercely debated in the two years since it had been announced. He hoped in *Miranda* "to explore some facets of the problems thus exposed of applying the privilege against self-incrimination to in-custody interrogation, and to give concrete constitutional guidelines for law enforcement agencies and courts to follow."[28]

Warren emphatically denied that *Escobedo* and *Miranda* were departures from the Court's prior decisions. Instead, they were "an application of principles long recognized and applied in other settings." The American Founders, drawing on tenets stretching back through centuries of English jurisprudence, sought to ensure that the terrible majesty of the state would not force suspects to incriminate themselves when faced with zealous police practices. Even when police officers exercise restraint, the potential for abuse is ever-present. As Warren explained, "questions put to [a suspect] may assume an inquisitorial character [and] the temptation to press the witness unduly, to browbeat him if he be timid or reluctant, to push him into a corner, and to entrap him into fatal contradictions" would always

Earl Warren, Chief Justice of the U.S. Supreme Court, authored the majority opinion in *Miranda v. Arizona*. (Historical & Special Collections, Harvard Law School Library)

exist unless the courts provided a bright-line rule governing the nature of questioning.[29]

The coercive nature of police interrogations can be intimidating to citizens, many of whom are uneducated and ignorant of their constitutional rights. If these rights are to have any meaning, Warren explained, a suspect must be informed of their existence. Otherwise, a defendant's Fifth Amendment right against self-incrimination and Sixth Amendment right to an attorney are only theoretical. He concluded that "the person in custody must, prior to interrogation, be clearly informed that he has the right to remain silent, and that anything he says will be used against him in court; he must be clearly informed that he has the right to consult with a lawyer and to have the lawyer with him during interrogation, and that, if he is indigent, a lawyer will be appointed to represent him."[30]

As a practical matter, the police must not only inform a suspect of his or her rights, but cease the interrogation if the suspect requests counsel. "If the individual indicates in any manner, at any time prior to or during questioning, that he wishes to remain silent, the interrogation must cease," Warren explained. "If the individual states that he wants an attorney, the interrogation must cease until an attorney is present. At that time, the individual must have an opportunity to confer with the attorney and to have him present during any subsequent questioning."[31]

Justice Tom Clark concurred in part and dissented in part. "It is with regret that I find it necessary to write in these cases," he explained. "However, I am unable to join the majority because its opinion goes too far on too little, while my dissenting brethren do not go quite far enough. Nor can I join in the Court's criticism of the present practices of police and investigatory agencies as to custodial interrogation." Clark was worried that developing a bright-line rule would not take into account the nuances involved in a custodial interrogation and therefore inadvertently hamper police investigations as a result. Clark urged his brethren to be "on guard against the promulgation of doctrinaire rules."[32]

In lieu of a bright-line rule, Clark recommended the justices follow the "totality of the circumstances" test the Court articulated in a 1963 case, *Haynes v. Washington*. In that case, Justice Arthur Goldberg outlined broad parameters for determining whether an interrogation passed constitutional muster. "Under the 'totality of circumstances' rule of which my Brother Goldberg spoke in *Haynes*, I would consider in each case whether the police officer, prior to custodial interrogation, added the warning that the suspect might have counsel present at the interrogation, and, further, that a court would appoint one at his request if he was too poor to employ counsel," Clark suggested. "In the absence of warnings, the burden would be on the State to prove that counsel was knowingly and intelligently waived or that, in the totality of the circumstances, including the failure to give the necessary warnings, the confession was clearly voluntary."[33]

Justice John Marshall Harlan II, joined by Justices Potter Stewart and Byron White, dissented. "I believe the decision of the Court represents poor constitutional law and entails harmful consequences for the country at large," he noted at the outset. "How serious these consequences may prove to be, only time can tell. But the basic flaws in the Court's justification seem to me readily apparent now, once all sides of the problem are considered."[34]

Harlan contended that the majority opinion sought to reduce the pressures of a custodial interrogation so that a confession obtained during intensive questioning would be voluntarily given and reliably accurate. Yet the nature of an interrogation is always coercive. A person, guilty or innocent, subjected to aggressive examination by police officers investigating a crime no doubt will be fearful and experience no small measure of discomfort. "Without at all subscribing to the generally black picture of police conduct painted by the Court, I think it must be frankly recognized at the outset that police questioning allowable under due process precedents may inherently entail some pressure on the suspect, and may seek advantage in his ignorance or weaknesses," Harlan observed. Because the feelings of pressure invariably exist, requiring a pro forma recitation of a suspect's constitutional rights will not lessen the pressure. Such a requirement will only frustrate the efforts of police officers to investigate and solve criminal cases. "What the Court largely ignores is that its rules impair, if they will not eventually serve wholly to frustrate, an instrument of law enforcement that has long and quite reasonably been thought worth the price paid for it," Harlan complained.[35]

The lack of a constitutional warning should not obviate a confession if the statement was obtained through means consistent with due process of law. "All four of the cases involved here present express claims that confessions were inadmissible not because of coercion in the traditional due process sense, but solely because of lack of counsel or lack of warnings concerning counsel and silence," the incredulous justice observed. "For the reasons stated in this opinion, I would adhere to the due process test and reject the new requirements inaugurated by the Court."[36]

In Harlan's view, the majority opinion in *Miranda* was judicial activism at its worst. It hindered good police work and did not genuinely protect criminal defendants from coercion. "In conclusion," he wrote, "nothing in the letter or the spirit of the Constitution or in the precedents squares with the heavy-handed and one-sided action that is so precipitously taken by the Court in the name of fulfilling its constitutional responsibilities."[37]

Justice Byron White, joined by Justices Harlan and Stewart, took issue with Chief Justice Warren's contention that the *Miranda* decision was rooted in a long tradition of Anglo-American jurisprudence. "The proposition that the privilege against self-incrimination forbids in-custody interrogation without the warnings specified in the majority opinion and without a clear waiver of counsel has no significant support in the history of the privilege or in the language of the Fifth Amendment," White wrote.[38]

After reviewing applicable cases to bolster his argument, White speculated on the reasons the court majority resolved to create new law beyond the text of the Constitution and court precedents. "The obvious underpinning of the Court's decision is a deep-seated distrust of all confessions," he opined. "This is the not so subtle overtone of the opinion—that it is inherently wrong for the police to gather evidence from the accused himself. And this is precisely the nub of this dissent."[39]

Echoing Justice Harlan's concern that the majority opinion harmed police investigations without providing concomitant benefits to suspects, White observed that *Miranda* raised as many questions as it answered:

> Today's decision leaves open such questions as whether the accused was in custody, whether his statements were spontaneous or the product of interrogation, whether the accused has effectively waived his rights, and whether nontestimonial evidence introduced at trial is the fruit of statements made during a prohibited interrogation, all of which are certain to prove productive of uncertainty during investigation and litigation during prosecution. For all these reasons, if further restrictions on police interrogation are desirable at this time, a more flexible approach makes much more sense than the Court's constitutional straitjacket, which forecloses more discriminating treatment by legislative or rulemaking pronouncements.[40]

With the U.S. Supreme Court decision in June 1966, Ernesto Miranda won his appeal, but he was not a free man. He was retried with assistance from defense counsel. Ironically, the defendant who had challenged his confession inadvertently hurt his case during the interregnum between the first and second trials by allegedly confessing his guilt. He was engaged in a bitter fight with his common-law wife, Twila Hoffman, over custody of their daughter. Hurt and angry, Hoffman chose to strike back at her tormentor by cooperating with prosecutors at the second trial. She told investigators that Miranda had confessed the rape to her.

The second trial commenced on February 15, 1967. The crucial issue was whether a common-law wife could testify about conversations she had had with her husband. John J. Flynn again represented Miranda. During a hearing in Judge Lawrence K. Wren's chambers, Flynn vigorously argued that such a confession should not be admitted into evidence. The judge disagreed. A spouse cannot be compelled to testify against the other spouse, but he or she may voluntarily choose to do so.

The original confession to police was inadmissible, but with the second confession available to the jury, Miranda's conviction was virtually assured. Nonetheless, prosecutors left nothing to chance. They summoned multiple witnesses to build a case against their man. No one was shocked when the jury convicted Miranda. Sentenced to serve 20 to 30 years, he was incarcerated for five years until he was released on parole in 1972.[41]

Having become something of a celebrity owing to the famous case that bore his name, Ernesto Miranda eked out a modest living signing police *Miranda*-waiver cards for money. A deeply troubled man, he still found himself adrift. He occasionally picked up odd jobs and constantly ran into trouble with law enforcement. The end of his life was ignominious, as might be expected. He died on January 31, 1976, at the age of 34 during a brawl in a seedy Phoenix night spot, the La Amapola Bar. Eseziquiel Moreno, a Mexican national, stabbed Miranda to death during an argument. Moreno successfully fled the scene, but police apprehended his accomplice, Fernando Rodriguez Zamora. Cognizant of the new legal requirements, the arresting officers "Mirandized" the suspect. After hearing his rights read to him, Zamora wisely elected to remain silent.[42]

As for its impact on criminal procedure, the *Miranda* decision became one of the best known landmark cases in the American legal system. Owing to countless police dramas and other television shows throughout the years, virtually every man, woman, and child of a certain age recognizes the *Miranda* warnings. Although the wording varies slightly among jurisdictions, the warnings usually consist of informing a suspect in custody that he or she has the right to remain silent, that anything the suspect says can be used against him or her in a court of law, that the suspect has the right to have an attorney present before and during the questioning, and that the suspect has the right to have an attorney appointed to represent him or her before and during the questioning if he or she cannot afford to hire an attorney.[43]

Critics of the decision feared that requiring *Miranda* warnings would hamper police interrogations and severely undermine the criminal justice system. Republican presidential candidate Richard

Nixon urged Congress to enact the Omnibus Crime Control Act of 1968 to obviate the ruling, denouncing the *Miranda* decision's "legal technicalities" because the opinion "very nearly rules out 'confession' as an effective" law enforcement tool. During the Reagan administration, Attorney General Edwin Meese characterized *Miranda* as "infamous" and "a derelict on the waters of the law." Meese argued that overturning the case would be "among the most important achievements of this administration." One commentator called the case "the most reviled decision ever issued by the Supreme Court in a criminal case."[44]

Within academic circles, a cottage industry arose among lawyers and scholars who traded barbs over the positive and negative effects of the *Miranda* rule.[45] After careful study, law professor Richard Leo concluded that the dire predictions of criminals being turned loose in the streets following *Miranda* have not been supported by the data. In his estimation, 75 percent of criminal defendants waive their right to remain silent or be represented by an attorney and, in fact, they talk to police. Leo argued that if proponents of reform genuinely want to fix the problems of coerced confessions and determining when *Miranda* rights have been waived, they should pressure the courts to require electronic videotaping of custodial interrogations as a matter of due process of law.[46]

Some defenders suggest that *Miranda* warnings, properly given, actually benefit the police. As Justice David Souter noted in *Missouri v. Seibert*, a 2004 U.S. Supreme Court case:

> *Miranda* conditioned the admissibility at trial of any custodial confession on warning a suspect of his rights: failure to give the prescribed warnings and obtain a waiver of rights before custodial questioning generally requires exclusion of any statements obtained. Conversely, giving the warnings and getting a waiver has generally produced a virtual ticket of admissibility; maintaining that a statement is involuntary even though given after warnings and voluntary waiver of rights requires unusual stamina, and litigation over voluntariness tends to end with the finding of a valid waiver.[47]

Time and again, Congress and the courts have failed to overturn *Miranda*, despite the continued unpopularity of the decision. As of this writing, *Dickerson v. United States* is the most famous case where the high court might have rejected the *Miranda* requirements and chose not to do so. Writing for a 7–2 majority in 2000, Chief Justice William Rehnquist expressly declined to overrule the 1966 case. He noted that Congress does not possess the authority to overrule *Miranda*, as it attempted to do by enacting the Omnibus Crime Control Act in 1968. Only the U.S. Supreme Court can decide matters involving constitutional interpretation. As for overturning *Miranda*, Rehnquist recognized that the Court might reach a different decision if the case were decided in 2000 instead of 1966. "Whether or not we would agree with *Miranda*'s reasoning and its resulting rule, were we addressing the issue in the first instance, the principles of *stare decisis* weigh heavily against overruling it now," he observed. "*Miranda* has become embedded in routine police practice to the point where the warnings have become part of our national culture. . . ." According to the chief justice:

> While we have overruled our precedents when subsequent cases have undermined their doctrinal underpinnings . . . we do not believe that this has happened to the *Miranda* decision. If anything, our subsequent cases have reduced the impact of the *Miranda* rule on legitimate law enforcement while reaffirming the decision's core ruling that unwarned statements may not be used as evidence in the prosecution's case in chief.[48]

Despite the decision's continued vitality, as the chief justice noted, "subsequent cases have reduced the impact of the *Miranda* rule on legitimate law enforcement." In other words, *Miranda* needed to be modified but it was not necessary to throw out the entire rule. In cases decided after 1966, Rehnquist intimated, the high court already had ameliorated some of the more burdensome effects.[49]

Miranda proponents agree with Rehnquist that later cases blunted *Miranda*'s impact, but supporters do not view the changes as positive developments. For supporters of a liberal interpretation of constitutional criminal procedure, subsequent cases chipped away at the efficacy of the warnings and undermined civil liberties in the process. A 1971 case, *Harris v. New York*, allowed prosecutors to introduce a confession obtained without a *Miranda* warning into court to impeach a defendant's testimony. The majority reasoned that the admission of the statement into evidence was not being used to prove the facts about whether the defendant committed the crime. Instead, the statement was introduced to attack his or her credibility when testimony in court contradicted a prior inconsistent statement.[50] In a 1984 case,

New York v. Quarles, the Supreme Court carved out a public safety exception to the *Miranda* requirement. If a police officer in the field apprehends a suspect and needs vital, immediate information from the suspect to protect public safety, the officer need not read the suspect his or her rights "in the heat of battle."[51] In *Berghuis v. Thompkins*, the U.S. Supreme decided that a suspect who simply refuses to speak has not invoked his or her right to remain silent. Ironically, silence is not tantamount to "constitutional silence." A suspect must speak up and inform police that he is exercising his right to remain silent. Thus, a confession uttered after a suspect has been provided with *Miranda* warnings but before the suspect has stated that he or she chooses to remain silent and desires a lawyer to be present is admissible in court.[52]

The courts no doubt will continue to shape *Miranda* well into the future, but this observation is axiomatic. The law requires continual adjustments as time and circumstances change—to say nothing of changes among justices serving on the U.S. Supreme Court. As discussed throughout this book, criminal procedure evolves as society and technology evolve. In the American criminal justice system, landmark cases arise from seemingly routine circumstances that challenge preconceived notions as well as past concepts, procedures, and precedents.

NOTES

1. Liva Baker, *Miranda: Crime, Law and Politics* (New York: Atheneum, 1983), 9–10.

2. Colin Evans, "Ernesto Miranda Trials: 1963 & 1967," in *Great American Trials: From Salem Witchcraft to Rodney King*, Edward W. Knappman, editor (Detroit, Mich.: Visible Ink Press, a Division of Gale Research, Inc., 1994), 505; Gary L. Stuart, *Miranda: The Story of America's Right to Remain Silent* (Tucson: University of Arizona Press, 2004), 5.

3. Baker, *Miranda*, 7; Stuart, *Miranda*, 3.

4. Stuart, *Miranda*, 3.

5. Baker, *Miranda*, 3–5; Evans, "Ernesto Miranda Trials," 505; Richard Rogers, "A Little Knowledge Is a Dangerous Thing. . . Emerging *Miranda* Research and Professional Roles for Psychologists," *American Psychologist* 63, 8 (November 2008): 777; Stuart, *Miranda*, 4.

6. Baker, *Miranda*, 6; Stuart, *Miranda*, 4.

7. Evans, "Ernesto Miranda Trials," 505; Stuart, *Miranda*, 4–5.

8. Baker, *Miranda*, 9; Evans, "Ernesto Miranda Trials," 505; Stuart, *Miranda*, 4–5.

9. Stuart, *Miranda*, 5.
10. Evans, "Ernesto Miranda Trials," 505; Stuart, *Miranda*, 6–7.
11. Evans, "Ernesto Miranda Trials," 505; Michael S. Lief and H. Mitchell Caldwell, "You Have the Right to Remain Silent," *American Heritage* 57, 4 (August/September 2006): 48–50; Rogers, "A Little Knowledge Is a Dangerous Thing," 777; Stuart, *Miranda*, 6–7.
12. Rogers, "A Little Knowledge Is a Dangerous Thing," 777; Stuart, *Miranda*, 7.
13. Quoted in Stuart, *Miranda*, 7.
14. Evans, "Ernesto Miranda Trials," 505–6; Rogers, "A Little Knowledge Is a Dangerous Thing," 777; Stuart, *Miranda*, 7–8.
15. Rogers, "A Little Knowledge Is a Dangerous Thing," 778; Stuart, *Miranda*, 11.
16. Baker, *Miranda*, 20–23; Rogers, "A Little Knowledge Is a Dangerous Thing," 778; Stuart, *Miranda*, 15–22.
17. Baker, *Miranda*, 24; Evans, "Ernesto Miranda Trials," 506–07; Stuart, *Miranda*, 22.
18. *State v. Arizona*, 401 P.2d 721 (1965).
19. Baker, *Miranda*, 61; Stuart, *Miranda*, 41–43.
20. Baker, *Miranda*, 384; Liane J. Jackson, "Turning *Miranda* 'Upside Down'?," *ABA Journal* 96, 9 (September 2010): 20–21; Stuart, *Miranda*, 53.
21. The facts of the three companion cases are summarized in Stuart, *Miranda*, 24–26. See also Fred P. Graham, "High Court Puts New Curb on Powers of the Police to Interrogate Suspects," *New York Times* (June 14, 1966): A1.
22. *Miranda v. Arizona*, 384 U.S. 436, 444 (1966). See also Patrick A. Malone, "'You Have the Right to Remain Silent': *Miranda* after Twenty Years," *American Scholar* 55, 3 (Spring 1986): 367–68; William T. Pizzi and Morris B. Hoffman, "Taking *Miranda's* Pulse," *Vanderbilt Law Review* 58, 3 (April 2005): 815–17.
23. Ronald J. Allen, "*Miranda*'s Hollow Core," *Northwestern University Law Review* 100, 1 (Special Issue 2006): 72–74; Stuart, *Miranda*, 63–76.
24. *Escobedo v. Illinois*, 378 U.S. 478 (1964). See also 384 U.S. 436, 440; Baker, *Miranda*, 135, 384; Stuart, *Miranda*, 58, 148.
25. Allen, "*Miranda*'s Hollow Core," 71–85; Richard A. Leo, "The Impact of *Miranda* Revisited," *Journal of Law & Criminology* 86, 3 (Spring 1996): 621–94; Malone, "You Have the Right to Remain Silent," 367–80.
26. Baker, *Miranda*, 145; Stuart, *Miranda*, 70.
27. 384 U.S. 436, 439.
28. 384 U.S. 436, 441–42.
29. 384 U.S. 436, 442–44.
30. 384 U.S. 436, 437.
31. 384 U.S. 436, 473–74.
32. 384 U.S. 436, 499, 501.
33. 384 U.S. 436, 503. See also *Haynes v. Washington*, 373 U.S. 503 (1963).

34. 384 U.S. 436, 504.
35. 384 U.S. 436, 515, 516.
36. 384 U.S. 436, 524.
37. 384 U.S. 436, 525–26.
38. 384 U.S. 436, 526.
39. 384 U.S. 436, 537, 538.
40. 384 U.S. 436, 545.
41. Baker, *Miranda*, 193, 291; Stuart, *Miranda*, 93.
42. Baker, *Miranda*, 408; Evans, "Ernesto Miranda Trials," 507; Stuart, *Miranda*, 96–99, 149, 186.
43. Rogers, "A Little Knowledge Is a Dangerous Thing," 777. The literature on *Miranda*'s impact has been voluminous. See, for example, Paul G. Cassell, "*Miranda*'s 'Negligible' Effect on Law Enforcement: Some Skeptical Observations," *Harvard Journal of Law & Public Policy* 20, 2 (Winter 1997): 327–46; Floralynn Einesman, "Confessions and Culture: The Interaction of *Miranda* and Diversity," *Journal of Criminal Law & Criminology* 90, 1 (Fall 1999): 1–47; Fred P. Graham, "Curb on Police Questions Is Ruled Not Retroactive; Supreme Court Says Limits Placed on Interrogation Last Monday Apply Only to Trials after That Date," *New York Times* (June 21, 1966): A1; Arthur Krock, "In the Nation: The Wall between Crime and Punishment," *New York Times* (June 14, 1966): A46.
44. The Omnibus Crime Control and Safe Streets Act of 1968 (Pub.L. 90–351, 82 Stat. 197, enacted June 19, *1968*, codified at 42 U.S.C. § 3711). Nixon and Meese are quoted in Kit Kinports, "The Supreme Court's Love-Hate Relationship with *Miranda*," *Journal of Criminal Law & Criminology* 101, 2 (Spring 2011): 377. See also Baker, *Miranda*, 200–208; Evans, "Ernesto Miranda Trials," 508; Fred E. Inbau, "Overreaction—The Mischief of *Miranda v. Arizona*," *Journal of Criminal Law & Criminology* 89, 4 (Summer 1999): 1449–64; Leo, "The Impact of *Miranda* Revisited," 622–24; "*Miranda* Needs No Improvement," *New York Times* (January 10, 1986): A26. The commentator on *Miranda*'s poor reception was Malone, "You Have the Right to Remain Silent," 367.
45. See, for example, the conversations among scholars in the pages of the *Journal of Criminal Law & Criminology*. Paul G. Cassell, "Protecting the Innocent from False Confessions and Lost Confessions—And from *Miranda*," *Journal of Criminal Law & Criminology* 88, 2 (Winter 1998): 497–556; Richard A. Leo and Richard J. Ofshe, "Using the Innocent to Scapegoat *Miranda:* Another Reply to Paul Cassell," *Journal of Criminal Law & Criminology* 88, 2 (Winter 1998): 557–77.
46. Leo, "The Impact of *Miranda* Revisited," 624, 653.
47. *Missouri v. Seibert*, 542 U.S. 600, 608–09 (2004). See also Brian K. Payne and Victoria M. Time, "Support for *Miranda* among Police Chiefs: A Qualitative Examination," *American Journal of Criminal Justice* 25, 1 (Fall 2000): 65–76.

48. *Dickerson v. United States*, 530 U.S. 428, 443–44 (2000).

49. See, for example, Edward Walsh, "High Court Upholds *Miranda* Rights; Rehnquist Calls Warnings Part of 'National Culture,'" *The Washington Post* (June 27, 2000): A1.

50. *Harris v. New York*, 401 U.S. 222 (1971).

51. *New York v. Quarles*, 467 U.S. 649 (1984).

52. *Berghuis v. Thompkins* 130 S.Ct. 2250 (2010). See also Michael L. Vander Giessen, "*Berghuis v. Thompkins:* The Continued Erosion of *Miranda*'s Protections," *Gonzaga Law Review* 46, 1 (2011): 189–214.

CHAPTER 9
Katz v. United States (1967) and the Right to Privacy

Katz v. United States was a landmark case holding that electronic surveillance cannot be used to gather evidence in a criminal proceeding without a warrant. The justices of the U.S. Supreme Court expanded privacy rights by extending Fourth Amendment protections to this burgeoning area of the law. According to the Court majority, if the Constitution is designed to shield its citizens from the power and might of the state, the warrant requirement of the Fourth Amendment must be reinterpreted to keep pace with changing law enforcement tactics and evolving technologies.[1]

Privacy rights and the limits of searches and seizures affected by the Fourth Amendment have been recurring themes throughout American legal history. The parameters of a permissible search have been problematic because court opinions have evolved as societal values and technological progress have evolved. In a 1928 case, *Olmstead v. United States* (see Chapter 3), a bare majority of the U.S. Supreme Court concluded that warrantless wiretapping did not constitute an unreasonable search or seizure under the Fourth Amendment because no physical invasion had occurred. Justice Louis D. Brandeis's eloquent dissent championing individual privacy rights in *Olmstead* served as a crucial foundation for *Katz v. United States,* which revisited the concept of wiretapping evidence and the Fourth Amendment.[2]

Charles B. Katz was a consummate gambler who frequently used the telephone to contact associates throughout the country. By the mid-1960s, he was a leading basketball handicapper in the United States. He lived in an apartment on Sunset Boulevard but was careful to conduct business away from the premises. To avoid detection, Katz would leave his building and wander onto Sunset to use one of three nearby telephone booths in the 8200 block to place bets. By transmitting gambling wagers from Los Angeles to Boston to Miami, he violated federal antigambling laws and attracted attention from many sources, including the Federal Bureau of Investigation (FBI).

In February 1965, the FBI received a tip that Katz would use a public telephone to speak with his confederates. Because he alternated among the three telephone booths, agents devised a means for recording his calls on the correct telephone at the correct time. To reduce the permutations and combinations of possible calls, they contacted the telephone company and arranged to place one phone out of service. Afterward, the agents installed electronic eavesdropping equipment on the exterior of the two remaining telephone booths where Katz typically made his phone calls. An undercover agent watched Katz's apartment to determine when he left the premises.

The plan worked as expected. The FBI observed and recorded Katz's telephone calls from the two working telephones from February 19 through February 25, with the exception of February 22. A routine developed. When Katz left his apartment, the agent assigned to watch him gave a "high sign" to a nearby agent. The second agent turned on the recording device, which captured Katz's conversation as he used the telephone to transmit gambling information across state lines. Based on the recordings, the FBI arrested Katz and charged him on an eight-count indictment. The agents had no search warrant to record Katz's telephone conversations, but under the *Olmstead* case, a warrant was unnecessary because the agents had not physically invaded the telephone booth.[3]

At trial in the District Court for the Southern District of California (now the Central District of California), the prosecution presented an expert witness to interpret what the recordings revealed because the wiretaps captured only Katz's part of the conversations. According to Joseph Gunn from the Administrative Vice Division of the Los Angeles Police Department, the defendant's jargon incontrovertibly demonstrated that he was engaged in illegal interstate gambling. Seemingly cryptic comments such as "Give me Duquesne minus seven for a nickel" referred to a bet placed on a college game and the amount based on the point spread. It was damning evidence.[4]

A well-known criminal defense attorney, Burton Marks, represented Katz at trial. Marks knew he could not argue persuasively that the conversations had been misinterpreted. Therefore, he challenged the constitutionality of the wiretap by arguing that a person should enjoy the same rights to privacy when he closes the door to a telephone booth as he enjoys inside his home. Marks's point was well taken, although he erroneously stated in his written motion before the court that "a man has as much right to bet alone in a public telephone booth as in his own home." Instead of "bet alone," he meant "be alone." The typographical error caused Marks and his client consternation before the court, and the judge denied his motion to suppress the evidence gained via the wiretap. Under the *Olmstead* precedent, Marks probably would have lost the motion even if he had not slipped up in the paperwork. Not surprisingly, Katz was convicted. The Ninth Circuit Court of Appeals affirmed the trial court's judgment, citing *Olmstead v. United States* as the controlling precedent.[5]

Marks agreed to file a petition for certiorari with the U.S. Supreme Court. Each side reiterated the assertions from trial. On his client's behalf, Marks contended that federal authorities had violated Katz's Fourth Amendment rights against unreasonable searches and seizures owing to the use of the electronic eavesdropping devices without first obtaining a warrant from a magistrate or judge. The government argued that the placement of the devices on the exterior of the telephone booth did not constitute a physical intrusion into the booth and was not a Fourth Amendment search. Consequently, Katz's rights were not violated.[6]

As with so many cases discussed in this book, the petitioner's attorneys faced a difficult hurdle, for they were arguing against a multitude of precedents. In the past, the U.S. Supreme Court had relied on the trespass doctrine, which held that a "search" necessitating a warrant under the Fourth Amendment requires physical penetration of a constitutionally protected location. In addition to *Olmstead*, several prominent cases supported this reasoning. In *Goldman v. United States*, a case factually similar to *Katz*, federal agents had placed listening devices against a wall leading to the defendant's office. The devices recorded the defendant's conversations, which served as the basis for prosecution. The Supreme Court permitted the recordings to be entered into evidence because the agents had not physically broken into the defendant's office. They simply used electronic devices to amplify his conversations.[7]

In *Silverman v. United States*, by contrast, police officers entered the defendant's property and placed a "spike mike" listening device on the premises. Hiding in a vacant house next door, they recorded conversations made inside the defendant's house. In that case, the U.S. Supreme Court held that the defendant's Fourth Amendment rights had been violated because the police had trespassed onto his property. The bright-line rule beginning with *Olmstead* was clear and unequivocal: if physical invasion occurred, the evidence would be excluded, but if officers could capture the conversations without trespassing on the defendant's property, the evidence would be admissible in court.[8]

Even bright-line rules are not inviolable. The world of the 1960s was radically different than the world of the 1920s. When Prohibition agents had tape-recorded the enterprising young bootlegger Roy Olmstead's telephone conversations in the mid-1920s, the technology was comparatively new. Reviewing courts did not view the use of eavesdropping equipment as especially invasive of privacy for most Americans. By the 1960s, the use of telephones and electronic media had increased markedly. The idea that law enforcement personnel could surreptitiously collect information on citizens' conversations—provided they did not trespass onto a suspect's property—absent a warrant appeared increasingly anachronistic. Such a cramped view of the Fourth Amendment would surely diminish the rights of ordinary Americans.[9]

The U.S. Supreme Court agreed to hear the *Katz* case and consider two salient issues. First, is physical intrusion into a so-called constitutionally protected area required to constitute a search for Fourth Amendment purposes? Second, does a right to privacy extend to a telephone booth and other public places? In considering these questions, the Court ruled 7–1 to overturn Katz's conviction. Justice Potter Stewart, joined by Justices Brennan, Douglas, Fortas, Harlan, Warren, and White, wrote the majority opinion. Only Justice Black dissented. Justice Douglas, joined by Justice Brennan, filed a separate concurrence, as did Justices Harlan and White. Justice Thurgood Marshall did not participate.[10]

According to Justice Stewart, the issues in the case were inappropriately framed. "We decline to adopt this formulation of the issues. In the first place, the correct solution of Fourth Amendment problems is not necessarily promoted by incantation of the phrase 'constitutionally protected area.' Secondly, the Fourth Amendment cannot be translated into a general constitutional 'right to privacy.' That Amendment protects individual privacy against certain kinds of governmental intrusion, but its protections go further, and often have nothing to do with privacy at all."[11] Stewart believed that cases involving Fourth Amendment searches should not be characterized by whether the place is protected by the Constitution. "Because of the misleading way the issues have been formulated, the parties have attached great significance to the characterization of the telephone booth from which the petitioner placed his calls," he wrote. In a famous sentence, he observed, "For the Fourth Amendment protects people, not places."[12]

In crafting a memorable phrase, Justice Stewart obfuscated the point. Undoubtedly, the amendment protects people, but the place is important in determining when people can reasonably expect to enjoy privacy. The analysis depends on where they are at the time the expectation occurs. A person can reasonably expect to enjoy privacy when he or she converses inside his or her home. The same conversation undertaken on a subway platform where hundreds of people mill about will be less private. To ensure privacy, a person must take steps to protect his or her conversations when he or she is in a public setting. Thus, although the Fourth Amendment clearly protects people instead of things, the level of protection depends on other factors, including the time, place, and circumstances. As Stewart observed about a suspect, "What he seeks to preserve as private, even in an area accessible to the public, may be constitutionally protected."[13]

The respondent argued that a glass telephone booth does not afford complete privacy because passersby can look inside and see a person using the telephone. Justice Stewart agreed, but added, "What he sought to exclude when he entered the booth was not the intruding eye—it was the uninvited ear." Absolute privacy is not the issue. The question is whether the suspect sought a measure of privacy in closing the door to the telephone booth. Justice Stewart eloquently explained that Charles Katz's expectations were different from Roy Olmstead's expectations because the world had changed over time. "One who occupies [a telephone booth], shuts the door behind him, and pays the toll that permits him to place a call is surely entitled to assume that the words he utters into the mouthpiece will not be broadcast to the world. To read the Constitution more narrowly is to ignore the vital role that the public telephone has come to play in private communication."[14]

This case was fact determinative; that is, the nature of Katz's actions—he stepped inside a telephone booth, closed the door, and sought to speak on the telephone without anyone else overhearing the conversation—indicated that he expected a measure of privacy. A physical intrusion is not necessary for the law enforcement activity to constitute a Fourth Amendment search. "We conclude that the underpinnings of *Olmstead* and *Goldman* have been so eroded by our subsequent decisions that the 'trespass' doctrine there enunciated can no longer be regarded as controlling," Stewart explained in closing. "The Government's activities in electronically listening to and recording the petitioner's words violated the privacy upon which he justifiably relied while using the telephone booth, and thus constituted a 'search and seizure' within the meaning of the Fourth Amendment."[15]

Although he joined the majority opinion, Justice Douglas felt "compelled to reply to the separate concurring opinion of my Brother White, which I view as a wholly unwarranted green light for the Executive Branch to resort to electronic eavesdropping without a warrant in cases which the Executive Branch itself labels 'national security' matters."[16] Douglas was worried that White's attempt to carve out a warrant exception for crimes deemed to be "treason" would open the door for all manner of constitutional mischief. "There is, so far as I understand constitutional history, no distinction under the Fourth Amendment between types of crimes," Douglas noted. "Article III, § 3, gives 'treason' a very narrow definition, and puts restrictions on its proof. But the Fourth Amendment draws no lines between various substantive offenses."[17]

Justice John Marshall Harlan II's concurrence in *Katz* has become the most famous opinion from that case. Harlan agreed with the majority that the Fourth Amendment protects people, not places, but he noted that places are important, nonetheless. A closed telephone booth is similar to a home and, as discussed in *Weeks v. United States* (see Chapter 2), a search warrant is required before authorities can demand entry to the premises. An open field, by contrast, is not protected.

Harlan argued that the analysis of whether a warrantless search is constitutional should turn on whether the suspect has an expectation of privacy. To that end, he observed that expectations of privacy can be determined by relying on a two-pronged test with a subjective component and an objective component. "My understanding of the rule that has emerged from prior decisions is that there is a twofold requirement, first that a person have exhibited an actual (subjective) expectation of privacy and, second, that the expectation be one that society is prepared to recognize as 'reasonable.'"[18]

Applying this analytical framework to the *Katz* case, Harlan believed the defendant met both prongs of the test. A person who enters a telephone booth subjectively expects his or her telephone conversation will be private. Society should be prepared to recognize this fact. A telephone booth may be available for any citizen who chooses to use it, but it is not analogous to an open field, where no privacy expectation exists. When the citizen enters the telephone booth and shuts the door, he or she is walling himself or herself off from other people in a specific attempt to ensure a measure of privacy.

Justice John Marshall Harlan's concurring opinion in *Katz v. United States* laid the groundwork for the Court's interpretation of a "reasonable expectation" of privacy. (Library of Congress)

Harlan explained that the *Goldman* case, which upheld the *Olmstead* rule that physical penetration is required before the Fourth Amendment applies, should be overruled. "This case requires us to reconsider *Goldman*, and I agree that it should now be overruled," he wrote. "Its limitation on Fourth Amendment protection is, in the present day, bad physics as well as bad law, for reasonable expectations of privacy may be defeated by electronic as well as physical invasion." In a footnote, Harlan added, "I also think that the course of development evinced by [precedents leading back to *Olmstead*] and today's decision must be recognized as overruling *Olmstead v. United States*, 277 U.S. 438, which essentially rested on the ground that conversations were not subject to the protection of the Fourth Amendment."[19]

Justice Byron White also filed a concurring opinion. Although he agreed with the Court majority, White was a law-and-order judge, formerly deputy attorney general in the Kennedy administration. "I agree that the official surveillance of petitioner's telephone conversations in a public booth must be subjected to the test of reasonableness under the Fourth Amendment and that, on the record now before us, the particular surveillance undertaken was unreasonable absent a warrant properly authorizing it," he wrote.[20] Having said this, White did not want the majority opinion to be interpreted broadly to require a search warrant in all instances where law enforcement officials relied on wiretaps. "This application of the Fourth Amendment need not interfere with legitimate needs of law enforcement," he explained. In some cases, electronic surveillance can be undertaken absent a search warrant. For example, when a criminal suspect converses with a confidential informant, as long as the informant knows of the wiretap, a warrant is unnecessary. "When one man speaks to another, he takes all the risks ordinarily inherent in so doing, including the risk that the man to whom he speaks will make public what he has heard," White contended. "The Fourth Amendment does not protect against unreliable (or law-abiding) associates."[21] He also believed that wiretaps used in the interests of national security should not be subject to the same requirements as wiretaps employed in the ordinary course of law enforcement. "We should not require the warrant procedure and the magistrate's judgment if the President of the United States or his chief legal officer, the Attorney General, has considered the requirements of national security and authorized electronic surveillance as reasonable." This was the comment that upset Justice Douglas and compelled him to pen a separate concurrence.[22]

Justice Black wrote the lone dissent. He believed his brethren were rewriting the Fourth Amendment. "If I could agree with the Court that eavesdropping carried on by electronic means (equivalent to wiretapping) constitutes a 'search' or 'seizure,' I would be happy to join the Court's opinion," he wrote. "My basic objection is two-fold: (1) I do not believe that the words of the Amendment will bear the meaning given them by today's decision, and (2) I do not believe that it is the proper role of this Court to rewrite the Amendment in order 'to bring it into harmony with the times,' and thus reach a result that many people believe to be desirable."[23]

The words of the amendment indicate that the Constitution protects tangible things, which do not include electronic surveillance. Anticipating the objection that the Founders could not have known how technology would develop and therefore they did not include wiretaps, Black explained that wiretaps were not the issue. "A conversation overheard by eavesdropping, whether by plain snooping or wiretapping, is not tangible and, under the normally accepted meanings of the words, can neither be searched nor seized," he wrote. He conceded, "While I realize that an argument based on the meaning of words lacks the scope, and no doubt the appeal, of broad policy discussions and philosophical discourses on such nebulous subjects as privacy, for me, the language of the Amendment is the crucial place to look in construing a written document such as our Constitution."[24]

Applying the Fourth Amendment to nontangible future conversations can lead to confusing legal problems the majority opinion does not address. The Fourth Amendment requires a warrant to be issued only when the attesting officer's oath or affirmation is accompanied by a statement "particularly describing the place to be searched and the persons or things to be seized." Black asked rhetorically, "How can one 'describe' a future conversation, and, if one cannot, how can a magistrate issue a warrant to eavesdrop one in the future? It is argued that information showing what is expected to be said is sufficient to limit the boundaries of what later can be admitted into evidence; but does such general information really meet the specific language of the Amendment, which says 'particularly describing'? Rather than using language in a completely artificial way, I must conclude that the Fourth Amendment simply does not apply to eavesdropping."[25]

Eavesdropping, an ancient practice, has existed for centuries even if electronic surveillance is new. The Framers of the Constitution could have written the language of the Fourth Amendment to include eavesdropping in the warrant requirement had they chosen to do so. In his characteristically inimitable manner, Black bluntly assessed the Court's overreaching in *Katz.* "No one, it seems to me, can read the debates on the Bill of Rights without reaching the conclusion that its Framers and critics well knew the meaning of the words they used, what they would be understood to mean by others, their scope and their limitations." Yet the activist Warren Court ignored the plain meaning of the words. "Under these circumstances, it strikes me as a charge against their scholarship, their common sense and their candor to give to the Fourth Amendment's language the eavesdropping meaning the Court imputes to it today."[26]

Black examined the Court's pre-*Katz* precedents, which exempted evidence obtained through wiretaps from the warrant requirement, and concluded the earlier cases were more in line with the Framers' intent for the Fourth Amendment than was the majority opinion in *Katz*. Focusing especially on *Olmstead v. United States*, the justice observed, "In holding that the interception of private telephone conversations by means of wiretapping was not a violation of the Fourth Amendment, this Court, speaking through Mr. Chief Justice Taft, examined the language of the Amendment and found, just as I do now, that the words could not be stretched to encompass overheard conversations."[27]

As a matter of policy, the court may extend the warrant requirement to include evidence procured through electronic eavesdropping, but that policy is not rooted in the language of the Fourth Amendment. "This Court has adopted an exclusionary rule to bar evidence obtained by means of such intrusions," he argued. "As I made clear in my dissenting opinion in *Berger v. New York*, 388 U.S. 41, 76, I continue to believe that this exclusionary rule formulated in *Weeks v. United States*, 232 U.S. 383, rests on the 'supervisory power' of this Court over other federal courts and is not rooted in the Fourth Amendment."[28]

After admonishing the Court to cease its efforts to expand the Constitution beyond the Framers' intent in a misguided effort to craft public policy—"With this decision the Court has completed, I hope, its rewriting of the Fourth Amendment"—Justice Black concluded his opinion with a summary of the law against unreasonable searches and seizures.[29] He wrote:

> The Fourth Amendment protects privacy only to the extent that it prohibits unreasonable searches and seizures of "persons, houses, papers, and effects." No general right is created by the Amendment so as to give this Court the unlimited power to hold unconstitutional everything which affects privacy. Certainly the Framers, well acquainted as they were with the excesses of governmental power, did not intend to grant this Court such omnipotent lawmaking authority as that. The history of governments proves that it is dangerous to freedom to repose such powers in courts.[30]

Justice Black was correct that *Katz* represented a departure from the U.S. Supreme Court's previous cases involving privacy and electronic surveillance. One commentator subsequently observed that the opinion "bears the marks of a quintessential *political* compromise, with both sides getting something they wanted—one side, the overthrow of the overly restrictive *Olmstead* decision; the other, a clear statement of the essential legality of electronic surveillance."[31] The Prohibition-era bootlegger Roy Olmstead, discussed in Chapter 3, was vindicated in his assumption that the Fourth Amendment warrant requirement applied to information obtained from wiretaps, albeit the reinterpretation was almost four decades after he transported whiskey through the Pacific Northwest. The Court finally abandoned the trespass doctrine, that aged warhorse that had served Fourth Amendment jurisprudence for decades. In its place, the justices carved out a "portable" view of privacy. Individuals are protected wherever they travel in the United States since the amendment applies to people and not places. The characterization of the place remains a consideration, but owing to Justice Harlan's articulation of the two-pronged expectation of privacy test in his concurrence, the analysis hinges on whether an individual had a subjective expectation of privacy and whether society would agree objectively with that conclusion in a specific context.[32]

Although *Katz* remains good law as of this writing, the matter of electronic surveillance and Fourth Amendment protections is hardly settled. Congress has enacted many statutes detailing the manner in which electronic devices can be used to collect evidence for a criminal proceeding. Title III of the Omnibus Crime Control and Safe Streets Act of 1968, the Electronic Communications and Privacy Act of 1986, and the Communications Assistance for Law Enforcement Act of 1994 are among the best known laws in this area. Congress passed and President George W. Bush signed the Uniting and Strengthening America by Providing Appropriate Tools Required to Intercept and Obstruct Terrorism Act of 2001 in response to the terrorist attacks of September 11, 2001. The act, among other things, expanded the U.S. government's authority to search through electronic records without having to obtain a search warrant in the interests of national security. Each of these congressional responses to crime and terrorism remain highly contested.[33]

In the meantime, the U.S. Supreme Court continues to delineate the parameters of when electronic surveillance can and cannot be performed consistent with the strictures of the Fourth Amendment. In 2012, the high court considered the warrantless use of portable electronic devices—in this case, global positioning systems (GPS) on automobiles—and whether individuals can be monitored using such devices. In *United States v. Jones* (2012), a unanimous court held that when law enforcement officers attach a GPS device to a vehicle to monitor the vehicle's movements, this action constitutes a search under the Fourth Amendment. Accordingly, a warrant or a valid, recognized exception to the warrant requirement is necessary.[34]

Katz v. United States is not the last word on what constitutes a valid search under the Fourth Amendment, nor should it be. The digital world is ever-changing. Despite the concern that Justice Black voiced in his *Katz* dissent, the meaning of the Fourth Amendment is not frozen in 1791, when it was ratified. In *Katz*, a majority of the Court chose, rightly or wrongly, to reinterpret the requirements of the Fourth Amendment as society and technology evolved.[35]

NOTES

1. Christopher R. Brennan, "*Katz* Cradle: Holding on to Fourth Amendment Parity in an Age of Evolving Electronic Communication," *William & Mary Law Review* 53, 5 (April 2012): 1804; Sue Carter Collins, "The Case of *Katz v. United States* (1967)," in *Criminal Procedure and the Supreme Court: A Guide to the Major Decisions on Search and Seizure, Privacy, and Individual Rights*, Rolando V. Del Carmen and Craig Hemmens, editors (Lanham, Md.: Rowman & Littlefield, 2010), 9–25.

2. *Katz v. United States*, 389 U.S. 347 (1967). See also Tom McInnis, "The Changing Definition of Search or Seizure," *Insights on Law & Society* 11, 2 (May 2011): 10–13; Peter Winn, "*Katz* and the Origins of the 'Reasonable Expectation of Privacy' Test," *McGeorge Law Review* 40, 1 (2009): 1–2.

3. 389 U.S. 347, 348. See also Harvey A. Schneider, "*Katz v. United States:* The Untold Story," *McGeorge Law Review* 40, 1 (2009): 13–14.

4. Collins, "The Case of *Katz v. United States* (1967)," 10; Schneider, "*Katz v. United States*," 14.

5. 389 U.S. 347, 348. See also Schneider, "*Katz v. United States*," 14; Winn, "*Katz* and the Origins of the 'Reasonable Expectation of Privacy' Test," 10.

6. 389 U.S. 347, 349–55. See also Winn, "*Katz* and the Origins of the 'Reasonable Expectation of Privacy' Test," 1–4, 10–12.

7. *Goldman v. United States*, 316 U.S. 129 (1942). See also Judge Kevin Emas and Tamara Pallas, "*United States v. Jones:* Does *Katz* Still Have Nine Lives?," *St. Thomas Law Review* 24, 2(2012): 118–22; Henry R. Fradella, Weston J. Morrow, Ryan G. Fischer, and Connie Ireland, "Quantifying *Katz:* Empirically Measuring 'Reasonable Expectations of Privacy' in the Fourth Amendment Context," *American Journal of Criminal Law* 38, 3 (Summer 2011): 291–94; Melanie Reid, "*United States v. Jones:* Big Brother and the 'Common Good' versus the Fourth Amendment and Your Right to Privacy," *Tennessee Journal of Law and Policy* 9, 1 (Spring 2013): 14.

8. *Silverman v. United States*, 365 U.S. 505 (1961). See also Emas and Pallas, "*United States v. Jones:* Does *Katz* Still Have Nine Lives?," 124–25; Reid, "*United States v. Jones*," 14.

9. See, for example, Brennan, "*Katz* Cradle," 1804; Reid, "*United States v. Jones*," 14–16.

10. 389 U.S. 347. See also Collins, "The Case of *Katz v. United States* (1967)," 10–11; Winn, "*Katz* and the Origins of the 'Reasonable Expectation of Privacy' Test," 2–3.

11. 389 U.S. 347, 350.

12. 389 U.S. 347, 351.

13. 389 U.S. 347, 351.

14. 389 U.S. 347, 352.

15. 389 U.S. 347, 353. See also Collins, "The Case of *Katz v. United States* (1967)," 10–11.

16. 389 U.S. 347, 359.

17. 389 U.S. 347, 360.

18. 389 U.S. 347, 361. See also Collins, "The Case of *Katz v. United States* (1967)," 14; Reid, "*United States v. Jones*," 15; Winn, "*Katz* and the Origins of the 'Reasonable Expectation of Privacy' Test," 6–10.

19. 389 U.S. 347, 362.

20. 389 U.S. 347, 362–63.

21. 389 U.S. 347, 363.

22. 389 U.S. 347, 364.

23. 389 U.S. 347, 364. See also Collins, "The Case of *Katz v. United States* (1967)," 11–12.

24. 389 U.S. 347, 365.

25. 389 U.S. 347, 366.

26. 389 U.S. 347, 366.

27. 389 U.S. 347, 367.

28. 389 U.S. 347, 369.

29. 389 U.S. 347, 373.

30. 389 U.S. 347, 374.

31. Winn, "*Katz* and the Origins of the 'Reasonable Expectation of Privacy' Test," 4. Emphasis in the original.

32. Collins, "The Case of *Katz v. United States* (1967)," 12–15; Emas and Pallas, "*United States v. Jones:* Does *Katz* Still Have Nine Lives?," 125–30; McInnis, "The Changing Definition of Search or Seizure," 10–13; Winn, "*Katz* and the Origins of the 'Reasonable Expectation of Privacy' Test," 10–13.

33. The Omnibus Crime Control and Safe Streets Act of 1968 (Pub.L. 90–351, 82 Stat. 197, enacted June 19, 1968, codified at 42 U.S.C. § 3711, et seq.); the Electronic Communications and Privacy Act of 1986 (ECPA) (Pub L. 99–508, 100 Stat. 1848, enacted October 21, 1986, codified at 18 U.S.C. § 2510, et seq.); the Communications Assistance for Law Enforcement Act of 1994 (CALEA) (Pub. L. No. 103–414, 108 Stat. 4279, enacted October 25, 1994, codified at 47 USC §1001 et seq.); Uniting and Strengthening America by Providing Appropriate Tools Required to Intercept and Obstruct Terrorism Act of 2001 (USA PATRIOT) (Pub. L. 107–56, 115 Stat. 272, enacted October 26, 2001, codified at 18 USC §2712, 31 USC §5318A,

15 USC §1681v, 8 USC §1226A, 18 USC §1993, 18 USC §2339, 18 USC §175b, 50 USC §403–5b, 51 USC §5103a).

34. *United States v. Jones*, 132 S.Ct. 945 (2012).

35. Collins, "The Case of *Katz v. United States* (1967)," 15–25; Emas and Pallas, "*United States v. Jones:* Does *Katz* Still Have Nine Lives?," 116–217; McInnis, "The Changing Definition of Search or Seizure," 10–13; Winn, "*Katz* and the Origins of the 'Reasonable Expectation of Privacy' Test," 10–13.

CHAPTER 10

Terry v. Ohio (1968) and the Stop-and-Frisk Search

At 62 years of age, Officer Martin J. McFadden had not seen everything life can throw at a man, but he had seen much. Having spent more than three decades of his law enforcement career policing the streets of Cleveland, Ohio, he had developed an uncanny knack for spotting suspicious activity. Around 2:30 on the afternoon of October 31, 1963, he witnessed a scene that convinced him that he must intervene to foil a potential burglary. In doing so, he triggered a series of events culminating in one of the most important Supreme Court cases in American legal history.[1]

The plainclothes officer patrolled on foot near the corner of Euclid Avenue and Huron Road in Cleveland during that Halloween afternoon, less than a month before President Kennedy was murdered. McFadden was scanning the crowd of people in search of shoplifters and pickpockets reputed to prowl the area. As he walked his beat, the officer spied two men standing in front of a store. Based on his long experience working in law enforcement, he thought their behavior warranted a second look. The officer later explained he "had developed routine habits of observation over the years," which involved close scrutiny of individuals acting in an odd manner. He would "stand and watch people or walk and watch people at many intervals of the day."[2]

Something about those two fellows appeared out of place. He had never seen either individual previously, nor did he find their dress unusual. They wore topcoats, a standard garment for a chilly autumn afternoon in northern Ohio. Despite their unremarkable appearance, McFadden believed "they didn't look right to me at the time," even though they were only standing in front of the store when he first encountered them. Asked to explain how he reached such a conclusion, McFadden was noncommittal. "I really don't know," he said. Critics later surmised the officer was suspicious of the two men because they were black, but McFadden never indicated that race was a factor in the investigation.[3]

McFadden kept an eye on the two men from a distance of between 300 and 400 feet for approximately 10 minutes. As he watched, they performed a ritual. One man walked down the street, peered into a storefront window, and continued walking. He then returned to his colleague and the two fellows conferred. The second man repeated the actions of the first. McFadden's report, which he filed that same day, commented that the men performed the ritual "about three times each." During a suppression hearing a year later, McFadden estimated the men acted in this bizarre manner "at least four or five times apiece." On another occasion, he estimated they paced back and forth between four and six times. At trial, he testified to a different number: "about four trips, three to four trips, maybe four to five trips, maybe a little more; it might be a little less. I don't know. I didn't count the trips."[4]

The number of times the men walked back and forth in front of the store would become crucial in the resultant case because the question was whether their actions were suspicious enough to suggest that a burglary might occur. No crime had been committed, but Officer McFadden believed the men were "casing a job" in preparation for breaking in and stealing merchandise. In most instances, a police officer must possess probable cause that a crime has occurred to detain an individual for questioning and possible arrest. As the Supreme Court would discuss in *Terry v. Ohio*, the case arising out of Officer McFadden's actions that day, a lesser standard will justify a brief detention, but the officer must be able to articulate reasonable grounds for his suspicion.[5]

While the officer observed their actions, the two men welcomed a third fellow, a white man. The three associates engaged in a conversation. If race had not played a role until that time, it seemed to be important after the third man appeared. Cleveland in 1963 was a segregated city. Whites and blacks usually did not mix. McFadden's suspicions deepened. At the conclusion of the conversation, the two black men walked away from the white man. Moments later, the three congregated again in front of Zucker's, a men's clothing store. Convinced that criminal activity was afoot, the officer decided he must act.[6]

McFadden approached the trio, identified himself as a police officer, and asked the men to disclose their names. They mumbled incoherently, obviously uncomfortable with the request. The two black men were John W. Terry and Richard D. Chilton. The white man was Carl Katz. Although he lacked probable cause, Officer McFadden believed the suspicious circumstances allowed him to perform a brief pat down. He grabbed John Terry, spun him around, and felt the outside portion of Terry's clothing. McFadden discovered that Terry carried a .38-caliber revolver in the left breast pocket of his overcoat. Unable to remove the gun, the officer ordered the three men to step inside Zucker's store. As they entered, McFadden stripped Terry's coat off and retrieved the gun.

McFadden ordered the three men to face the wall and raise their hands. After patting down the other men, the officer found that Chilton also carried a .38-caliber handgun, but Katz was unarmed. As Chief Justice Earl Warren subsequently explained the facts:

> The officer testified that he only patted the men down to see whether they had weapons, and that he did not put his hands beneath the outer garments of either Terry or Chilton until he felt their guns. So far as appears from the record, he never placed his hands beneath Katz' outer garments. Officer McFadden seized Chilton's gun, asked the proprietor of the store to call a police wagon, and took all three men to the station, where Chilton and Terry were formally charged with carrying concealed weapons.[7]

Katz was held for two days as a "suspicious person" but released for lack of evidence.[8]

While the two defendants awaited trial, they sought to suppress the incriminating evidence on the grounds that Officer McFadden did not possess probable cause and the men never consented to a search. Using the same defense attorney, Terry and Chilton filed a joint motion in the Cuyahoga County Court of Common Pleas to exclude the guns from evidence. The prosecutor initially argued that Officer McFadden's actions were part of a search incident to a lawful arrest, but the trial judge concluded it "would be stretching the facts beyond reasonable comprehension" to allow the guns to be admitted into evidence using such a justification. The officer did not have probable cause to detain the men; therefore, finding the guns after the detention occurred would have to rely on another rationale. The trial court found exactly such a rationale, concluding that an experienced police officer could briefly detain people who "were conducting themselves suspiciously" and, to ensure his own safety, could pat down their outer clothing in search of weapons. As Chief Justice Warren later observed, "The court distinguished between an investigatory 'stop' and an arrest, and between a 'frisk' of the outer clothing for weapons and a full-blown search for evidence of crime. The frisk, it held, was essential to the proper performance of the officer's investigatory duties, for, without it, 'the answer to the police officer may be a bullet, and a loaded pistol discovered during the frisk is admissible.'"[9]

After the court denied the motion to suppress, the defendants stood trial and were convicted. They appealed. The Ohio Supreme Court affirmed the convictions. When the defendants appealed again, the U.S. Supreme Court granted certiorari to hear John Terry's case. Richard Chilton died after the Court agreed to hear the case but before a decision was rendered. Thus, Terry became the sole petitioner.[10]

Chief Justice Warren, in his majority opinion, which was joined by Justices Black, Brennan, Stewart, Fortas, and Marshall, summarized the issue succinctly: "The question is whether, in all the circumstances of this on-the-street encounter, his [i.e., defendant John Terry's] right to personal security was violated by an unreasonable search and seizure." Recognizing the case "thrusts to the fore difficult and troublesome issues regarding a sensitive area of police activity," the chief justice explained that the matter was at its core a reiteration of the perennial debate between the needs of the police to rely on an "escalating set of flexible responses" and the rights of a citizen to live free from government intervention. The outcome depended on "the specific justification for any intrusion upon protected personal security, coupled with a highly developed system of judicial controls."[11]

The chief justice observed that police officers must decide matters in the field under enormous pressure with little time for reflection. On some occasions, their decisions hold life-or-death consequences. Although officers of the law indisputably must be held to high legal standards, a reviewing court must be "mindful of the limitations of the judicial function in controlling the myriad daily situations in which policemen and citizens confront each other on the street." Second-guessing a discretionary judgment call can paralyze the carefully crafted law enforcement system. The role of the courts, therefore, is to balance the competing values of government authority and individual freedom. In Warren's words:

> Courts which sit under our Constitution cannot and will not be made party to lawless invasions of the constitutional rights of citizens by permitting unhindered governmental use of the fruits of such invasions. Thus, in our system, evidentiary rulings provide the context in which the judicial process of inclusion and exclusion approves some conduct as comporting with constitutional guarantees and disapproves other actions by state agents. A ruling admitting evidence in a criminal trial, we recognize, has the necessary effect of legitimizing the conduct which produced the evidence, while an application of the exclusionary rule withholds the constitutional imprimatur.[12]

Warren rejected the idea that a policeman stopping and frisking a person in a street encounter falls outside the purview of the Fourth Amendment because the individual has not been "searched" or "seized." A person who is detained for a period of time prior has been "seized" even if he or she is not arrested and transported to the police station to face criminal charges. "And it is nothing less than sheer torture of the English language to suggest that a careful exploration of the outer surfaces of a person's clothing all over his or her body in an attempt to find weapons is not a 'search,'" the chief justice reasoned.[13]

The Fourth Amendment allows for *reasonable* searches and seizures. According to Warren, the crucial question is whether the search and seizure in a stop-and-frisk encounter are characterized as "reasonable." The analysis requires a two-fold discussion. First, the court must examine the facts of a case and determine the governmental interest served by the brief detention. Second, the police officer involved in the case must be able to articulate the factual basis that led to the stop. The court will apply a "reasonable person" standard: would a reasonable person facing the same circumstances as the officer believe the detention was necessary?[14]

"Applying these principles to this case, we consider first the nature and extent of the governmental interests involved," the chief justice wrote. Crime prevention and detection are legitimate governmental interests—in fact, they are the primary responsibilities of law enforcement officers. When an experienced police officer witnesses a person engage in a suspicious activity, he has a duty to investigate. In this case, the officer saw the "men pace alternately along an identical route, pausing to stare in the same store window roughly 24 times" before conferring with a third confederate. "It would have been poor police work indeed for an officer of 30 years' experience in the detection of thievery from stores in this same neighborhood to have failed to investigate this behavior further."[15]

Some commentators have questioned whether the facts in the case were as indisputable as Chief Justice Warren assumed. The actions of the men that day may not have been "suspicious" to a reasonable person.[16] Setting aside that issue, Warren contended that a more important question was at stake. "The crux of this case, however, is not the propriety of Officer McFadden's taking steps to investigate petitioner's suspicious behavior," he argued, "but, rather, whether there was justification for McFadden's invasion of Terry's personal security by searching him for weapons in the course of that investigation."[17]

Warren conceded, "Even a limited search of the outer clothing for weapons constitutes a severe, though brief, intrusion upon cherished personal security, and it must surely be an annoying, frightening, and perhaps humiliating experience."[18] Nonetheless, police officers interact with citizens on a daily basis and, upon occasion, the officer may realize that something is wrong. If forced to wait until he had probable cause before undertaking a search or seizure, the officer would be placed in an untenable position. The person with whom he was interacting might draw a weapon, thereby endangering the officer as well as public safety. In Warren's opinion, an officer must possess the authority to act on the basis of more than a whim even if less than probable cause. He remarked that "a perfectly reasonable apprehension of danger may arise long before the officer is possessed of adequate information to justify taking a person into custody for the purpose of prosecuting him for a crime."[19] The goal is to ensure that "there must be a narrowly drawn authority to permit a reasonable search for weapons for the protection of the police officer" or law enforcement officials will be hampered in their work.[20]

In reviewing McFadden's actions on Halloween Day 1963, Warren agreed that the officer made a valid judgment call under the circumstances:

> Thus, when Officer McFadden approached the three men gathered before the display window at Zucker's store, he had observed enough to make it quite reasonable to fear that they were armed, and nothing in their response to his hailing them, identifying himself as a police officer, and asking their names served to dispel

that reasonable belief. We cannot say his decision at that point to seize Terry and pat his clothing for weapons was the product of a volatile or inventive imagination, or was undertaken simply as an act of harassment; the record evidences the tempered act of a policeman who, in the course of an investigation, had to make a quick decision as to how to protect himself and others from possible danger, and took limited steps to do so.[21]

At the conclusion of his opinion, Warren affirmed Terry's conviction but noted that case-by-case adjudication always would be required in lieu of the court announcing a bright-line rule. The facts surrounding the police–citizen encounter are crucial in determining the reasonableness, or lack thereof, of the stop and frisk. A noncustodial detention by a police officer does not rise to the level of unreasonable government intrusion if the incident amounts to a brief, "reasonable" stop. Despite the fact that Terry and his co-defendant were "seized" by Officer McFadden—and such a "seizure" normally would require probable cause pursuant to the Fourth Amendment—in this case the pat down was not a full-blown search. The Fourth Amendment does not prohibit warrantless searches, only "unreasonable" warrantless searches. Nothing in the U.S. Constitution undermines the ability of law enforcement personnel to investigate, detect, and prevent criminal activity. The *Terry* ruling balances the privacy interests of individuals with the needs of law enforcement personnel.[22]

Justice John Marshall Harlan II filed a concurrence. He remarked, "I unreservedly agree with the Court's ultimate holding in this case," but he suggested the majority opinion contained a few gaps. "Since the question in this and most cases is whether evidence produced by a frisk is admissible, the problem is to determine what makes a frisk reasonable."[23] Harlan argued, "I would make it perfectly clear that the right to frisk in this case depends upon the reasonableness of a forcible stop to investigate a suspected crime." If the stop is reasonable, the officer may take steps to ensure his safety as well as the safety of others. "There is no reason why an officer, rightfully but forcibly confronting a person suspected of a serious crime, should have to ask one question and take the risk that the answer might be a bullet."[24]

In this instance, the patrolman met the standard for a reasonable stop. "Officer McFadden had no probable cause to arrest Terry for anything, but he had observed circumstances that would reasonably lead an experienced, prudent policeman to suspect that Terry was

Terry v. Ohio **allowed police officers acting on reasonable suspicion to stop and frisk suspects even if the officers lack probable cause of criminal activity. The brief detention can escalate into a full custodial arrest. In this photograph, New York City police officers pat down a suspect during a citizen encounter in 1973. Despite this scene, a police officer does not customarily draw a weapon unless the officer fears for his safety. (The Granger Collection, New York)**

about to engage in burglary or robbery," Harlan contended. "His justifiable suspicion afforded a proper constitutional basis for accosting Terry, restraining his liberty of movement briefly, and addressing questions to him, and Officer McFadden did so." Based on Terry's behavior—he mumbled and did not satisfactorily answer the officer's inquiries—McFadden suspected the man might be engaged in a crime, and perhaps he was armed. "Once that forced encounter was justified . . . the officer's right to take suitable measures for his own safety followed automatically."[25]

Justice Byron White also concurred. He began his opinion by objecting to the majority opinion's obiter dicta regarding limits on the exclusionary rule. Afterward, White explained that a police officer can ask a question of anyone walking down the street, but "the person stopped is not obliged to answer, answers may not be compelled, and refusal to answer furnishes no basis for an arrest." If the policeman possesses additional facts suggesting the commission of a crime is imminent, he can briefly detain the person. "In my view, it is temporary detention, warranted by the circumstances, which chiefly justifies the protective frisk for weapons."[26] White concluded by observing that "constitutional rights are not necessarily violated if pertinent questions are asked and the person is restrained briefly in the process."[27]

In a blistering dissent, Justice William O. Douglas expressed concern that the Court's decision would erode the concept of "probable cause." By allowing a police officer to detain a person for a stop-and-frisk pat down, the court majority provided law enforcement officials with the power denied to a magistrate who must sign off on a warrant based on probable cause. "To give the police greater power than a magistrate is to take a long step down the totalitarian path," Douglas argued, albeit histrionically. "Perhaps such a step is desirable to cope with modern forms of lawlessness. But if it is taken, it should be the deliberate choice of the people through a constitutional amendment."[28]

Recognizing the fear of crime and the seemingly lawless mood prevalent in the United States in that pivotal year of 1968, Justice Douglas sympathized with the desire to provide the police with enhanced authority. "There have been powerful hydraulic pressures throughout our history that bear heavily on the Court to water down constitutional guarantees and give the police the upper hand. That hydraulic pressure has probably never been greater than it is today," he acknowledged. "Yet if the individual is no longer to be sovereign, if the police can pick him up whenever they do not like the cut of his jib, if they can 'seize' and 'search' him in their discretion, we enter a new regime. The decision to enter it should be made only after a full debate by the people of this country."[29]

Since 1968, when the *Terry* case was announced, the courts have recognized essentially three types of law enforcement stops. The first is the casual and mutually consensual interaction between an individual and a police officer. When the individual desires to disengage, the encounter ends. The second type is an investigative stop where the police officer does not possess probable cause that a crime has been committed, as was the case in *Terry*. In such situations, the police officer can briefly detain the individual and even pat down the detainee if the officer suspects the person is hiding a weapon. Although probable cause is lacking, the police officer is justified in brief, noncustodial detention as long as he can articulate a particularized, objective, reasonable basis for believing that criminal activity may be underway. The *Terry* case preserves the warrant requirement while also allowing police officers to use discretion in protecting the community from criminal activity. The third stop involves an arrest and is permissible as long as the police officer has probable cause or possesses an arrest warrant issued by a duly authorized judicial official such as a magistrate. In limited instances, exigent circumstances may provide an exception to the warrant requirement.[30]

As frequently happens when the U.S. Supreme Court announces an opinion, reactions to *Terry v. Ohio* were, and remain, mixed. Some commentators were worried that the case left numerous practical questions unanswered. Judge Michael R. Juviler wrote, "After the *Terry* opinions were filed, we felt perhaps like the makers of the hydrogen bomb. What had we created? What had we contributed to? Would this lead to further racial divisions, police abuse, police 'testifying?'"[31] In 1988, Professor Edwin J. Butterfoss of Hamline University School of Law remarked, "Because the issue of when a seizure occurred was not decided in *Terry*, the precise contours of the 'nonseizure' category identified by the Court were left undefined."[32]

The imprecision in the case opened the door to unintended mischief. "Despite reversing precedent, *Terry* and its Supreme Court progeny allowed police officers to rely upon their reasonable suspicions to conduct searches only under narrow conditions," Professor Brando Simeo Starkey of Villanova University School of Law wrote. "Lower courts, however, have enlarged *Terry* beyond recognition. Indeed, police officers now have wide latitude to stop and frisk suspects."[33]

The wide latitude left to police officers could result in intentionally or unintentionally biased citizen detentions. "In *Terry v. Ohio*, the Supreme Court sanctioned police investigations of individuals based on nothing more than an officer's 'reasonable suspicions,'" Professor L. Song Richardson of American University observed in 2012. "The problem is that implicit biases may cause police officers to pay more attention to Blacks than Whites and to interpret the behaviors of Blacks as suspicious more readily than the identical behaviors of Whites."[34] Professor Starkey agreed that race may become a factor in *Terry* stops. "As the trajectory of American race relations predicts, minorities, particularly males in lower-income communities, have complained of police harassment in the wake of *Terry*," he argued. "Indeed, Blacks and Hispanics contend that police officers stop and frisk them even when no 'reasonable' basis for doing so exists. It seems that 'reasonableness' highly correlates to melanin."[35]

Professor Starkey's conclusion is especially harsh. Other observers have found the *Terry* standard to be a flexible tool for law enforcement officers and unrelated to racial animus. Reflecting on the case three decades later, Professor Stephen A. Saltzburg of George Washington University School of Law wrote in a law review article that "*Terry*'s stop and frisk rule as developed over the past 30 years has evolved to a practically ideal approach for governing law enforcement efforts to deal with a range of potentially criminal conduct without unnecessarily interfering with the liberty of ordinary people." Unlike some Supreme Court doctrines that are unworkable in the field, the *Terry* rule has stood the test of time because it recognizes the vagaries that police officers encounter as they interact with members of the public. "Because of *Terry* and its progeny, law enforcement officers can act before crime occurs to protect society, and they can do so without compromising the probable cause standard that governs arrests and warrants."[36]

Chief Justice Warren did not use the term "reasonable suspicion" in his majority opinion, but Justice Harlan referred to the concept.[37] In any case, after 1968, "reasonable suspicion" became a shorthand means of describing the totality of articulable facts that suggest to an experienced police officer that criminal activity may be imminent. The Fourth Amendment jurisprudence after *Terry v. Ohio* defined some of the myriad circumstances that constitute reasonable suspicion as well as the parameters of a *Terry* search. For example, *Minnesota v. Dickerson*, a 1993 case, broadened the *Terry* rule beyond merely searching for weapons during a pat down. The Court held that a police officer conducting a lawful *Terry* search can seize contraband (in this case, crack cocaine) even if the contraband is not a weapon.[38] Seven years later, in *Illinois v. Wardlow*, the U.S. Supreme Court decided that a person fleeing from police in an area known for drug trafficking when the police did not initiate contact beforehand creates the reasonable suspicion necessary to justify a *Terry* stop.[39] In *Hiibel v. Sixth Judicial District Court of Nevada*, a 2004 case, the Court decided by a 5–4 vote that a state statute requiring a suspect to disclose his name when stopped by a police officer did not violate the Fourth Amendment if the statute justified the original stop on the basis of reasonable and articulable suspicion of criminal activity.[40]

Terry v. Ohio has been, and will remain, a controversial case because it modified the standards governing police–citizen interactions under the Fourth Amendment. Critics charge that the case initiated a gradual process of bleeding together probable cause and reasonable suspicion in favor of aggressive law enforcement. The two standards effectively have become one, which means that probable cause has been watered down so that police officers can stop "suspicious" individuals on any convenient pretext. For their part, *Terry* supporters argue that the case did not lessen the traditional probable cause standard. Instead, it added a category of police–citizen engagement between a mere whim and the more exacting probable cause requirement. Supporters believe that *Terry* provides law enforcement officers with the flexible tools necessary to combat crime, protect their own safety as well as the safety of others, and safeguard Fourth Amendment guarantees.

NOTES

1. *Terry v. Ohio*, 392 U.S. 1, 5 (1968).
2. Quoted in Lewis R. Katz, "*Terry v. Ohio* at Thirty-Five: A Revisionist View," *Mississippi Law Journal* 74, 2 (2004): 429. See also 392 U.S. 1, 5; Nicholas R. Alioto, "Unreasonable Differences: The Dispute Regarding the Application of *Terry* Stops to Completed Misdemeanor Crimes," *St. John's Law Review* 83, 3 (Summer 2009): 951; Stephen A. Saltzburg, "*Terry v. Ohio:* A Practically Perfect Doctrine," *St. John's Law Review* 72, 3 (Summer-Fall 1998): 912–13.
3. Quoted in Katz, "*Terry v. Ohio* at Thirty-Five," 429. See also 392 U.S. 1, 5.
4. Quoted in Katz, "*Terry v. Ohio* at Thirty-Five," 429–30.
5. In his majority opinion in *Terry*, Chief Justice Warren wrote, "The two men repeated this ritual alternately between five and six times apiece—in all, roughly a dozen trips." 392 U.S. 1, 6. The nature of the suspects' actions, clearly one of the pivotal parts of the case, could never be accounted for accurately in any account.
6. 392 U.S. 1, 5–6. See also Tiffany D. Corona, "A Public Safety Approach: Reconciling *Terry* with Individual Rights," *McGeorge Law Review* 41, 4 (October 2010): 908; Katz, "*Terry v. Ohio* at Thirty-Five," 431.
7. 392 U.S. 1, 7.
8. Katz, "*Terry v. Ohio* at Thirty-Five," 431–32; Saltzburg, "*Terry v. Ohio,*" 913–14.

9. 392 U.S. 1, 7–8. See also Saltzburg, "*Terry v. Ohio*," 914–15.
10. 392 U.S. 1, 8.
11. 392 U.S. 1, 10–11.
12. 392 U.S. 1, 13.
13. 392 U.S. 1, 16.
14. 392 U.S. 1, 21–22.
15. 392 U.S. 1, 23.
16. See, for example, Corona, "A Public Safety Approach," 908–12; Katz, "*Terry v. Ohio* at Thirty-Five," 429–33; Brando Simeo Starkey, "A Failure of the Fourth Amendment & Equal Protection's Promise: How the Equal Protection Clause Can Change Discriminatory Stop and Frisk Policies," *Michigan Journal of Race & Law* 18, 1 (Fall 2012): 134–35.
17. 392 U.S. 1, 23.
18. 392 U.S. 1, 24–25.
19. 392 U.S. 1, 26–27.
20. 392 U.S. 1, 27.
21. 392 U.S. 1, 28.
22. 392 U.S. 1, 29–31.
23. 392 U.S. 1, 31.
24. 392 U.S. 1, 33.
25. 392 U.S. 1, 33–34. See also Saltzburg, "*Terry v. Ohio*," 927–28.
26. 392 U.S. 1, 34.
27. 392 U.S. 1, 35.
28. 392 U.S. 1, 38. See also Saltzburg, "*Terry v. Ohio*," 929.
29. 392 U.S. 1, 39.
30. The literature on this point is voluminous. See, for example, Susan Bandes, "*Terry v. Ohio* in Hindsight: The Perils of Predicting the Past," *Constitutional Commentary* 16, 3 (Winter 1999): 491–97; Aidan Taft Grano, "Casual or Coercive? Retention of Identification in Police-Citizen Encounters," *Columbia Law Review* 113, 5 (June 2013): 1285–86.
31. Hon. Michael R. Juviler, "A Prosecutor's Perspective," *St. John's Law Review* 72, 3–4 (Summer-Fall 1998): 743–44.
32. Edwin J. Butterfoss, "Bright Line Seizures: The Need for Clarity in Determining When Fourth Amendment Activity Begins," *Journal of Criminal Law & Criminology* 79, 2 (Summer 1988): 437.
33. Starkey, "A Failure of the Fourth Amendment & Equal Protection's Promise," 135.
34. L. Song Richardson, "Police Efficiency and the Fourth Amendment," *Indiana Law Journal* 87, 3 (Summer 2012): 1151.
35. Starkey, "A Failure of the Fourth Amendment & Equal Protection's Promise," 135. See also David Cole, "The Usual Suspects," *The Nation* 294, 27/28 (July 2/9, 2012): 4–6.
36. Saltzburg, "*Terry v. Ohio*," 974.

37. 392 U.S. 1, 32.
38. *Minnesota v. Dickerson*, 508 U.S. 366 (1993).
39. *Illinois v. Wardlow*, 528 U.S. 119 (2000).
40. *Hiibel v. Sixth Judicial District Court of Nevada*, et al., 542 U.S. 177 (2004).

CHAPTER 11

Chimel v. California (1969) and Searches Incident to Arrest

On the afternoon of September 13, 1965, three police officers arrived at Ted Chimel's home in Santa Ana, California. They brought a warrant authorizing them to arrest Chimel for allegedly burglarizing a coin shop, but they did not possess a search warrant for the premises. When the officers knocked on the door, they identified themselves to Chimel's wife and asked if they could come inside. She agreed even though her husband was not at home when the police arrived. The officers waited 10 or 15 minutes until Chimel returned from work.

As the suspect stepped inside the house, an officer handed him the arrest warrant and asked for permission to "look around" the premises. Chimel strenuously objected. In response, the officer told him that "on the basis of the lawful arrest," law enforcement officials would conduct a search regardless of his objections.

Chimel's wife accompanied the officers as they searched the three-bedroom house as well as the attic, the garage, and a small workshop. In some areas, the police performed a perfunctory search, but in other rooms they instructed Mrs. Chimel to open drawers and "physically move contents of the drawers from side to side." At the end of the 45-minute search, the officers removed medals, tokens, and several other objects they believed to have been stolen during the suspected burglary.

Prosecutors eventually charged Ted Chimel with burglary and introduced the items seized during the search as evidence against him. Chimel argued the items had been seized illegally because the officers had not obtained a valid search warrant. The trial court disagreed, and Chimel was convicted. On appeal, both the California Court of Appeal and the California Supreme Court agreed that the officers should have obtained a search warrant beforehand; however, because the arresting officers had obtained the arrest warrant "in good faith" and they had possessed sufficient information to constitute probable cause for the petitioner's arrest, the arrest had been lawful. Consequently, the search was incident to a lawful arrest.[1]

The case raised a long-standing issue in criminal procedure. The Fourth Amendment indicates that a warrant is necessary before law enforcement officials reasonably can search for evidence of criminality. Yet throughout the years, the courts have recognized the need for exceptions to the warrant requirement. Interactions between law enforcement officials and the public often happen quickly and with little advance notice. Police officers cannot be expected to apply for a warrant in the field when circumstances necessitate swift and decisive action. Requiring a warrant in every instance would be unworkable and would hamper criminal investigations.[2]

An examination of the historical record indicates the origins of the search-incident-to-an-arrest rule are murky. The Framers of the Constitution, suspicious of centralized authority, erred on the side of denying or limiting discretionary authority to government officials whenever possible. They had experienced the vagaries of an obdurate government exercising seemingly arbitrary power against the citizenry, and they had no desire to replicate the whole nasty business. Why replace a faraway tyrant such as England's King George III with a homegrown variety that could engage in greater mischief than the king he supplanted? The new sovereign, after all, would be ensconced on native soil.[3]

Searches and seizures without a warrant were limited in the Founding period to arrestees who were subsequently convicted of a felony. The after-the-fact justification made for an awkward arrangement as law enforcement authorities could not know whether the arrest was legitimate until a court or jury pronounced it so. Authorities could only arrest persons suspected of committing a misdemeanor after the officer witnessed the offense and the crime also breached the public peace. An officer who failed to comply with such strictures could find himself haled before a civil court and facing a lawsuit for trespass or false imprisonment. The dire consequences for a mistake created a powerful disincentive for a police officer to arrest a citizen without a warrant absent overwhelmingly compelling circumstances indicating the guilt of the accused.[4]

American constables on patrol during the 18th century served in a part-time capacity. In most places, the post paid poorly and afforded its occupants limited prestige. The position was akin to a night watchman who kept his eyes open for signs of criminal activity but was not expected to participate in law enforcement. It was little wonder, therefore, that police officers seldom launched criminal investigations or arrested suspects. If investigations and arrests were limited in number and scope, the question of searches incident to arrest was not pressing.

In rare instances where an arrest occurred, the issue of whether a police officer could search the suspect at the time of the arrest was never clear. As a practical matter, the officer would disarm a person taken into custody, but a search for weapons or evidence of criminality in the immediate vicinity of the suspect was not expected. Even when the officer conducted a search, he sought physical evidence of stolen property. Owing to the limited forensics of the 18th and 19th centuries, police officers did not search for evidence, such as fingerprints, DNA, and bodily fluids, commonly used to establish a criminal case in a later era.

By the middle of the 19th century, as citizens became concerned about a crime rate that grew in proportion to the rise in urbanization, larger U.S. cities organized professional police forces. Courts increasingly recognized the concept of exigent circumstances that created probable cause to arrest suspects without a warrant, a change that significantly broadened police power. Societal expectations evolved. Law enforcement officers were no longer supposed to be night watchmen who passively observed the area and reported on wrongdoing. They were tasked with serving and protecting the public. Aggressively policing the community meant patrolling neighborhoods to prevent crime, investigating leads to detect crime, and arresting suspects, followed by prosecuting defendants, to punish crime.[5]

Late in the 19th century, legal commentators ruminated on the appropriate parameters for searching persons placed under arrest. As a leading treatise writer, Joel Prentiss Bishop, observed in 1895, an officer could "safely keep an arrested prisoner," which meant the officer was justified in searching the arrestee, if "from violent conduct or other reason he fears an attempt to escape." The search was limited to ensuring the person in custody was not harboring a weapon. If the arresting officer found a weapon, he could take it. The arresting officer was not justified in seizing additional evidence unless it directly pertained to the case for which the suspect was being arrested. In instances where an arrestee was not armed and the officer had no reasonable belief that the person possessed a weapon, a search was impermissible. A person detained for "disorderly drunkenness" was the quintessential example of a case where a search incident to arrest was unnecessary. "In the absence of any special reason, the officer should not take anything from the prisoner's custody" under such circumstances, Bishop advised.[6]

The first modern case on a search incident to an arrest occurred during the World War I era. In *Weeks v. United States*, discussed in Chapter 2 of this book, the U.S. Supreme Court ruled on whether a defendant's private papers could be seized without a warrant.[7] In the opinion, the Court included dictum indicating that a search incident to an arrest sometimes is permissible:

> What, then, is the present case? Before answering that inquiry specifically, it may be well by a process of exclusion to state what it is not. It is not an assertion of the right on the part of the government always recognized under English and American law, to search the person of the accused when legally arrested, to discover and seize the fruits or evidences of crime. This right has been uniformly maintained in many cases.[8]

The Court reiterated the point 11 years later in *Carroll v. United States*. Writing for the majority, Chief Justice William Howard Taft explained, "When a man is legally arrested for an offense, whatever is found upon his person or in his control which it is unlawful for him to have and which may be used to prove the offense may be seized and held as evidence in the prosecution."[9] Taft's statement was the first clear articulation of the general rule on searches incident to arrest, but it was not the last. Justice Butler wrote for the majority in *Agnello v. United States* that "the right without a search warrant contemporaneously to search persons lawfully arrested while committing crime and to search the place where the arrest is made in order to find and seize things connected with the crime as its fruits or as the means by which it was committed, as well as weapons and other things to effect an escape from custody is not to be doubted."[10]

In another case decided during the 1920s, *Marron v. United States*, the Supreme Court considered a matter where police arrived at the defendant's leased property to look for paraphernalia associated with manufacturing liquor. As they searched the premises in accordance with a valid search warrant, they discovered a ledger that was not listed on the warrant. Officers seized the ledger and it was admitted into evidence. In reviewing the case, the high court held that the officers "had a right without a warrant contemporaneously to search the place in order to find and seize the things used to carry on the criminal enterprise." Although the defendant did not have the ledger in his hand or pocket when he was arrested, "it was nonetheless a part of the outfit or equipment actually used to commit the offense" and "it was in his immediate possession and control."[11]

Marron broadened the area that could be searched when a suspect was placed under arrest, but the Court was not always consistent in applying the rule. In *Go-Bart Importing Company v. United States*, for example, the Court decided a case involving a bootlegging company during the Prohibition era. When law enforcement personnel arrived at the office to arrest the company's officers, the police had secured an arrest warrant but not a search warrant. They seized a ledger and admitted it into evidence. The facts were similar to the *Marron* case, yet the Court found the seizure to be improper in *Go-Bart* because the items seized were not part of the ongoing offense of manufacturing illegal liquor, nor was an offense involving the ledger committed in the presence of the arresting officer.[12]

Similarly, in *United States v. Lefkowitz*, another Prohibition case, the Court excluded material seized without a search warrant from desk drawers during an arrest. "Save as given by that warrant and as lawfully incident to its execution, the officers had no authority over respondents or anything in the room," Justice Butler wrote for the Court.[13] Later in the opinion, he distinguished *Lefkowitz* from *Marron*. "Here, the searches were exploratory and general, and made solely to find evidence of respondents' guilt of the alleged conspiracy or some other crime. Though intended to be used to solicit orders for liquor in violation of the act, the papers and other articles found and taken were, in themselves, unoffending."[14]

The confusion continued in additional cases. *Harris v. United States* involved, once again, arrests without a search warrant. In this instance, the defendant was suspected of violating the Mail Fraud Statute and the National Stolen Property Act. Five federal agents arrested him and searched his apartment for five hours. During the investigation, they found a sealed envelope marked "personal papers" buried beneath clothes inside a bureau drawer. The officers tore open the envelope to discover draft cards belonging to the United States. Possession of the cards violated the Selective Training and Service Act of

1940. The defendant was convicted. On appeal, the U.S. Supreme Court held that the evidence was admissible because the "search was not a general exploration, but was specifically directed to the means and instrumentalities by which the crimes charged had been committed."[15]

Despite the differing outcomes in multiple cases, the Supreme Court was reluctant to announce a bright-line rule on how far the search incident to an arrest extended. In a 1948 case, Justice Murphy, writing for the majority, suggested that the results depended on each specific set of facts. He cautioned against allowing a widespread search, seemingly a retreat from the *Harris* decision a year earlier:

> A search or seizure without a warrant as an incident to a lawful arrest has always been considered to be a strictly limited right. It grows out of the inherent necessities of the situation at the time of the arrest. But there must be something more in the way of necessity than merely a lawful arrest. The mere fact that there is a valid arrest does not *ipso facto* legalize a search or seizure without a warrant. [Citation omitted.] Otherwise, the exception swallows the general principle, making a search warrant completely unnecessary wherever there is a lawful arrest.[16]

In *United States v. Rabinowitz*, Justice Minton wrote for the majority in a case involving the arrest of a forger. Arriving with an arrest warrant but no search warrant, police officers rifled through the suspect's desk, safe, and file cabinet of his one-room office for over an hour and a half. Following his conviction, Rabinowitz appealed on the grounds that the search was beyond the scope of a search incident to an arrest. Distinguishing *Go-Bart* and *Lefkowitz* from that case, Justice Minton explained, "Those cases condemned general exploratory searches, which cannot be undertaken by officers with or without a warrant. In the instant case, the search was not general or exploratory for whatever might be turned up. Specificity was the mark of the search and seizure here. There was probable cause to believe that respondent was conducting his business illegally." In Minton's opinion, formulating an inviolable rule for undertaking a valid search incident to arrest is impossible owing to myriad circumstances. "What is a reasonable search is not to be determined by any fixed formula. The Constitution does not define what are 'unreasonable' searches, and, regrettably, in our discipline, we have no ready litmus paper test. The recurring questions of the reasonableness of searches must find resolution in the facts and circumstances of each case."[17] The case came to stand for the proposition that police officers could search the area around a suspect's control without a search warrant if the arrest itself was justified. Beyond that small point, general guidance was lacking.[18]

By the 1960s, given the confusing back-and-forth nature of the Court's prior decisions on how far a warrantless search could extend when a suspect was being arrested, justices on the U.S. Supreme Court recognized that more definitive guidance was needed even if developing a "fixed formula" was impossible. They needed a suitable vehicle, and Ted Chimel's case appeared to fit the bill. They granted certiorari to address the question of what constitutes a valid search incident to an arrest, hoping to outline the scope and justification for such searches.[19]

Justice Potter Stewart wrote for a 7–2 majority. "This case raises basic questions concerning the permissible scope under the Fourth Amendment of a search incident to a lawful arrest," he wrote.[20] After reviewing the facts, Justice Stewart acknowledged that the "decisions of this Court bearing upon that question have been far from consistent" and the Court needed to provide guidance on a muddled area of the law.[21] To remedy past defects, the justice described the permissible scope for a search incident to an arrest as the "grabbable" area in the suspect's immediate vicinity. If a person under arrest can be searched for weapons to protect the officer's safety, "the area into which an arrestee might reach in order to grab a weapon or evidentiary items must, of course, be governed by a like rule." In Stewart's view, "A gun on a table or in a drawer in front of one who is arrested can be as dangerous to the arresting officer as one concealed in the clothing of the person arrested. There is ample justification, therefore, for a search of the arrestee's person and the area 'within his immediate control'—construing that phrase to mean the area from within which he might gain possession of a weapon or destructible evidence." A search beyond the arrestee's "grabbable" area is not justified. "Such searches, in the absence of well recognized exceptions, may be made only under the authority of a search warrant. The 'adherence to judicial processes' mandated by the Fourth Amendment requires no less."[22]

Ted Chimel's case involved a clearly impermissible search because the arresting officers conducted a lengthy, wide-ranging scavenger hunt. In reversing the conviction, Stewart explained that any other result would blur the distinction between an arrest warrant and a search warrant, obviating the intent of the Fourth Amendment in the process. "Application of sound Fourth Amendment principles to the

In *Chimel v. California,* Justice Potter Stewart, pictured here, wrote, "There is ample justification . . . for a search of the arrestee's person and the area 'within his immediate control,'" but rummaging through the entire house without a search warrant is constitutionally impermissible. (Library of Congress)

facts of this case produces a clear result," he concluded. "The search here went far beyond the petitioner's person and the area from within which he might have obtained either a weapon or something that could have been used as evidence against him. There was no constitutional justification, in the absence of a search warrant, for extending the search beyond that area. The scope of the search was, therefore, 'unreasonable' under the Fourth and Fourteenth Amendments, and the petitioner's conviction cannot stand."[23]

Justice John Marshall Harlan II concurred in the Court's opinion. In keeping with his concern for federalism principles, Harlan worried that the result might overly burden state courts. "We simply do not know the extent to which cities and towns across the Nation are prepared to administer the greatly expanded warrant system which will be required by today's decision; nor can we say with assurance that, in each and every local situation, the warrant requirement plays an essential role in the protection of those fundamental liberties protected against state infringement by the Fourteenth Amendment," he wrote.[24] Nonetheless, while the "federal-state factor has not been an easy one for me to resolve," Harlan reconciled his position by observing that "in the last analysis, I cannot in good conscience vote to perpetuate bad Fourth Amendment law." In other words, he agreed with the majority opinion that limits must be placed on the area properly searched incident to arrest even if the decision caused hardships for state law enforcement and judicial officers.[25]

Justice White, joined by Justice Black, dissented. Rather than clarifying the law surrounding a search incident to an arrest, the instant case obfuscates, White contended. "Few areas of the law have been as subject to shifting constitutional standards over the last 50 years as that of the search 'incident to an arrest,'" he remarked. "There has been a remarkable instability in this whole area, which has seen at least four major shifts in emphasis. Today's opinion makes an untimely fifth."[26]

White explained that a police officer who arrives on the premises possessing a valid arrest warrant has probable cause to be there. If the officer determines that exigent circumstances exist after he lawfully arrives on the scene, he is justified in moving beyond the strict terms of the arrest warrant because he has acquired probable cause for a wider search. White sought to ease the burden on law enforcement officials when they are arresting a suspect by maximizing flexibility. In his view, "It seems to me unreasonable to require the police to leave the scene in order to obtain a search warrant when they are already legally there to make a valid arrest, and when there must almost always be a strong possibility that confederates of the arrested man will in the meanwhile remove the items for which the police have probable cause to search."[27]

Before the officers arrived at his house that day, Ted Chimel had obliquely alerted other people that he had burglarized the coin shop. Such admissions against interest were sufficient to establish probable cause. Moreover, although the record was not explicit on the point, in all likelihood, Chimel also told his wife about his illicit activities. If the officers had arrested Chimel, removed him from the house, acquired a search warrant, and returned to look for evidence, the wife probably would have removed the incriminating materials in the interim.[28]

Justice White agreed with the majority opinion insofar as it permitted the arresting officers to search for evidence in the defendant's immediate vicinity, but he believed the Court did not allow law enforcement personnel sufficient discretionary authority:

> Like the majority, I would permit the police to search the person of a suspect and the area under his immediate control either to assure the safety of the officers or to prevent the destruction of evidence. And like the majority, I see nothing in the arrest alone furnishing probable cause for a search of any broader scope. However, where, as here, the existence of probable cause is independently established and would justify a warrant for a broader search for evidence, I would follow past cases and permit such a search to be carried out without a warrant, since the fact of arrest supplies an exigent circumstance justifying police action before the evidence can be removed, and also alerts the suspect to the fact of the search so that he can immediately seek judicial determination of probable cause in an adversary proceeding, and appropriate redress.[29]

White argued that his approach would not violate the Fourth Amendment because he was not arguing in favor of expanding the scope of the search. "The issue in this case is not the breadth of the search, since there was clearly probable cause for the search which was carried out," he explained. "No broader search than if the officers had a warrant would be permitted. The only issue is whether a search warrant was required as a precondition to that search. It is agreed that such a warrant would be required absent exigent circumstances. I would hold that the fact of arrest supplies such an exigent circumstance, since the police had lawfully gained entry to the premises to effect the arrest and since delaying the search to secure a warrant would have involved the risk of not recovering the fruits of the crime."[30]

In White's estimation, by excluding the evidence found in the search of Chimel's home, the majority was not providing necessary Fourth Amendment protection for criminal defendants. Persons arrested pursuant to a valid search warrant already had surrendered a measure of individual liberty. The effect of the *Chimel* decision was to hinder police in fighting crime. Allowing the law to err on the side of a search would not harm a defendant who wished to challenge a search incident to arrest; he would still have an opportunity to do so when he was brought before a judge. Promulgating a rule limiting searches incident to arrest to a "grabbable" area creates more mischief than it corrects, White concluded.[31]

Despite Justice White's concern that the majority opinion "makes an untimely fifth" shift in jurisprudence on searches incident to arrest, the *Chimel* rule seems relatively clear. It was certainly an improvement over the muddled jurisprudence that preceded the case—although applying the rule to areas outside the home, especially involving automobiles, provided to be problematic and controversial.[32] Nonetheless, *Chimel* was another clarification, albeit an incomplete one, of the parameters in criminal procedure announced by the Warren Court. It would be the last. The day *Chimel* was announced—June 23, 1969—was also Earl Warren's last day as chief justice. With his retirement, a new era dawned. Warren E. Burger, President Nixon's selection as Warren's successor, eventually would lead the high court in a new direction away from expanding criminal procedure rights for defendants and toward a new age of law and order.[33]

NOTES

1. The facts of the case can be found in multiple sources. See, for example, *Chimel v. California*, 395 U.S. 752, 753–54 (1969); Kelly A. Deters, "The 'Evaporation Point': *State v. Sykes* and the Erosion of the Fourth Amendment through the Search-Incident-to-Arrest Exception," *Iowa Law Review* 92, 5 (July 2007): 1907; Chelsea Oxton, "The Search Incident to Arrest Exception Plays Catch Up: Why Police May No Longer Search Cell Phones Incident to Arrest without a Warrant," *Creighton Law Review* 43, 4 (June 2010): 1164–65; Myron Moskovitz, "A Rule in Search of a Reason: An Empirical Reexamination of *Chimel*and *Belton*," *Wisconsin Law Review* 2002, 3 (2002): 658.

2. 395 U.S. 752, 753–60.

3. On the Founders and the original purpose of the Fourth Amendment, see Carolyn N. Long, "The Origins of the Fourth Amendment," *Insights on Law & Society* 11, 2 (May 2011): 4–29; Stephen J. Schulhofer, *More Essential Than Ever: The Fourth Amendment in the Twenty-First Century* (New York and Oxford: Oxford University Press, 2012). The literature on the Founders and their fears concerning oppressive governmental authority is voluminous. See, for example, Martin Diamond, "Democracy and *The Federalist:* A Reconsideration of the Framers' Intent," *American Political Science Review* 53,

1 (March 1959): 52–68; James A. Dorn, "The Scope of Government in a Free Society," *Cato Journal* 32, 3 (Fall 2012): 629–42; Vincent Ostrom, *The Political Theory of a Compound Republic: Designing the American Experiment*, 8th ed. (Lanham, Md.: Lexington Books, 2008).

4. Wayne A. Logan, "An Exception Swallows a Rule: Police Authority to Search Incident to Arrest," *Yale Law & Policy Review* 19, 2 (2001): 385–90; Seth W. Stoughton, "Modern Police Practices: *Arizona v. Gant*'s Illusory Restriction of Vehicle Searches Incident to Arrest," *Virginia Law Review* 97, 7 (November 2011): 1731–32.

5. Much has been written about crime and punishment in 19th-century America. See, for example, Roger Lane, "Urban Police and Crime in Nineteenth-Century America," *Crime & Justice* 2, 1 (1980): 1–43; Logan, "An Exception Swallows a Rule," 385–88.

6. Quoted in Logan, "An Exception Swallows a Rule," 388.

7. Sara M. Corradi, "Be Reasonable! Limit Warrantless Searches Smart Phone Searches to *Gant*'s Justification for Searches incident to Arrest," *Case Western Reserve Law Review* 63, 3 (Spring 2013): 45; Stoughton, "Modern Police Practices," 1731–32.

8. *Weeks v. United States*, 232 U.S. 383, 392 (1914).

9. *Carroll v. United States*, 267 U.S. 132, 158 (1925).

10. *Agnello v. United States*, 269 U.S. 20, 30 (1925).

11. *Marron v. United States*, 275 U.S. 192, 199 (1927).

12. *Go-Bart Importing Company v. United States*, 282 U.S. 344 (1931).

13. *United States v. Lefkowitz*, 285 U.S. 452, 463 (1932).

14. 285 U.S. 452, 465.

15. *Harris v. United States*, 331 U.S. 145, 153 (1947).

16. *Trupiano v. United States*, 334 U.S. 699, 708 (1948).

17. *United States v. Rabinowitz*, 339 U.S. 56, 62–63 (1950).

18. 395 U.S. 752, 760.

19. 395 U.S. 752, 755.

20. 395 U.S. 752, 753.

21. 395 U.S. 752, 755.

22. 395 U.S. 752, 763.

23. 395 U.S. 752, 768.

24. 395 U.S. 752, 769.

25. 395 U.S. 752, 769–70.

26. 395 U.S. 752, 770.

27. 395 U.S. 752, 774.

28. 395 U.S. 752, 774–75.

29. 395 U.S. 752, 780.

30. 395 U.S. 752, 781.

31. 395 U.S. 752, 782–83.

32. See for example, *New York v. Belton*, 453 U.S. 454 (1981) and *Arizona v. Gant*, 556 U.S. 332 (2009).

33. The literature in this field is voluminous. See, for example, Vincent Blasi, *The Burger Court: The Counter-Revolution That Wasn't* (New Haven, Conn.: Yale University Press, 1983); Ed Cray, *Chief Justice: A Biography of Earl Warren* (New York: Simon & Schuster, 1997), 511–14; Charles A. Johnson, "Personnel Change and Policy Change on the U.S. Supreme Court," *Social Science Quarterly* 62, 4 (December 1981): 751–57; "The Legacy of the Warren Court," *Time* 94, 1 (July 4, 1969): 64–67; William A. Taggart and Matthew R. DeZee, "A Note on Substantive Access Doctrines in the U.S. Supreme Court: A Comparative Analysis of the Warren and Burger Courts," *Western Political Quarterly* 38, 1 (March 1985): 84–93.

CHAPTER 12

United States v. Leon (1984) and a Good Faith Exception to the Exclusionary Rule

The exclusionary rule has become an integral feature of 21st-century American criminal procedure. Yet it exists as a much-maligned, controversial judicial doctrine, especially in cases where police officers acted in good faith while searching for evidence, only to discover after the fact that a warrant was defective. The U.S. Supreme Court confronted the issue directly in *United States v. Leon*, which created a "good faith" exception to the exclusionary rule. When officers have obtained a search warrant from a neutral magistrate and relied on the warrant to justify an evidentiary search, the material they collect can be admitted into court without violating the Fourth Amendment.[1]

The *Leon* case began in August 1981 in Burbank, California, when an informant "of unproven reliability" notified police officers that two associates, "Armando" and "Patsy," were dealing drugs, primarily cocaine and methaqualone, from a residence located at 620 Price Drive. The tip was extremely detailed. The informant also recounted an episode from five months earlier when Patsy had sold methaqualone and displayed a shoebox filled with cash. The informant further explained that Patsy and Armando kept only a small amount of drugs at the residence. They stored larger quantities at a secondary location.

Acting on the tip, police officers launched an investigation at the Price Drive location and at two other residences. As a result of the property surveillance, they discovered that the cars parked on Price Drive belonged to Armando Sanchez, who had been arrested previously for marijuana possession, and Patsy Stewart, who did not have a criminal record. A variety of characters visited the residence, presumably to buy drugs, while officers staked out the house. Two men with a history of drug use, Ricardo Del Castillo and Alberto Leon, especially captured the attention of the police. Officers investigated Leon's background and discovered a drug arrest dating back to 1980. Based on this observation as well as corroboration from a second informant, the lead officers presented an affidavit to a judge and secured a search warrant to examine three separate premises as well as several automobiles. Officer Cyril Rombach of the Burbank Police Department, an experienced narcotics officer, prepared a warrant application to search 620 Price Drive, 716 South Sunset Canyon, 7902 Via Magdalena, and automobiles registered to each suspect as well several other items at those locations. In September 1981, after several deputy district attorneys reviewed the application, Officer Rombach submitted it to a state superior court judge. The judge issued the search warrant.

As expected, Officer Rombach and his team found a cache of illegal drugs and other items, suggesting that illegal activity had occurred. Leon and the other suspects were indicted on federal drug offenses in the District Court for the Central District of California and charged with conspiracy to possess and distribute cocaine and additional substantive counts.[2]

At a pretrial suppression hearing, the defendants challenged the admissibility of the evidence on the grounds that the search warrant was deficient because the affidavit did not establish probable cause as a matter of law. The informant was not known to be reliable and, therefore, should not have been used as a source in the warrant application. Government attorneys argued that even if the warrant was deficient, the police believed it was legally sufficient and relied on the validity of the judge's decision in good faith. Owing to this good faith, the evidence that police seized during the searches should not be suppressed at trial. The district court recognized the officers' good faith, but refused to carve out an exception to the exclusionary rule. The evidence was suppressed. The court of appeals affirmed this decision, emphasizing not only that the informant was unreliable, but his information about drug deals at the Price Drive location was also "fatally stale" because he had observed the transactions months earlier.[3]

In reviewing the case, the U.S. Supreme Court did not consider the question of whether the search warrant established probable cause because that was not the issue submitted to the court. Instead, the question was "whether the Fourth Amendment exclusionary rule should be modified so as not to bar the admission of evidence seized in reasonable, good faith reliance on a search warrant that is subsequently held to be defective."[4] Justice White, joined by Justices Burger, Blackmun, Powell, Rehnquist, and O'Connor, wrote the majority opinion.

After reviewing the facts of the case and outlining the Supreme Court's long history involving the exclusionary rule, White noted that the concept was created by judges deciding cases; it was not a "necessary corollary" to the Fourth Amendment, despite occasional language to that effect in previous cases. If the rule was not a specific requirement found in the Fourth Amendment, judges and justices could interpret the doctrine in myriad ways. Specifically, a case affecting the exclusionary rule should "be resolved by weighing the costs and benefits of preventing the use in the prosecution's case in chief of inherently trustworthy tangible evidence obtained in reliance on a search warrant issued by a detached and neutral magistrate that ultimately is found to be defective."[5]

In White's view, whatever its virtues, the exclusionary rule must not be rigidly applied so as to bar the use of evidence obtained by officers acting in reasonable reliance on a search warrant issued by a detached, neutral magistrate—even if the warrant later was found to be invalid. Law enforcement officials are not judges, nor are they able to discern all the legal nuances pertaining to the Fourth Amendment; that is the role of a judicial officer. In an ordinary case, a police officer cannot be expected to question the magistrate's probable cause determination or his judgment that the form of the warrant is technically sufficient. Once the warrant is issued, there is literally nothing more the policeman can do to comply with the law. Penalizing the officer for the magistrate's error, rather than his own, cannot logically deter Fourth Amendment violations, which was the original purpose of the exclusionary rule. (This assessment presupposes that the officer provided complete and accurate information in the original warrant application.)[6]

Thus, a majority of the Court decided that the exclusionary rule should be applied when a Fourth Amendment violation has been "substantial and deliberate," but an exception can be made by weighing the costs and benefits of preventing the use of inherently trustworthy tangible evidence. "We conclude that the marginal or nonexistent benefits produced by suppressing evidence obtained in objectively reasonable reliance on a subsequently invalidated search warrant cannot justify the substantial costs of exclusion," White explained.[7]

Justice Harry Blackmun penned a concurrence to explain why "I believe that the rule announced today advances the legitimate interests of the criminal justice system without sacrificing the individual

Writing for a majority of the U.S. Supreme Court in *United States v. Leon*, Justice Byron White, pictured here, carved out a "good faith" exception to the controversial exclusionary rule. (Library of Congress)

rights protected by the Fourth Amendment."[8] Although he substantially agreed with the majority opinion, Blackmun wanted to ensure that law enforcement officials did not abuse a "good faith" exception. "If it should emerge from experience that, contrary to our expectations, the good faith exception to the exclusionary rule results in a material change in police compliance with the Fourth Amendment, we shall have to reconsider what we have undertaken here. The logic of a decision that rests on untested predictions about police conduct demands no less."[9]

Blackmun viewed the exclusionary rule as a constantly evolving judicial construct. "If a single principle may be drawn from this Court's exclusionary rule decisions, from *Weeks* through *Mapp v. Ohio*, 367

U.S. 643 (1961), to the decisions handed down today, it is that the scope of the exclusionary rule is subject to change in light of changing judicial understanding about the effects of the rule outside the confines of the courtroom," he wrote. Because it is not a strict Fourth Amendment requirement, the rule is adaptable, as it should be, to ensure that law enforcement officials can search for evidence, as necessary. Yet the rule also can limit the scope of the search, which means that the flexible nature of the doctrine can both help and impede the police. "It is incumbent on the Nation's law enforcement officers, who must continue to observe the Fourth Amendment in the wake of today's decisions, to recognize the double-edged nature of that principle," Blackmun concluded.[10]

Justice William Brennan wrote a lengthy, vehement dissent, remarking that during the past decade, "in case after case, I have witnessed the Court's gradual but determined strangulation of the rule." As the justices have recognized multiple exceptions to the exclusionary rule, they have undermined its efficacy. Eventually, as the exceptions proliferate, the exclusionary rule will cease to exist. Unlike Justice Blackmun, who argued that the flexibility of the rule was a positive feature, Brennan worried that the Court's desire to allow a good faith exception eroded constitutional protections in the interests of expedient law enforcement. "It now appears that the Court's victory over the Fourth Amendment is complete," he lamented.[11]

Brennan especially attacked the majority opinion's discussion of costs and benefits. "The Court seeks to justify this result on the ground that the 'costs' of adhering to the exclusionary rule in cases like those before us exceed the 'benefits.' But the language of deterrence and of cost/benefit analysis, if used indiscriminately, can have a narcotic effect. It creates an illusion of technical precision and ineluctability."[12] The justice explained that the Court is lured into a constitutional quagmire, so to speak. The Founders recognized that "the task of combating crime and convicting the guilty will in every era seem of such critical and pressing concern that we may be lured by the temptations of expediency into forsaking our commitment to protecting individual liberty and privacy. It was for that very reason that the Framers of the Bill of Rights insisted that law enforcement efforts be permanently and unambiguously restricted in order to preserve personal freedoms."[13]

Aside from pragmatic concerns about police officers searching for evidence and citing their good faith should the warrant prove to be defective, Brennan's larger fear was that the Court's analysis was fundamentally flawed. The majority's dismissive characterization of the exclusionary rule as merely a judicial creation not fundamentally rooted in the language of the Fourth Amendment rationalized all manner of abuse. Brennan acknowledged that the rule is nowhere to be found in the Bill of Rights, but such an observation, in addition to being trite, misses the point. The Constitution is not a compendium of people's rights or an exhaustive enumeration of government limitations. It is an outline, a blueprint for distinguishing the parameters between individual freedom and government authority. The Constitution left it to the judiciary to interpret its provisions in the context of specific legal questions.[14]

Brennan argued that the development of the exclusionary rule was an attempt by judges and justices to apply the Fourth Amendment to law enforcement and thereby hold officers accountable. The majority opinion in *Leon* "rests ultimately on an impoverished understanding of judicial responsibility in our constitutional scheme" because it assumes that "the substantive protections of the Fourth Amendment are wholly exhausted at the moment when police unlawfully invade an individual's privacy, and thus no substantive force remains to those protections at the time of trial when the government seeks to use evidence obtained by the police."[15] Not so, Brennan contended. Judges and justices must ensure that the Fourth Amendment protects the citizenry from police overreaching, which means "the courts therefore cannot be absolved of responsibility for the means by which evidence is obtained."[16]

In early decisions on the exclusionary rule beginning with *Weeks v. United States*, "the Court plainly understood that the exclusion of illegally obtained evidence was compelled not by judicially fashioned remedial purposes, but rather by a direct constitutional command."[17] In later cases, beginning with *Wolf v. Colorado*, the Court moved away from this reasoning. *Wolf* allowed the admission of illegally seized evidence as long as the court devised another manner of protecting a citizen's Fourth Amendment rights. This decision began the trend of eroding the exclusionary rule and, by extension, the Fourth Amendment.[18]

In overruling the *Wolf* case, *Mapp v. Ohio* appeared to restore the original understanding of the exclusionary rule. Yet in the years after *Mapp*, the Court gradually drifted away from the argument that the rule undergirds a Fourth Amendment "constitutional command." Other rationales for the rule were cited and thereafter denigrated, especially the "deterrence" argument. Some judges and justices accept the notion that the exclusionary rule is a means of deterring police officers from illegally searching for evidence. If deterrence is the central rationale, the exclusionary rule can be modified or perhaps eliminated if police misconduct can be deterred in some other manner. When the rationale is no longer tied to a constitutional command, however, considerations of costs and benefits, such as in the *Leon* majority opinion, also can, and probably will, occur.[19] The problem is that "the Court's decisions over the past decade have made plain that the entire enterprise of attempting to assess the benefits and costs of the exclusionary rule in various contexts is a virtually impossible task for the judiciary to perform honestly or accurately. Although the Court's language in those cases suggests that some specific empirical basis may support its analyses, the reality is that the Court's opinions represent inherently unstable compounds of intuition, hunches, and occasional pieces of partial and often inconclusive data."[20]

Brennan discussed several cases where the Court relied on the deterrence rationale and yet cited empirical evidence to explain why deterrence was ineffective. In Brennan's opinion, arguing the deterrence rationale and thereafter attacking the concept is tantamount to building a straw man only to tear it down. "By remaining within its redoubt of empiricism and by basing the rule solely on the deterrence rationale, the Court has robbed the rule of legitimacy. A doctrine that is explained as if it were an empirical proposition, but for which there is only limited empirical support, is both inherently unstable and an easy mark for critics," Brennan observed.[21]

Examining the *Leon* case without considering the deterrence rationale and the cost–benefit analysis suggests the search warrant should never have been issued. Probable cause was lacking. The officer's application was based on information that was months old and supplied by an unreliable informant. "Stripped of the authority of the warrant, the conduct of these officers was plainly unconstitutional—it amounted to nothing less than a naked invasion of the privacy of respondents' homes without the requisite justification demanded by the Fourth Amendment," Brennan wrote. "In order to restore the Government to the position it would have occupied had this unconstitutional search not occurred, therefore, it was necessary that the evidence be suppressed."[22]

Justice Brennan feared the *Leon* decision was a slippery slope where Fourth Amendment protections were eroded as the definition of "good faith" expanded in subsequent cases. He remarked that "although the Court's decisions are clearly limited to the situation in which police officers reasonably rely upon an apparently valid warrant in conducting a search, I am not at all confident that the exception unleashed today will remain so confined."[23] When a clarion call rings out for elected officials to combat crime, "the relaxation of Fourth Amendment standards seems a tempting, costless means of meeting the public's demand for better law enforcement. In the long run, however, we as a society pay a heavy price for such expediency." Yet Brennan closed his opinion on a positive note about the possibility of the court reinstating Fourth Amendment rights in future cases. "Once lost, such rights are difficult to recover. There is hope, however, that in time this or some later Court will restore these precious freedoms to their rightful place as a primary protection for our citizens against overreaching officialdom."[24]

Justice John Paul Stevens concurred in part and dissented in part. He opened his opinion with an ironic observation. "The Court assumes that the searches in these cases violated the Fourth Amendment, yet refuses to apply the exclusionary rule because the Court concludes that it was 'reasonable' for the police to conduct them." Stevens believed the anomalous result was absurd. "In my opinion, an official search and seizure cannot be both 'unreasonable' and 'reasonable' at the same time."[25]

Stevens also expressed concern that the Court had carved out a general "good faith" exception to the exclusionary rule when it could have decided the case without doing so. Factually, *Leon* was a close case, and it was not altogether clear that the search warrant was valid. When a court uses a case with muddled facts as a vehicle for broad judicial construction, "it can only encourage the perception that it is pursuing its own notions of wise social policy, rather than adhering to its judicial role."[26]

Justice Stevens devoted considerable attention to the majority opinion's assertion that police officers should be able to rely in good faith on the issuance of a search warrant by a magistrate. "Until today, that has plainly not been the law; it has been well settled that, even when a magistrate issues a warrant, there is no guarantee that the ensuing search and seizure is constitutionally reasonable," Stevens wrote. "Law enforcement officers have long been on notice that, despite the magistrate's decision, a warrant will be invalidated if the officers did not provide sufficient facts to enable the magistrate to evaluate the existence of probable cause responsibly and independently. Reviewing courts have always inquired into whether the magistrate acted properly in issuing the warrant—not merely whether the officers acted properly in executing it."[27] In drafting the Fourth Amendment, the Framers focused on "the unreasonable issuance of warrants," not on whether a police officer thought the warrant was sufficient.[28] "The Court's view that it is consistent with our Constitution to adopt a rule that it is presumptively reasonable to rely on a defective warrant is the product of constitutional amnesia."[29]

As for the deterrence argument, even if Justice Brennan was wrong that deterrence was not a major historical rationale for the Fourth Amendment, the Court's analysis of the issue was flawed. If zealous police officers are determined to search for evidence with little regard for citizen rights, they can game the system. "Under the majority's new rule, even when the police know their warrant application is probably insufficient, they retain an incentive to submit it to a magistrate, on the chance that he may take the bait. No longer must they hesitate and seek additional evidence in doubtful cases."[30]

At the conclusion of his opinion, Stevens admitted that the exclusionary rule is controversial because it seems to allow guilty defendants to go free on a legal technicality. "It is, of course, true that the exclusionary rule exerts a high price—the loss of probative evidence of guilt," he acknowledged. "But that price is one courts have often been required to pay to serve important social goals. That price is also one the Fourth Amendment requires us to pay, assuming as we must that the Framers intended that its strictures 'shall not be violated.'"[31]

In *Massachusetts v. Sheppard*, a case argued and decided the same day as *Leon*, the court applied the good faith exception to the exclusionary rule under a fact setting almost identical to the *Leon* case. Justice White again wrote the majority opinion. "Having already decided that the exclusionary rule should not be applied when the officer conducting the search acted in objectively reasonable reliance on a warrant issued by a detached and neutral magistrate that subsequently is determined to be invalid . . . the sole issue before us in this case is whether the officers reasonably believed that the search they conducted was authorized by a valid warrant," he wrote.[32] The defense argued that the search warrant had failed to meet the Fourth Amendment requirement that it stated "with particularity" what officers were searching for; therefore, the evidence should be excluded. Citing the good faith exception announced in *Leon*, the U.S. Supreme Court allowed the evidence to be admitted. In White's opinion, "the police conduct in this case clearly was objectively reasonable and largely error-free. An error of constitutional dimensions may have been committed with respect to the issuance of the warrant, but it was the judge, not the police officers, who made the critical mistake." A police officer is entitled to rely on the judge's decision to issue a search warrant.[33] "Suppressing evidence because the judge failed to make all the necessary clerical corrections despite his assurances that such changes would be made will not serve the deterrent function that the exclusionary rule was designed to achieve," White explained. "Accordingly, federal law does not require the exclusion of the disputed evidence in this case."[34]

With *Leon* and *Sheppard*, it was clear that the Supreme Court was willing to provide more leeway to law enforcement officials even in cases where a magistrate had issued a defective search warrant. What was not clear was whether the Court would be willing to expand the exception to include good faith reliance on other sources, such as a statute.[35] Many commentators writing after 1984 argued that the *Leon* rule, while ostensibly clear in the specific context of a search warrant issued by a judicial officer, left the door open for abuse. One observer noted that "the Supreme Court has shown a proclivity for expanding the good faith exception beyond the context of reasonable reliance on a search warrant in some circumstances."[36] Another commentator suggested that "cases decided after *Leon* have begun to establish certain patterns and it appears that some of the worst fears of the dissenting Justices in *Leon* are coming true."[37] In still another commentator's view, "the full perimeters of the *Leon* holding continue to bewilder courts and litigants."[38]

Illinois v. Krull, decided three years after *Leon*, tested whether the good faith exception extended beyond a magistrate's issuance of a search warrant. In *Krull*, an Illinois state statute permitted police officers to enter the premises of an automotive repair shop or wrecking yard "at any reasonable time during the night or day" to inspect records regarding automobile ownership. A search warrant was not required for an "examination of the premises of the licensee's established place of business for the purpose of determining the accuracy of required records." On July 5, 1981, a police officer appeared at Action Iron & Metal Inc., a Chicago-based automotive wrecking yard, and asked to inspect the books. When the operators could not locate the records, the officer asked for permission to walk around the yard. After he received permission, the officer discovered that several automobiles were stolen. He arrested the operators. In an unrelated case, the federal court invalidated the state statute a day after the *Krull* search because the law violated the Fourth Amendment prohibition on unreasonable searches and seizures. In a 5–4 opinion, with Justice Blackmun writing for the majority, the U.S. Supreme Court determined the exclusionary rule did not apply when a police officer searched for evidence under a statute authorizing warrantless administrative searches and the statute subsequently was found to violate the Fourth Amendment. Because the officer acted based on "objectively reasonable reliance," the evidence should not be suppressed. The law was valid at the time the search occurred.[39]

In 1995, the high court once again considered the parameters of the good faith exception. In *Arizona v. Evans,* a patrolman witnessed the driver of an automobile traveling the wrong way on a one-way street. When the officer stopped the motorist, the officer learned the man's license had been suspended. Afterward, the officer entered information about the driver into a computer console inside the patrol car. The driver's record indicated that an outstanding misdemeanor arrest warrant existed, so the officer promptly took the suspect into custody. While the man was handcuffed, he dropped a marijuana cigarette. A search of the car incident to the arrest uncovered a bag of marijuana beneath the driver's seat. The police officer subsequently learned that the outstanding arrest warrant had been quashed but was never properly removed from the record. At trial, the defendant moved to suppress the evidence because it was found while the driver was arrested based on a quashed arrest warrant. In a 7–2 opinion, with Chief Justice Rehnquist writing the majority opinion, the U.S. Supreme Court held that the exclusionary rule did not apply since the officer acted in good faith by acting on the arrest warrant. The error occurred owing to a clerk's failure to record that the arrest warrant had been quashed.[40]

In *Herring v. United States* (2009), a case factually similar to *Evans,* an investigator in the Coffee County, Alabama, Sheriff's Department asked a department clerk to check whether any outstanding warrants existed for a man who had arrived to retrieve an impounded pickup truck. The clerk of Coffee County called a clerk in a neighboring county and learned that an outstanding arrest warrant existed for the man asking about the truck. Based on that information, the officer arrested the man. In searching the arrestee's vehicle, the officer found firearms and methamphetamine. Within 15 minutes of the original call, the clerk from the neighboring county called back to say the original information was incorrect. The outstanding arrest warrant was invalid.

On appeal, the defendant argued that he should never have been arrested since the warrant was invalid. Because the arrest was improper, the evidence seized during a search of his vehicle should be inadmissible. The U.S. Supreme Court disagreed. By a 5–4 vote, with Chief Justice John Roberts authoring the majority opinion, the Court again expanded the good faith exception. In affirming the conviction, Roberts noted, "To trigger the exclusionary rule, police conduct must be sufficiently deliberate that exclusion can meaningfully deter it, and sufficiently culpable that such deterrence is worth the price paid by the justice system. As laid out in our cases, the exclusionary rule serves to deter deliberate, reckless, or grossly negligent conduct, or in some circumstances recurring or systemic negligence. The error in this case does not rise to that level." The clerk from the neighboring county caused the error, not the arresting officer.[41]

As discussed in previous chapters of this book, the exclusionary rule has been, and likely will remain, a controversial constitutional doctrine because it applies at the intersection between freedom and authority. Law enforcement officers must possess the tools to combat crime, but they must also obey the strictures of the Fourth Amendment if individuals are to live in a free society. The exclusionary rule is the judiciary's means for ensuring that government agents stay within the Fourth Amendment guidelines. When officers of the law collect evidence outside of the guidelines, the question is whether the material collected is the fruit of the poisonous tree or whether it can be rehabilitated and admitted at trial. Because the Constitution is silent on the remedies for a violation, this area of the law will always be contested because reasonable minds can differ on the value of excluding evidence when it is acquired through mistake or accident.

NOTES

1. *United States v. Leon*, 468 U.S. 897 (1984). See also Robert M. Bloom, "*United States v. Leon* and Its Ramifications," *University of Colorado Law Review* 56, 1 (Winter 1985): 247–63.

2. 468 U.S. 897, 901–2. See also Robert L. Misner, "Limiting *Leon:* A Mistake of Law Analogy," *The Journal of Law & Criminology* 77, 3 (Fall 1986): 510–11.

3. 468 U.S. 897, 903. See also Rebecca Davis, "The Good Faith Exception in a Computerized Society: State Court Reactions to *U.S. v. Leon* and *Arizona v. Evans,*" *The Justice Professional* 12, 1 (June 1998): 49–50.

4. 468 U.S. 897, 905.

5. 468 U.S. 897, 907.

6. The original purpose of the exclusionary rule is a matter of fierce debate. Aside from the opinions in *Leon,* see also Craig M. Bradley, "The 'Good Faith Exception' Cases: Reasonable Exercises in Futility," *Indiana Law Journal* 60, 2 (Spring 1984): 287–304; Kenneth J. Melilli, "What Nearly a Quarter Century of Experience Has Taught Us about *Leon* and 'Good Faith,'" *Utah Law Review* 2008, 2 (2008): 519–62.

7. 468 U.S. 897, 922.
8. 468 U.S. 897, 927.
9. 468 U.S. 897, 928.
10. 468 U.S. 897, 928.
11. 468 U.S. 897, 928–29.
12. 468 U.S. 897, 929.
13. 468 U.S. 897, 929–30.
14. 468 U.S. 897, 932–33.
15. 468 U.S. 897, 935.
16. 468 U.S. 897, 937.
17. 468 U.S. 897, 938–39.
18. 468 U.S. 897, 939. See also *Weeks v. United States*, 232 U.S. 383 (1914); *Wolf v. Colorado*, 338 U.S. 25 (1949).
19. 468 U.S. 897, 938–41.
20. 468 U.S. 897, 942. See also *Mapp v. Ohio*, 367 U.S. 643 (1961).
21. 468 U.S. 897, 943.
22. 468 U.S. 897, 944.
23. 468 U.S. 897, 959.
24. 468 U.S. 897, 960.
25. 468 U.S. 897, 961.
26. 468 U.S. 897, 963.
27. 468 U.S. 897, 969.
28. 468 U.S. 897, 971.
29. 468 U.S. 897, 972.
30. 468 U.S. 897, 974.
31. 468 U.S. 897, 979.
32. *Massachusetts v. Sheppard*, 468 U.S. 981, 987–88 (1984). See also Bradley, "The 'Good Faith Exception' Cases," 287–90; Matthew Allan Josephson, "To Exclude or Not to Exclude: The Future of the Exclusionary Rule after *Herring v. United States*," *Creighton Law Review* 43, 1 (December 2009): 182–83.
33. 468 U.S. 981, 990.
34. 468 U.S. 981, 990–91.
35. The literature on the *Leon* repercussions is voluminous. See, for example, Albert W. Alschuler, "'Close Enough for Government Work': The Exclusionary Rule after *Leon*," *The Supreme Court Review* 1984, 1 (1984): 309–58; Bloom, "*United States v. Leon* and Its Ramifications," 247–63; Lawrence Crocker, "Can the Exclusionary Rule Be Saved?," *The Journal of Criminal Law & Criminology* 84, 2 (Summer 1993): 310–51; Steven B. Duke, "Making *Leon* Worse," *The Yale Law Journal* 95, 7 (June 1986): 1405–23; Andrew W. Taslitz, "The Expressive Fourth Amendment: Rethinking the Good Faith Exception to the Exclusionary Rule," *Mississippi Law Journal* 76, 2 (2006): 483–593.
36. Derik T. Fettig, "When 'Good Faith' Makes Good Sense: Applying *Leon*'s Exception to the Exclusionary Rule to the Government's Reasonable

Reliance on Title III Wiretap Orders," *Harvard Journal on Legislation* 49, 2 (Summer 2012): 383.

37. Misner, "Limiting *Leon*," 507.

38. Melilli, "What Nearly a Quarter Century of Experience Has Taught Us about *Leon* and 'Good Faith,'" 520.

39. *Illinois v. Krull*, 480 U.S. 340 (1987). See also Josephson, "To Exclude or Not to Exclude," 183–84; Melilli, "What Nearly a Quarter Century of Experience Has Taught Us about *Leon* and 'Good Faith,'" 521.

40. *Arizona v. Evans*, 514 U.S. 1 (1995). See also Davis, "The Good Faith Exception in a Computerized Society," 45–63; Josephson, "To Exclude or Not to Exclude," 184–85.

41. *Herring v. United States*, 555 U.S. 135, 143 (2009). See also Yale Kamisar, "In Defense of the Search and Seizure Exclusionary Rule," *Harvard Journal of Law & Public Policy* 26, 1 (Winter 2003): 119–40; Wayne R. LaFave, "The Smell of *Herring:* A Critique of the Supreme Court's Latest Assault on the Exclusionary Rule," *The Journal of Criminal Law & Criminology* 99, 3 (Spring 2009): 757–87.

CHAPTER 13

California v. Hodari D. (1991) and Determining When a "*Seizure*" Occurs

Around 10:00 P.M. on the evening of April 18, 1988, an unmarked brown Dodge police car cruised through an Oakland, California, neighborhood known for high crime and low living. Adorned in street clothes (save for blue jackets embossed with the word "Police" on the back), Officers Brian McColgin and Jerry Pertoso, veterans of the Oakland Police Department's Narcotics Task Force, patrolled for signs of suspicious behavior or illegal activity. The men were familiar with the neighborhood, having made narcotics arrests in the area on numerous occasions. They did not have to search far and wide that April evening.

As their vehicle rounded the corner of Foothill Boulevard and 63rd Avenue, the officers noticed a group of four or five young black males huddled around a red compact car parked near the curb. When the Dodge was approximately 40 yards away, the sudden appearance of an unfamiliar vehicle startled the youths. In an instant, the group scattered. The red car roared to life, racing from the neighborhood at a high rate of speed. Although the policemen did not recognize the individuals and had not witnessed illegal activity, the group's reaction suggested that the young men were engaged in illicit trade.

Officer McColgin pulled to the curb so that his partner could jump from the car and set off on foot. Afterward, McColgin drove the Dodge south on 63rd Avenue. The officers intended to detain as many of the young men as they could find to ask about their activities. First, they had to apprehend someone.

As the group scattered, Pertoso chose to follow two young men. It was a footrace he could not win. When the officer saw he probably could not catch the fleeing suspects directly, he realized he could outsmart the fellows and thereby apprehend at least one person. He followed a circuitous route onto a parallel street. There he came face to face with the suspect later identified as Hodari D. Hodari was looking back when the officer approached him and, therefore, did not see Pertoso until they were approximately 11 feet apart. Recognizing he was about to be apprehended, Hodari, using "an underhand scooping motion," threw a small object away as though he wanted to rid himself of incriminating evidence. The object landed near an adjacent house. Seconds later, Pertoso tackled and arrested the young man. After handcuffing Hodari and radioing for assistance, Officer Pertoso discovered the adolescent had $130 in cash inside his pockets as well as a pager. The object he tossed away, which resembled a rock, turned out to be crack cocaine.[1]

Because he was a minor child, Hodari was brought before a California juvenile court. His attorney moved to suppress the crack cocaine from evidence because it constituted the fruit of an illegal seizure. The juvenile court denied the defendant's motion without providing a written opinion. On appeal, the central issue was not whether the police officers possessed reasonable suspicion or probable cause to justify stopping Hodari. Instead, the outcome turned on whether a "seizure" has occurred if a fleeing person refuses to stop when commanded to do so by a police officer. The State Court of Appeal reversed, holding that Hodari had been "seized" at the moment he saw Pertoso running toward him because the officer's actions could be "reasonably perceived" as an intrusion on Hodari's freedom of movement. Consequently, the evidence gathered after the seizure was "unreasonable" under the Fourth Amendment because the defendant's rights had not been protected.[2]

The U.S. Supreme Court typically analyzes Fourth Amendment cases by examining the facts of a case to discern the point at which an individual is "seized." It is a crucial determination because an encounter between a person and a police officer that fails to meet the legal definition of a "seizure" does not trigger Fourth Amendment protections. A police officer approaching a person walking down the street and asking a question has not seized the person, in the words of the U.S. Supreme Court in *Terry v. Ohio*, unless "the officer, by means of physical force or show of authority, has in some way restrained the liberty of a citizen."[3]

Before Officer Pertoso chased down Hodari D. on that April night in 1988, a series of cases had carved out the parameters of a police officer–citizen encounter when reasonable suspicion or probable cause does not exist. In *Brown v. Texas* (1979), for example, two police officers attempted to question a man in a neighborhood where frequent drug sales occurred, but the man refused to cooperate. The officers arrested him for violating a statute that required citizens to identify themselves when approached by the police. In striking down the conviction, the U.S. Supreme Court held that police officers can legally approach a person, but if the person refuses to cooperate and the officers will not allow him or her to leave, the person has been "seized." The Fourth Amendment applies at the moment of the seizure, and the officer must possess reasonable suspicion or probable cause to justify the detention.[4]

During the same term, the high court decided *United States v. Mendenhall* (1980), a crucial case that developed a test for determining when a seizure has occurred. The case originated when two Drug Enforcement Administration (DEA) officers inside the Detroit Metropolitan Airport asked a woman, Sylvia Mendenhall, to produce identification and a plane ticket because she matched portions of a drug courier profile. After she produced a driver's license bearing one name (Sylvia Mendenhall) and a plane ticket in another name (Annette Ford), the agents asked if she would accompany them to a DEA office in the airport. She complied without protest. Once she was inside the room, Mendenhall consented to a search. A female officer found two packages hidden beneath her clothing; consequently, the suspect was arrested for heroin possession. At trial, Mendenhall claimed she had been seized at the moment the DEA agents approached her. If she was seized before she consented to the search, the evidence should be excluded because the "consent" was not voluntary.[5]

The U.S. Supreme Court disagreed and upheld Mendenhall's conviction. In his majority opinion, Justice Potter Stewart articulated a standard that subsequently became known as the *Mendenhall* test for a "seizure":

> We conclude that a person has been "seized" within the meaning of the Fourth Amendment only if, in view of all of the circumstances surrounding the incident, a reasonable person would have believed that he was not free to leave. Examples of circumstances that might indicate a seizure, even where the person did not attempt to leave, would be the threatening presence of several officers, the display of a weapon by an officer, some physical touching of the person of the citizen, or the use of language or

> tone of voice indicating that compliance with the officer's request might be compelled.[6]

Throughout the remainder of the 1980s, the Supreme Court applied the *Mendenhall* test to determine whether a seizure had occurred. In a 1983 case, *Florida v. Royer*, the Court considered facts similar to *Mendenhall*. Two undercover officers approached a man who fit the drug courier profile in an airport and asked to see identification. The names on the man's driver's license and his airline ticket did not match. As a result of this anomaly, the officers asked the suspect to follow them to an adjacent room away from the concourse. He said nothing, but accompanied them to the room. Once inside, the officers retrieved the man's luggage, searched inside, and found marijuana. Royer produced a key and unlocked the suitcase upon request, but an officer opened it. Relying on the *Mendenhall* test, the U.S. Supreme Court decided that Royer had been seized at the time the officers grabbed his identification, plane, ticket, and luggage. Royer never consented to the search because he no longer believed he could leave when the search occurred. A reasonable person would have interpreted the request to enter a small room away from the concourse as an official police demand restricting his or her freedom of movement. Because the officers did not have probable cause for the "extended conversation," the evidence they obtained was inadmissible in court.[7]

In *Immigration and Naturalization Service v. Delgado*, a 1984 case, INS agents entered a factory to survey employees about their citizenship. Although the agents blocked the exits, factory workers were permitted to roam throughout the factory. Four employees later sued, arguing they had been "seized" during the factory sweep. Writing for the majority, Justice William Rehnquist found that the employees had not been seized:

> The presence of agents by the exits posed no reasonable threat of detention to these workers while they walked throughout the factories on job assignments. Likewise, the mere possibility that they would be questioned if they sought to leave the buildings should not have resulted in any reasonable apprehension by any of them that they would be seized or detained in any meaningful way. Since most workers could have had no reasonable fear that they would be detained upon leaving, we conclude that the work forces as a whole were not seized.[8]

The Court did not reject the *Mendenhall* test in *Delgado*, despite Justice Brennan's vehement dissent that when the agents blocked the doors, they provided a "show of authority."[9] The Court still contended that the crucial determination was whether "in view of all of the circumstances surrounding the incident, a reasonable person would have believed that he was not free to leave." In *Delgado*, however, the Court majority believed that the facts did not demonstrate a show of authority since workers were not free to leave during employment hours regardless of whether government agents had entered the premises (assuming the workers wished to remain employed).[10]

In *Michigan v. Chesternut*, the Court again applied the *Mendenhall* test. A marked police car was making a routine patrol through a Detroit, Michigan, neighborhood when it came upon Michael Mose Chesternut. After Chesternut recognized the marked police car, he turned and ran. Curious about his reaction, the officers inside the car followed him for a short distance. During that time, they witnessed the young man tossing packets of an unknown substance from his pockets. When the police car stopped, an officer retrieved the packets and recognized codeine, an illegal substance. The officers arrested Chesternut for narcotics possession.[11]

Writing for the majority, Justice Blackmun relied on the *Mendenhall* test. "The test is necessarily imprecise," he admitted, "because it is designed to assess the coercive effect of police conduct, taken as a whole, rather than to focus on particular details of that conduct in isolation."[12] Nonetheless, despite its imprecision, the test provided a helpful framework for analyzing facts in case-by-case adjudication. "Applying the Court's test to the facts of this case, we conclude that respondent was not seized by the police before he discarded the packets containing the controlled substance." The officers had not stopped Chesternut at the time he discarded the drugs, nor had they provided a show of force such as flashing their lights, turning on the siren, or ordering the man to halt. "Although Officer Peltier referred to the police conduct as a 'chase,' and the Magistrate who originally dismissed the complaint was impressed by this description, the characterization is not enough, standing alone, to implicate Fourth Amendment protections," Blackmun explained.[13]

The *Mendenhall* test remained the most often-cited standard at the time the U.S. Supreme Court agreed to hear the *Hodari* case. *Hodari* appeared to be yet another garden-variety case to determine whether the defendant had been "seized" within the meaning of the Fourth

Amendment at the time he dropped the drugs. The outcome would depend on the factual context, as previous cases suggested, for if the young man had been seized at the time he tossed the crack cocaine, his constitutional rights would have been violated.[14]

Justice Antonin Scalia authored the short majority opinion, writing for a 7–2 majority of the U.S. Supreme Court. "From the time of the founding to the present, the word 'seizure' has meant a 'taking possession,'" Scalia contended. "For most purposes at common law, the word connoted not merely grasping, or applying physical force to, the animate or inanimate object in question, but actually bringing it within physical control."[15] For purposes of Fourth Amendment protections, however, the standard has been modified over time. To constitute a seizure of a person, there must be either the application of physical force, however slight, or, where that is absent, submission to a police officer's "show of authority" to restrain the subject's liberty.[16]

The facts in *Hodari D.* were different from the circumstances found in most prior cases. As Scalia observed, "Hodari was untouched by Officer Pertoso at the time he discarded the cocaine. His defense relies instead upon the proposition that a seizure occurs 'when the officer, by means of physical force or show of authority, has in some way restrained the liberty of a citizen.'" Yet such a proposition could not stand. The high court held that Hodari D. had not been seized. According to Justice Scalia, "No physical force occurred in this case since Officer Pertoso had not touched Hodari before the latter dropped the drugs."[17] Even if Pertoso's pursuit constituted a "show of authority," Hodari was not seized until he was tackled. Thus, the cocaine abandoned while he was running was not the fruit of a seizure. "The word 'seizure' readily bears the meaning of a laying on of hands or application of physical force to restrain movement, even when it is ultimately unsuccessful," Scalia argued. "It does not remotely apply, however, to the prospect of a policeman yelling 'Stop, in the name of the law!' at a fleeing form that continues to flee. That is no seizure."[18]

As for the *Mendenhall* test and a show of force by the police, Scalia distinguished *Hodari* from the earlier case:

> In seeking to rely upon that test here, respondent fails to read it carefully. It says that a person has been seized "only if," not that he has been seized "whenever"; it states a *necessary*, but not a *sufficient*, condition for seizure—or, more precisely, for seizure effected through a "show of authority." *Mendenhall* establishes

> that the test for existence of a "show of authority" is an objective one: not whether the citizen perceived that he was being ordered to restrict his movement, but whether the officer's words and actions would have conveyed that to a reasonable person.[19]

In other words, because Hodari did not yield to a show of force, no seizure occurred.

The opinion impressed some lawyers and academics as a strained attempt to support the law enforcement community. One commentator remarked that Justice Scalia's analysis significantly changed the *Mendenhall* analysis because it dramatically moved the point of "seizure." "The seizure was born only at the moment of touching or submission, i.e., cessation of movement, and only the events immediately preceding the touching or submission are considered under *Hodari D.*"[20]

Justice Antonin Scalia, pictured here, wrote for a majority of the U.S. Supreme Court in *California v. Hodari D.* that a "seizure," as that term is used in the Fourth Amendment, must have a physical component. (National Archives and Records Administration)

Because the majority decided a seizure had not occurred pursuant to the Fourth Amendment, the result was clear. "In sum, assuming that Pertoso's pursuit in the present case constituted a 'show of authority' enjoining Hodari to halt, since Hodari did not comply with that injunction, he was not seized until he was tackled," Scalia concluded. "The cocaine abandoned while he was running was, in this case, not the fruit of a seizure, and his motion to exclude evidence of it was properly denied." Accordingly, the high court reversed the opinion of the California Court of Appeal and remanded the case.[21]

Justice John Paul Stevens, joined by Justice Thurgood Marshall, filed a dissent. "The Court's narrow construction of the word 'seizure' represents a significant, and in my view, unfortunate, departure from prior case law construing the Fourth Amendment," he wrote.[22] Characterizing the majority's cramped, narrow definition of "seizure" as "profoundly unwise," Stevens contended that applicable legal precedents do not require a physical element for a citizen to be "seized" within the meaning of the Fourth Amendment. Stevens sardonically observed that "the Court assumes, without acknowledging, that a police officer may now fire his weapon at an innocent citizen and not implicate the Fourth Amendment—as long as he misses his target."[23]

Before reviewing the cases, Stevens plowed through the facts. At the moment Pertoso stepped from the vehicle and chased Hodari D., the officer did not possess a lawful reason for arresting the young man. Neither Officer Pertoso nor his partner had witnessed any criminal activity. A group of people congregating around a car and fleeing when they believed they were being watched did not create reasonable suspicion, much less probable cause, in Stevens's opinion. When Pertoso ran after Hodari D., the officer provided a "show of force" that constituted part of a "seizure" in the law. The suspect's decision to toss the crack cocaine was a direct consequence of the show of force. Although the arrest did not occur until after the police officer tackled the suspect in this case, "if the officer had succeeded in touching respondent before he dropped the rock—even if he did not subdue him—an arrest would have occurred." In Stevens's opinion, this fact was dispositive. "In that event (assuming the touching precipitated the abandonment), the evidence would have been the fruit of an unlawful common law arrest. The distinction between the actual case and the hypothetical case is the same as the distinction between the common law torts of assault and battery—a touching converts the former into the latter." By not recognizing this insight, the court majority mistakenly narrowed the Fourth Amendment interpretation.[24]

Stevens criticized the majority for failing to distinguish between an arrest and an attempted arrest. Justice Scalia analyzed the former, but the latter situation would have been more appropriate. Stevens explained that "the facts of this case do not describe an actual arrest, but rather, an unlawful attempt to take a presumptively innocent person into custody." Under common law standards, an attempted arrest in this fact setting would be illegal. "Thus, if the Court wants to define the scope of the Fourth Amendment based on the common law, it should look, not to the common law of arrest, but to the common law of attempted arrest, according to the facts of this case."[25]

After sifting through the facts, Stevens noted that the instant case narrowed the definition of "seizure" even as recent cases expanded it. He cited *Katz v. United States*, the 1967 opinion that defined electronic surveillance as a search or seizure absent trespass or a physical invasion.[26] In *Terry v. Ohio* a year later, the Court once again broadened the concept of seizure.[27] The *Terry* majority held that reasonable suspicion (without using the term) was a sufficient standard for a police officer to detain a citizen. By expanding the parameters of a constitutionally permissible detention, "the Court necessarily concluded that the word 'seizure' in the Fourth Amendment encompasses official restraints on individual freedom that fall short of a common law arrest. Thus, *Terry* broadened the range of encounters between the police and the citizen encompassed within the term 'seizure,' while at the same time, lowering the standard of proof necessary to justify a 'stop' in the newly expanded category of seizures now covered by the Fourth Amendment."[28]

Taken together, *Katz* and *Terry* clearly demonstrate that the Court has rejected the common law notion of "arrest" as defining the parameters of a "seizure" under the Fourth Amendment. If a person can be seized prior to arrest, as Stevens indicated, then Hodari D. was seized before the officer tackled him. If he was seized at the time he threw the cocaine, he was protected by the Fourth Amendment. The exclusionary rule prohibits evidence procured through a Fourth Amendment violation from being admitted into court. Consequently, Stevens believed that Hodari D.'s conviction should be reversed.[29]

As for the argument that a significant amount of time elapsed between Pertoso's show of force and the actual arrest, Stevens analogized the situation to an encounter when a police officer shouts "freeze," fires a warning shot, or turns on sirens and flashing lights to capture a citizen's attention. In each example, time may pass between the officer's show of force and a person's compliance. In Stevens's opinion, "the point at which the interaction between citizen and police officer becomes a seizure occurs, not when a reasonable citizen believes he or she is no longer free to go, but rather only after the officer exercises control over the citizen."[30]

It can be difficult to determine the specific moment when an officer exercises control over a suspect, but Stevens contended that case-by-case adjudication would be necessary to examine the facts in each instance. The law requires a reviewing court to analyze the facts to ensure that constitutional protections are afforded to the citizenry. In *Hodari D.*, for example, "if Officer Pertoso had succeeded in tackling respondent before he dropped the rock of cocaine, the rock unquestionably would have been excluded as the fruit of the officer's unlawful seizure. Instead, under the Court's logic-chopping analysis, the exclusionary rule has no application, because an attempt to make an unconstitutional seizure is beyond the coverage of the Fourth Amendment, no matter how outrageous or unreasonable the officer's conduct may be."[31]

Justice Stevens concluded by admitting that it was too soon to know the consequences of the majority opinion in *Hodari D.*, but it was possible that police officers could show force and intimidate citizens into surrendering their Fourth Amendment rights. "Some sacrifice of freedom always accompanies an expansion in the executive's unreviewable law enforcement powers. A court more sensitive to the purposes of the Fourth Amendment would insist on greater rewards to society before decreeing the sacrifice it makes today," he lamented.[32] "The Court's immediate concern with containing criminal activity poses a substantial, though unintended, threat to values that are fundamental and enduring."[33]

The case stirred considerable controversy and debate. One commentator concluded that the Supreme Court's opinion in *Hodari D.*, coupled with the opinion in *Florida v. Bostick*—which explained that the reasonable person test was whether a person "would feel free to disregard the questions and carry on with his business"—fundamentally altered American criminal procedure.[34] Maryland assistant attorney general Thomas K. Clancy commented in 1990 that "underpinning these decisions is a historic shift in judicial interpretation of the fourth amendment from favoring individual interests to promoting government interests."[35]

The legacy of *Hodari D.* is that a person who has been "seized" by submitting to a police officer's show of authority is protected by the Fourth Amendment. Assuming that probable cause or reasonable suspicion did not exist for the stop, the person can successfully move to suppress evidence acquired as a result of the stop. A person who does not submit to the show of authority but attempts to flee the scene is not protected by the Fourth Amendment. As one commentator remarked, reflecting Justice Stevens's position, "There is an element of unfairness in considering only 'successful seizures' as subject to the Fourth Amendment. Limiting the application of deterrence to successful seizures that lack constitutional basis is akin to only applying criminal penalties to successful crimes."[36]

Subsequent cases would struggle to discern the point at which Fourth Amendment protections apply during a specific citizen–police encounter. The difficulty with such case-by-case adjudication is that for all the supposed objectivity of the *Mendenhall* test and the theoretical precision of *Hodari D.*, a reviewing court must decide *after the fact* whether a reasonable person would have reacted to the presence of police in a particular manner in a specific situation. Should the person have stopped under these circumstances, or was he or she free to leave? For police officers in the field and persons suddenly confronted by a governmental authority, the situation is anything but clear.[37]

NOTES

1. *California v. Hodari D.*, 499 U.S. 621, 622–23 (1991). See also Michael E. Brooks, "Flight as Justification for Seizure: Supreme Court Rulings," *FBI Law Enforcement Bulletin* 69, 6 (June 2000): 31–32; Ethan Bronner, "Justices Enhance Police Power to Give Chase," *Boston Globe* (April 24, 1991); Timothy J. Devetski, "Fourth Amendment—Protection against Unreasonable Seizure of the Person: The New (?) Common Law Arrest Test for Seizure," *The Journal of Criminal Law & Criminology* 82, 4 (Winter 1992): 753–55; Jayme W. Holcomb, "Abandonment of Items Associated with the Person," *FBI Law Enforcement Bulletin* 76, 8 (August 2007): 27–28; Randolph Alexander Piedrahita, "A Conservative Court Says 'Goodbye to All That' and Forges a New Order in the Law of Seizure—*California v. Hodari D.*," *Louisiana Law Review* 52, 5 (May 1992): 1321–55.

2. 499 U.S. 621, 622–23. See also Devetski, "Fourth Amendment," 755–56; Linda Greenhouse, "Evidence a Fleeing Suspect Drops Is Ruled Legal," *New York Times* (April 24, 1991): A20.

3. *Terry v. Ohio*, 392 U.S. 1, 19 n.16 (1968). See also David K. Kessler, "Free to Leave—An Empirical Look at the Fourth Amendment's Seizure Standard," *The Journal of Criminal Law & Criminology* 99, 1 (Fall 2008): 51–88.

4. *Brown v. Texas*, 443 U.S. 47 (1979).

5. *United States v. Mendenhall*, 446 U.S. 544, 546–549 (1980).

6. 446 U.S. 544, 554. See also Piedrahita, "A Conservative Court Says 'Goodbye to All That' and Forges a New Order in the Law of Seizure," 1326–27.

7. *Florida v. Royer*, 460 U.S. 491, 503–05 (1983).

8. *Immigration and Naturalization Service v. Delgado*, 466 U.S. 210, 219 (1984).

9. 466 U.S. 210, 229.

10. Piedrahita, "A Conservative Court Says 'Goodbye to All That' and Forges a New Order in the Law of Seizure," 1329.

11. *Michigan v. Chesternut*, 486 U.S. 567, 569 (1988).

12. 486 U.S. 567, 573.

13. 486 U.S. 567, 574.

14. 499 U.S. 621, 622. See also Ruth Marcus, "Rights Discarded with Evidence, Court Says," *The Washington Post* (April 24, 1991): A4.

15. 499 U.S. 621, 624.

16. See, for example, Thomas K. Clancy, "The Future of Fourth Amendment Seizure Analysis after *Hodari D.* and *Bostick*," *American Criminal Law Review* 28, 4 (1990–1991): 802; Devetski, "Fourth Amendment," 757–58.

17. 499 U.S. 621, 625.

18. 499 U.S. 621, 626.

19. 499 U.S. 621, 628.

20. Piedrahita, "A Conservative Court Says 'Goodbye to All That' and Forges a New Order in the Law of Seizure," 1333.

21. 499 U.S. 621, 629. See also Bronner, "Justices Enhance Police Power to Give Chase"; Greenhouse, "Evidence a Fleeing Suspect Drops Is Ruled Legal," A20; Marcus, "Rights Discarded with Evidence, Court Says," A4; Holcomb, "Abandonment of Items Associated with the Person," 27–28; David A. Sklansky, "The Fourth Amendment and Common Law," *Columbia Law Review* 100, 7 (November 2000): 1754.

22. 499 U.S. 621, 629.

23. 499 U.S. 621, 630. See also Devetski, "Fourth Amendment," 760–62.

24. 499 U.S. 621, 630–31. See also Bronner, "Justices Enhance Police Power to Give Chase"; Greenhouse, "Evidence a Fleeing Suspect Drops Is Ruled Legal," A20.

25. 499 U.S. 621, 631–32.

26. *Katz v. United States*, 389 U.S. 347 (1967). See also Devetski, "Fourth Amendment," 760–61.

27. 392 U.S. 1 (1968). See also Devetski, "Fourth Amendment," 761.

28. 499 U.S. 621, 635–36.

29. 499 U.S. 621, 637–43.

30. 499 U.S. 621, 643.

31. 499 U.S. 621, 646.

32. 499 U.S. 621, 647–48.

33. 499 U.S. 621, 648. See also Devetski, "Fourth Amendment," 760–62.

34. *Florida v. Bostick*, 501 U.S. 429 (1991). See also Aidan Taft Grano, "Casual or Coercive? Retention of Identification in Police-Citizen Encounters," *Columbia Law Review* 113, 5 (June 2013): 1291–93.

35. Clancy, "The Future of Fourth Amendment Seizure Analysis after *Hodari D.* and *Bostick*," 799.

36. Piedrahita, "A Conservative Court Says 'Goodbye to All That' and Forges a New Order in the Law of Seizure," 1334.

37. Kessler, "Free to Leave," 54; Kathryn R. Urbonya, "Justice on the Run," *ABA Journal* 85, 10 (October 1999): 38.

CHAPTER 14

Hamdan v. Rumsfeld (2006) and Trial by Jury

Hamdan v. Rumsfeld was a U.S. Supreme Court case that arose in the wake of the September 11, 2001, terrorist attacks when the United States was engaged in a "war on terror." Afghani forces captured Salim Ahmed Hamdan, al-Qaeda founder Osama bin Laden's former chauffeur, in November 2001 and, eight months later, turned him over to U.S. forces. Satisfied that Hamdan was an enemy of the United States, officials dispatched the captive to the military prison in Guantánamo Bay, Cuba, where he languished. President George W. Bush eventually determined that Hamdan and other detainees could be tried by a military commission. In the meantime, the prisoner challenged his indefinite detention by filing a petition for a writ of habeas corpus and a writ of mandamus in federal district court. Before the district court ruled on the petition, Hamdan received a hearing from a military tribunal, which designated him an "unlawful enemy combatant." In a decision characterized as a "stinging rebuke" to President Bush and "a clear affirmation of the rule of law," the U.S. Supreme Court held that the president could not authorize the use of a military commission to try a defendant absent express authorization from Congress.[1]

Hamdan's case raised a host of questions about American criminal procedure in the post–September 11 era. When the U.S. government declares war on another country and engages in combat operations, the laws of war supplant the nation's criminal justice system insofar as enemy soldiers are concerned. The difficulty arises when an individual is a part of a group that does not represent a nation-state. In the amorphous war on terror, is a person hostile to U.S. interests a "terrorist" or an "unlawful enemy combatant" and does the use of such labels prevent the person from availing himself of the civilian criminal justice system? *Hamdan v. Rumsfeld* confronted these issues directly.[2]

The case began well before the September 11 terrorist attacks. Salim Ahmed Hamdan was born in Wadi Hadramawt, Yemen, in 1970 and raised as a Muslim. His father labored as a farmer and shopkeeper, while the family lived in a small mud-brick house jutting from a mountainside terrace. When Hamdan was seven years old, his mother died. Four years later, his father died. The child was sent to live with relatives in Mukalla, a port city of 100,000 on Yemen's southern coast. He left school around the same time, working odd jobs to earn his keep.[3]

In 1990, when he was 20 years old, Hamdan traveled to Sana'a, the capital of the new republic of Yemen. Earlier that year, the People's Democratic Republic of Yemen, a Marxist regime sometimes known as South Yemen, had been consolidated with the Yemen Arab Republic, or North Yemen, an Islamic state. Following unification, many Yemenis gravitated to the new, bustling capital city in hopes of finding work. Unfortunately for Hamdan, his limited education and marginal skills presented enormous, almost insuperable, barriers to securing gainful employment. He eventually found work as a driver at the city's Martyr's Mosque, a memorial to fallen soldiers constructed by the Yemeni government and a central gathering place. Around the same time, Hamdan married a young woman and began raising a family of daughters. It was a hardscrabble existence; he barely earned enough money to put food on the table. In time, he became one of the lost, desperate souls seeking a better life in the Arab world. With few opportunities available for advancement, he was vulnerable to anyone or anything that excited his imagination and offered him improved employment prospects. When Nasser al-Bahri, a man two years his junior but hailing from an affluent Saudi family, recruited Hamdan to join the al-Qaeda terrorist organization, the young father jumped at the chance. Hamdan was not especially religious or anti-Western, but he viewed the group as the means to an end of an improved life.[4]

Although Hamdan was married and raising daughters in Yemen, he traveled to Jalalabad, Afghanistan, with al-Bahri and 35 other recruits, mostly Yemenis and a few Saudis. The original plan was to enter Tajikistan to assist jihadists fighting on behalf of radical Muslims. After that scheme failed, Hamdan and his new colleagues met up with Osama bin Laden in the caves near Tora Bora. Not long after their initial meeting, Hamdan worked on an agricultural project for bin Laden until he became the al-Qaeda leader's driver. During his salad days,

Salim Hamdan earned about $200 a month, a princely sum for the impoverished Yemeni husband and father.[5]

At the time Hamdan met bin Laden in 1996, the Al-Qaeda founder already had made a name for himself as a charismatic fundamentalist and dedicated jihadist. The Saudi-born bin Laden was paying a steep price for his dedication, though. By the mid-1990s, he had been expelled from the Sudan, and the Saudi government had stripped him of his citizenship. To all outward appearances, he had been marginalized. Yet among the new adherents, he was an enormously appealing figure: tall, physically imposing, well spoken, and passionate in his excesses—a big, ambitious man sporting big, ambitious ideas with a penchant for creatively enforcing his will over others.

If bin Laden's rhetoric sounded melodramatic and his ambitions far exceeded his abilities, he was determined to build an organization that would bridge the gap between dreams and reality. Al-Qaeda would be his vehicle to capture headlines and strike fear into the hearts of his enemies. Long before Salim Ahmed Hamdan arrived on the scene, the organization had achieved a measure of infamy. The group's glory days were yet to come, but its roots stretched back to the 1980s.

After the Soviet Union invaded Afghanistan in 1979, young men from the Arab world joined the fight to liberate the mountainous nation from infidels, or nonbelievers. Young Osama bin Laden was not a soldier on the front lines, but he proved to be adept at using his extensive contacts and substantial financial resources to equip the rebel forces. He was well suited to the role as financier and organizational planner. The 17th child of between 54 and 57 offspring (the number varies) born to Mohammed bin Awad bin Laden, a billionaire Saudi construction tycoon with ties to the nation's royal family, Osama was the son of the great man's 10th wife, Hamida al-Attas (called Alia Ghanem). Osama inherited between $25 million and $30 million of his father's money when Mohammed died in a plane crash in September 1967.[6]

Bin Laden was reared as a fundamentalist Wahhabi Muslim. Wahhabism requires adherents to return to the pure form of Islam by removing tenets added to the religion since the first generation of Islam. The effort to return to Islam's true roots began in the 18th century when Muhammad ibn Abd al-Wahhab sought to filter out the corrupting influence of Western civilization and combat the spread of foreign religious ideas, especially the impiety practiced by Christian missionaries. As he matured to adulthood, Osama bin Laden became an enthusiastic Wahhabi Muslim, a zealot who grew ever more furious that Western culture was threatening fundamentalist values. Although he reputedly fought in one battle during the anti-Soviet campaign, the young Saudi was satisfied to work behind the scenes by assembling an intricate network of financiers that funneled money into the country to support guerilla activities. Known as the "Golden Chain," the network allowed bin Laden and his followers to equip and train the Afghan mujahedeen, or "holy warriors."[7]

The young zealot tended to see the world as dichotomous. A person was either a friend or a foe. Because the soldiers were encroaching on lands occupied by Muslims, the Soviet army was a foe. No effort must be spared to wage holy war against a foe.

During the holy struggle, bin Laden joined forces with Abdullah Azzam, a charismatic Palestinian and disciple of the fundamentalist, anti-Western Egyptian Muslim Sayyid Qutb. The two men created an organization known as the Bureau of Services (Mektab al Khidmat, or MAK) to funnel materiel into Afghanistan. After the rapidly imploding Soviet empire abandoned the fight in 1989, Azzam and bin Laden enjoyed immense prestige among their circle of fundamentalist admirers. To consolidate their gains, they set out to establish a base (known as al-Qaeda, or "the base") for future jihad, or a struggle against outsiders. Azzam initially served as the principal in MAK, while bin Laden stepped into the primary leadership role for the successor al-Qaeda organization. Although Azzam had served as bin Laden's mentor, the men later had a falling out about the appropriate role for al-Qaeda in the Arab world. On November 24, 1989, Azzam and two of his sons died as a result of a remote-controlled bomb explosion. Osama bin Laden assumed full control of his terrorist organization. Whether the protégé ordered the assassination of his former mentor remains a matter of speculation and debate to this day.[8]

During the early 1990s, bin Laden publicly lauded efforts to attack Western interests and undertook a series of steps to implement his fundamentalist vision of the world. The string of events began in 1992, when al-Qaeda issued a fatwa, or Islamic legal opinion, calling for jihad against the Western "occupation" of Islamic lands. Around this same period, bin Laden spoke of striking against the United States and thereby severing "the head of the snake."[9]

The decade witnessed a wave of al-Qaeda–sponsored and inspired violence. In December 1992, a bomb exploded at two hotels in Aden, Yemen, frequented by American military personnel.[10] At 12:18 P.M. on February 26, 1993, a truck bomb exploded in the parking garage of Tower One of the World Trade Center in New York City, killing six people and injuring more than 1,000. The blast ripped a hole in the building seven stories high. Ramzi Yousef, Mahmud Abouhalima, Mohammad Salameh Nidal Ayyad, Abdul Rahman Yasin, and Ahmad Ajaj, with financing from Yousef's uncle, Khalid Sheikh Mohammed (a key al-Qaeda member), planned and executed the 1993 attack.[11] A November 1995 car bomb exploded in Riyadh, Saudi Arabia, adjacent to a Saudi National Guard training facility and killed five Americans and two Indians. Although bin Laden and his group played no direct role, the four operatives who were caught and executed for the crime admitted that al-Qaeda had "inspired" their actions.[12] Al-Qaeda directly assisted in the bombing in the Khobar Towers building in Dhahran, Saudi Arabia, that killed 19 Americans and wounded 372 people on June 25, 1996.[13] On August 7, 1998, a suicide bomber detonated a bomb at the American Embassy in Nairobi, Kenya, killing 12 Americans and 201 other people, primarily Kenyan citizens who worked in the embassy offices. Four minutes later, a bomb erupted outside the American embassy in Dar es Salaam, Tanzania, killing 11 people and wounding 85 more.[14] On October 12, 2000, an American warship, the USS *Cole*, stopped to refuel in Aden, Yemen. Two Arab men in a skiff approached the destroyer. Smiling and waving, they appeared to be friendly locals. Unfortunately for the American sailors aboard the ship, the skiff was loaded with explosives. As it drew close, the small craft erupted into a huge fireball, tearing a 40-foot gash in the side of the *Cole* and killing 17 sailors. More than 40 were injured.[15] No one outside of bin Laden's network knew it at the time, but these events were dress rehearsals for an ambitious, large-scale assault that eventually became the terrorist attacks of September 11, 2001.

When he joined al-Qaeda in 1996, Salim Ahmed Hamdan could not plausibly argue he was oblivious to the group's goals. He may not have been involved in planning and operations, but he knew the founder's intentions were far from benign.[16] Throughout the 1990s, Osama bin Laden was directing the action and intricately involved in detailed planning. To ensure that no one mistook his intentions, on February 22, 1998, bin Laden issued a fatwa indicating that only one means existed to battle corrupting Western influences. He instructed all "genuine" Muslims "to kill the Americans and their allies—civilians and military" because it "is the individual duty for every Muslim who can do it in any country in which it is possible."[17]

Osama bin Laden was a frustrating, elusive presence to analysts working within the intelligence community, but most of the American public was unaware of the man until September 11, 2001. On that date, al-Qaeda operatives hijacked commercial airliners and used them as weapons to attack the World Trade Center in New York City and the Pentagon near Washington, D.C. Another plane probably headed for a target in the nation's capitol—possibly the White House or the Capitol building—crashed in a field outside of Shanksville, Pennsylvania. By day's end, almost 3,000 victims, mostly Americans, lay dead.[18]

In the aftermath of the attacks, Congress passed a joint resolution authorizing the president of the United States to "use all necessary and appropriate force against those nations, organizations, or persons he determines planned, authorized, committed, or aided the terrorist attacks . . . in order to prevent any future acts of international terrorism against the United States by such nations, organizations or persons." The president acted pursuant to the Authorization for Use of Military Force (AUMF) to declare that the Taliban regime in Afghanistan had supported al-Qaeda. U.S. armed forces entered that country to capture or kill responsible parties and to prevent future attacks. Salim Ahmed Hamdan was among the people captured during the ground operations.[19]

On November 13, 2001, President Bush also issued a comprehensive military order titled "Detention, Treatment, and Trial of Certain Non-Citizens in the War against Terrorism." The order applied to a noncitizen if the president determined "there is reason to believe" that he or she is now, or ever has been, a member of al-Qaeda or engaged in terrorist activities targeting the United States. An individual meeting those requirements "shall, when tried, be tried by military commission for any and all offenses triable by military commission that such individual is alleged to have committed, and may be punished in accordance with the penalties provided under applicable law, including imprisonment or death." The U.S. secretary of defense was authorized to appoint military commissions to try individuals subject to the military order. Later, John D. Altenburg Jr., a retired army major general and experienced military lawyer, was designated "Appointing Authority for Military Commissions."[20]

The president subsequently concluded that Hamdan and five other detainees at the Guantánamo detention camp were subject to the order and therefore could be tried by a military commission. In December 2003, five months after the president's determination, Hamdan was provided military counsel. Afterward, counsel demanded that the prisoner be afforded a speedy trial. Nonetheless, the case met with continuous delays. Despite the decision to try Hamdan before a military commission, officials decided that the Uniform Code of Military Justice (UCMJ) did not apply to an unlawful enemy combatant.[21]

Aggravated with the glacial pace of the proceedings, Hamdan, acting through his attorney, filed suit in the U.S. District Court for the Western District of Washington seeking a writ of habeas corpus and a writ of mandamus. Only after the district court suit was filed did government agents file charges seeking to retain jurisdiction for a military commission. On July 13, 2004, the U.S. government alleged that Hamdan represented a threat to the United States. The charges against the defendant contained 13 paragraphs, most of which did not pertain directly to Hamdan. The president's order of November 13, 2001, and his declaration of July 3, 2003, that Hamdan and five others were subject to the November 13 order were cited as the necessary legal authorization for a military commission to handle the case. The last two paragraphs of the charging document alleged that Hamdan "willfully and knowingly joined an enterprise of persons who shared a common criminal purpose and conspired and agreed with [a number of al-Qaeda members] to commit the following offenses triable by military commission: attacking civilians; attacking civilian objects; murder by an unprivileged belligerent; and terrorism." The document did not detail specific actions where the defendant participated in planning or carrying out terrorist attacks. Hamdan's overt acts were in aiding and abetting the al-Qaeda leadership. The government charged that between 1996 and his capture in November 2001, he had furthered a terrorist conspiracy by acting as Osama bin Laden's bodyguard and driver, arranging to transport weapons to be used by al-Qaeda operatives, driving bin Laden to al-Qaeda training camps, and receiving training in the camps.[22]

The U.S. District Court for the Western District of Washington transferred Hamdan's habeas corpus and mandamus petitions to the U.S. District Court for the District of Columbia. At approximately the same time, a Combatant Status Review Tribunal (CSRT) determined that Hamdan's detention at Guantánamo was justified because he was properly designated as an "unlawful enemy combatant."[23] When it eventually considered his petition, the district court countermanded the military tribunal and decided that Hamdan must be provided with a hearing to determine whether he was a prisoner of war under the Geneva Conventions before he could be tried by a military commission. On appeal, the Circuit Court of Appeals for the District of Columbia reversed the decision, finding that the Geneva Conventions could not be enforced in federal court and that the establishment of military tribunals had been authorized by Congress.[24]

The U.S. Supreme Court agreed to hear Hamdan's appeal. The question was "whether the military commission convened to try Hamdan has authority to do so, and whether Hamdan may rely on the Geneva Conventions in these proceedings."[25] Writing for the high court, Justice John Paul Stevens authored an opinion containing six parts. Justices Souter, Ginsburg, and Breyer joined in all six. Justice Kennedy joined in all except for Parts V and VI-D-iv.[26]

Stevens began Part I of the opinion by outlining Hamdan's arguments:

> His objection is that the military commission the President has convened lacks . . . authority, for two principal reasons: First, neither congressional Act nor the common law of war supports trial by this commission for the crime of conspiracy—an offense that, Hamdan says, is not a violation of the law of war. Second, Hamdan contends, the procedures that the President has adopted to try him violate the most basic tenets of military and international law, including the principle that a defendant must be permitted to see and hear the evidence against him.[27]

Stevens explained that "trial by military commission is an extraordinary measure raising important questions about the balance of powers in our constitutional structure." Where civil courts are operating and can adjudicate claims, they should be used to address judicial questions in lieu of relying on a military tribunal. "For the reasons that follow," Justice Stevens wrote, "we conclude that the military commission convened to try Hamdan lacks power to proceed because its structure and procedures violate both the [Uniform Code of Military Justice] and the Geneva Conventions. Four of us also conclude, see Part V, *infra*, that the offense with which Hamdan has been charged is not an 'offens[e] that by . . . the law of war may be tried by military commissions.'"[28]

In Part II, Steven denied the government's motion to dismiss the case owing to a lack of jurisdiction. In Part III, the Court refused to abstain from hearing the case while military proceedings were ongoing, explaining "under our precedent, abstention is not justified here. We therefore proceed to consider the merits of Hamdan's challenge."[29]

In Part IV of the opinion, Stevens emphatically rejected the idea that the Detainee Treatment Act of 2005 (DTA) or the AUMF authorized the president to allow military commissions to try detainees. "The military commission, a tribunal neither mentioned in the Constitution nor created by statute," he stated, "was born of military necessity."[30] Under exigent circumstances when civilian courts are not operating, a military commission may be appropriate, but those circumstances were not present here. Referring to *Ex Parte Quirin*, a 1942 case that allowed a military tribunal to try German saboteurs during World War II, Stevens distinguished that case from *Hamdan*. Aside from the fact that the United States signed and ratified the Geneva Conventions in 1949, seven years after *Quirin*, Congress had enacted a statute that authorized reliance on military commissions for the offenses outlined in the 1942 case. No such statutory authorization existed for *Hamdan*. "The Government would have us dispense with the inquiry that the *Quirin* Court undertook and find in either the AUMF or the DTA specific, overriding authorization for the very commission that has been convened to try Hamdan," Stevens wrote. "Neither of these congressional Acts, however, expands the President's authority to convene military commissions."[31]

Later in the opinion, Stevens explained that absent express congressional authorization, a military commission—assuming such a commission is authorized in the first place—must comply with the ordinary laws of the United States and the laws of war. The Geneva Conventions, as a part of the ordinary laws of war, can therefore be enforced by the Supreme Court, along with the statutory UCMJ. Moreover, excluding Hamdan from certain parts of his trial that were deemed classified by the military commission violated both of these sources of law, and the trial was therefore illegal.[32]

Justice Stephen G. Breyer, with whom Justice Kennedy, Justice Souter, and Justice Ginsburg joined, filed a short concurring opinion. Observing that the "Court's conclusion ultimately rests upon a single ground: Congress has not issued the Executive a blank check," Breyer denied that the majority opinion in *Hamdan* constrained the president's power to prevent or respond to a terrorist attack. "Indeed, Congress has denied the President the legislative authority to create military commissions of the kind at issue here. Nothing prevents the President from returning to Congress to seek the authority he believes necessary." According to Breyer, preventing the president from convening military commissions on his own authority enhances the "democratic means" at the core of the American republic. "The Constitution places its faith in those democratic means. Our Court today simply does the same."[33]

Justice Anthony Kennedy, with whom Justice Souter, Justice Ginsburg, and Justice Breyer joined as to Parts I and II, concurring in part, expressed his concerns about allowing the president to convene military commissions without a congressional check on his power. "Trial by military commission raises separation-of-powers concerns of the highest order," he wrote. "Located within a single branch, these courts carry the risk that offenses will be defined, prosecuted, and adjudicated by executive officials without independent review."[34] Common Article 3 of the Geneva Conventions of 1949 applied in *Hamdan*, Kennedy argued, because the United States had signed the treaty and was bound by the terms.[35] Under federal law, Congress deemed an Article 3 violation to be a war crime punishable by U.S. law.[36] Allowing special military commissions to be convened in some instances was authorized because Congress had established procedures for courts-martial under the UCMJ. "At a minimum a military commission like the one at issue—a commission specially convened by the President to try specific persons without express congressional authorization—can be 'regularly constituted' by the standards of our military justice system only if some practical need explains deviations from court-martial practice," Kennedy explained.[37] The government had failed to provide evidence of such a practical need. "Against this background, the Court is correct to conclude that the military commission the President has convened to try Hamdan is unauthorized."[38]

Justices Scalia, Thomas, and Alito dissented. Chief Justice John Roberts, who participated in the case while serving on the D.C. Circuit Court of Appeals, did not take part in the decision. In the first dissent, Justice Antonin Scalia argued that the Detainee Treatment Act unambiguously provided that "no court, justice, or judge" had jurisdiction to consider a habeas corpus petition from a Guantánamo Bay detainee.[39] Even cases pending as of December 30, 2005, when the statute went into effect, would be subject to the jurisdictional limitation. The majority opinion simply strained to construe the statute but offered no reliable precedents to bolster its arguments.[40] "A final but powerful indication of the fact that the Court has made a mess of this statute is the nature of the consequences that ensue," Scalia contended. According to the solicitor general, petitions had been filed on behalf of some 600 Guantánamo prisoners, which meant that a rule extending jurisdiction over such cases would strain judicial resources. "The Court's interpretation transforms a provision abolishing jurisdiction over *all* Guantanamo-related *habeas* petitions into a provision that retains jurisdiction over cases sufficiently numerous to keep the courts busy for years to come," Scalia wryly observed.[41]

Justice Clarence Thomas, with whom Justice Scalia joined, and with whom Justice Alito joined in all but Parts I, II–C–1, and III–B–2, filed a separate dissenting opinion. The justice argued that the Geneva Conventions should not be judicially enforceable in a U.S. federal court. Moreover, fighting terrorism should be left to the executive branch, especially in cases where Congress has provided explicit authority for the executive to act. Thomas observed that "the President's decision to try Hamdan before a military commission for his involvement with al-Qaeda is entitled to a heavy measure of deference. In the present conflict, Congress has authorized the President 'to use all necessary and appropriate force against those nations, organizations, or persons *he determines* planned, authorized, committed, or aided the terrorist attacks that occurred on September 11, 2001 . . . in order to prevent any future acts of international terrorism against the United States by such nations, organizations or persons.'"[42]

Justice Thomas discussed the use of military commissions to try "unlawful combatants" beyond simply courts-martial. In his view, the military commission charged with prosecuting Hamdan was "plainly 'regularly constituted' because such commissions have been employed throughout our history to try unlawful combatants for crimes against the law of war."[43] A military commission afforded a detainee ample legal protections. "In these circumstances, 'civilized peoples' would take into account the context of military commission trials against unlawful combatants in the war on terrorism, including the need to keep certain information secret in the interest of preventing future attacks on our Nation and its foreign installations so long as it did not deprive the accused of a fair trial."[44]

Justice Samuel Alito, with whom Justices Scalia and Thomas joined in Parts I–III, offered the final dissenting opinion. He agreed that the Court lacked jurisdiction to hear the case, but he wanted to add clarifying remarks. As Justice Alito dissected the case, the result depended on a relatively straightforward analysis:

> The holding of the Court, as I understand it, rests on the following reasoning. A military commission is lawful only if it is authorized by 10 U.S.C. §821; this provision permits the use of a commission to try "offenders or offenses" that "by statute or by the law of war may be tried by" such a commission; because no statute provides that an offender such as petitioner or an offense such as the one with which he is charged may be tried by a military commission, he may be tried by military commission only if the trial is authorized by "the law of war"; the Geneva Conventions are

> part of the law of war; and Common Article 3 of the Conventions prohibits petitioner's trial because the commission before which he would be tried is not "a regularly constituted court," Third Geneva Convention. . . .[45]

Common Article 3, Alito observed, imposes several requirements, including the provision "that the court be appointed or established in accordance with the appointing country's domestic law."[46] While the majority of the *Hamdan* court did not see a military commission as "a regularly constituted court," Alito disagreed. "In sum, I believe that Common Article 3 is satisfied here because the military commissions (1) qualify as courts, (2) that were appointed and established in accordance with domestic law, and (3) any procedural improprieties that might occur in particular cases can be reviewed in those cases."[47]

Despite the vehement dissents, Salim Hamdan had won his case. His victory in the U.S. Supreme Court meant that he would have to be tried in a civilian court—or so it seemed in the immediate aftermath. Because the majority opinion in the high court was not based on the Geneva Conventions, however, Congress responded by passing a bill to modify the UCMJ and thereby overcome the Court's objections. The Military Commissions Act of 2006 (MCA), signed into law by President George W. Bush on October 17, 2006, specifically authorized military commissions to try cases involving detainees classified as "unlawful enemy combatants." Such detainees were not allowed to file habeas corpus appeals in federal court. Habeas corpus petitions pending at the time the statute was enacted were stayed.[48]

As for Salim Ahmed Hamdan, he did not win his freedom. Despite his court victory and his five-year detention, he was charged with conspiracy as well as providing support for terrorism and held over for trial before a new military commission established under the MCA. His case was truly historic—the first American war crimes trial since World War II. While no one contended that the former al-Qaeda operative was a decision maker, his role as Osama bin Laden's driver meant that he had taken part in events that led to the September 11, 2001, terrorist attacks on American soil. Military prosecutors did not have to demonstrate that Hamdan was a high-ranking al-Qaeda operative to win. They only needed to demonstrate that he had furthered the cause of the terrorist conspiracy.[49]

Brought to trial in June 2007, Hamdan, along with a Canadian citizen, Omar Ahmed Khadr, won a significant legal victory when two military judges ruled that the defendants' CSRTs had not followed

Associated Press sketch artist Janet Hamlin drew this illustration of al-Qaeda founder Osama bin Laden's former chauffeur, Salim Ahmed Hamdan (far left), appearing at a U.S. military tribunal arraignment at the Guantánamo Bay U.S. naval base in Cuba on June 4, 2007. (AP Photo/Janet Hamlin, Pool)

the correct procedures necessary to classify the detainees as "unlawful enemy combatants."[50] Once again, the victory was short-lived. In December 2007, Hamdan was deemed to be an unlawful enemy combatant. Thereafter, he was tried before a six-member military jury. Although he was acquitted of the conspiracy charge, the defendant was sentenced to 66 months in prison for aiding al-Qaeda during his time as bin Laden's chauffeur. With credit for time served, he was eligible for release in January 2009.[51]

The U.S. government claimed it could still detain Hamdan indefinitely, but the case had dragged on for so long that prosecutors were weary from the proceedings and anxious to clear the docket. The Pentagon eventually transferred the prisoner to his native Yemen to serve out the remainder of his sentence. Despite his release in 2009, Hamdan continued to challenge his conviction, arguing that materially supporting terrorism was not considered a war crime at the time of his actions. In October 2012, a three-judge panel of the U.S. Court of Appeals for the D.C. Circuit unanimously agreed, overturning his conviction.[52]

Hamdan v. Rumsfeld was a landmark case where the U.S. Supreme Court wrestled with one of the most difficult issues in modern criminal procedure: the boundary between criminal defendants tried in a civilian court of law and unlawful enemy combatants tried before military commissions.[53] As the Supreme Court noted, relying on a military commission to try a criminal defendant is impermissible when the commission is not properly established and lacks the due process protections afforded to defendants in civilian courts.[54] If the history of American criminal procedure has taught us nothing else, it has demonstrated the importance of procedural protections as a necessary component of substantive justice. Even in extraordinary situations such as the horrific terrorist attacks in 2001, American criminal law is deeply rooted in procedural safeguards.

NOTES

1. Samuel Estreicher and Diarmuid O'Scannlain, "*Hamdan*'s Limits and the Military Commissions Act," *Constitutional Commentary* 23, 3 (Winter 2006): 403–7; Margaret Kohn, "Due Process and Empire's Law: *Hamdan v. Rumsfeld*," *Dissent* 54, 1 (Winter 2007): 5; Amy Quimby, "*Hamdan v. Rumsfeld:* Reviewing the Geneva Convention Rights of the Unlawful Enemy Combatants Detained at Gitmo," *Widener Law Journal* 17, 1 (Spring 2010): 318–19.

2. Eran Shamir-Borer, "Revisiting *Hamdan v. Rumsfeld*'s Analysis of the Laws of Armed Conflict," *Emory International Law Review* 21, 2 (2007): 601–4; Neal K. Katyal, Giorgio Bongiovanni, and Chiara Valentini, "Terrorism, Emergency Powers, and the Role of the U.S. Supreme Court: An Interview with Neal K. Katyal," *Ratio Juris.* 20, 4 (December 2007): 443–44;

3. Jonathan Mahler, *The Challenge: Hamdan v. Rumsfeld and the Fight over Presidential Power* (New York: Farrar, Strauss and Giroux, 2008), 4.

4. Mahler, *The Challenge*, 4–5; Michelle Shephard, "Bin Laden's Driver Talks," *Toronto Star* (August 17, 2009): A1.

5. Jonathan Mahler, "The Bush Administration vs. Salim Hamdan," *New York Times Magazine* (January 8, 2006): 44, 46; Mahler, *The Challenge*, 5–6; Jerry Markon, "Goal of the Hamdan Trial: Credibility; Prosecutors Seek Decisive Conviction of Former Driver," *The Washington Post* (July 27, 2008): A2; Shephard, "Bin Laden's Driver Talks," A1; Carol J. Williams, "Hamdan Helped Bin Laden Succeed, Agent Says," *Los Angeles Times* (July 26, 2008): A10.

6. See, for example, The Editors of Life, *Brought to Justice: Osama Bin Laden's War on America and the Mission That Stopped Him* (New York, Boston, and London: Little, Brown and Company, 2011), 19; Rohan Gunaratna, *Inside Al Qaeda: Global Network of Terror* (New York and London: Columbia University Press, 2002), 16; Lawrence Wright, *The Looming Tower: Al-Qaeda and the Road to 9/11* (New York: Knopf, 2006), 72.

7. The Editors of Life, *Brought to Justice*, 38; Pervez Hoodbhoy, "Afghanistan and the Genesis of Global Jihad," *Peace Research* 37, 1 (May 2005): 27–29; G. H. Jansen, *Militant Islam* (New York: Harper & Row, 1979), 87–88; National Commission on Terrorist Attacks upon the United States, *The 9/11 Commission Report* (New York and London: Norton, 2004), 55; Wright, *The Looming Tower*, 95–96, 99–100; Robin Wright, *Rock the Casbah: Rage and Rebellion across the Islamic World* (New York: Simon & Schuster, 2011), 49–50.

8. Zachary Abuza, "Tentacles of Terror: Al Qaeda's Southeast Asian Network," *Contemporary Southeast Asia* 24, 3 (December 2002): 429; The Editors of Life, *Brought to Justice*, 35, 37, 38, 43; Gunaratna, *Inside Al-Qaeda*, 21–23; Sohail Abdul Nasir, "Al Qaeda, Two Years On," *Bulletin of the Atomic Scientists* 59, 5 (September/October 2003): 34; National Commission on Terrorist Attacks upon the United States, *The 9/11 Commission Report*, 56; Wright, *The Looming Tower*, 129–33.

9. Ann M. Lesch, "Osama Bin Laden: Embedded in the Middle East Crises," *Middle East Policy* 9, 2 (June 2002): 85; National Commission on Terrorist Attacks upon the United States, *The 9/11 Commission Report*, 59–60.

10. National Commission on Terrorist Attacks upon the United States, *The 9/11 Commission Report*, 59–60; Wright, *The Looming Tower*, 188–89.

11. Abuza, "Tentacles of Terror," 441–42; Joseph T. McCann, *Terrorism on American Soil: A Concise History of Plots and Perpetrators from the Famous to the Forgotten* (Boulder, Colo.: Sentient Publications, 2006), 188–91; National Commission on Terrorist Attacks upon the United States, *The 9/11 Commission Report*, 71–72; Wright, *The Looming Tower*, 177–78.

12. The Editors of Life, *Brought to Justice*, 45, 48–49; Lesch, "Osama bin Laden," 85; National Commission on Terrorist Attacks upon the United States, *The 9/11 Commission Report*, 60.

13. Lesch, "Osama bin Laden," 85; National Commission on Terrorist Attacks upon the United States, *The 9/11 Commission Report*, 60; Wright, *The Looming Tower*, 237–39.

14. Bill Clinton, *My Life* (New York: Knopf, 2004), 797; Michael Doran, "The Pragmatic Fanaticism of al Qaeda: An Anatomy of Extremism in Middle Eastern Politics," *Political Science Quarterly* 117, 2 (Summer 2002): 183; The Editors of Life, *Brought to Justice*, 48–49; Lesch, "Osama bin Laden," 87; National Commission on Terrorist Attacks upon the United States, *The 9/11 Commission Report*, 70, 115–16; Benjamin Runkle, *Wanted Dead or Alive: Manhunts from Geronimo to Bin Laden* (New York: Palgrave-MacMillan, 2011),

160–61; Richard Sale, *Clinton's Secret Wars: The Evolution of a Commander in Chief* (New York: Thomas Dunne Books, St. Martin's Press, 2009), 295–96; Wright, *The Looming Tower*, 270–72.

15. Doran, "The Pragmatic Fanaticism of al-Qaeda," 183; The Editors of Life, *Brought to Justice*, 52; Fawaz A. Gerges, *The Rise and Fall of Al-Qaeda* (New York and Oxford: Oxford University Press, 2011), 68; Lesch, "Osama bin Laden," 87; McCann, *Terrorism on American Soil*, 277; National Commission on Terrorist Attacks upon the United States, *The 9/11 Commission Report*, 190–91; Runkle, *Wanted Dead or Alive*, 166–67; Wright, *The Looming Tower*, 319–20.

16. Hamdan admitted he overheard plans from time to time even if he was not an al-Qaeda decision maker. See, for example, Mahler, "The Bush Administration vs. Salim Hamdan," 46–48; Markon, "Goal of the Hamdan Trial," A2; Shephard, "Bin Laden's Driver Talks," A1; Williams, "Hamdan Helped Bin Laden Succeed, Agent Says," A10.

17. Quoted in Runkle, *Wanted Dead or Alive*, 160. See also Lesch, "Osama bin Laden," 87; McCann, *Terrorism on American Soil*, 276–77; National Commission on Terrorist Attacks upon the United States, *The 9/11 Commission Report*, 69; Sale, *Clinton's Secret Wars*, 295; Wright, *The Looming Tower*, 259–61.

18. See, for example, Julian Ku and John Yoo, "*Hamdan v. Rumsfeld:* The Functional Case for Foreign Affairs Deference to the Executive Branch," *Constitutional Commentary* 23, 2 (Summer 2006): 181–82; National Commission on Terrorist Attacks upon the United States, *The 9/11 Commission Report*, 71; Runkle, *Wanted Dead or Alive*, 1.

19. 48 U.S. 557, 568. See also Brian M. Christensen, "Extending *Hamdan v. Rumsfeld* to Combatant Status Review Tribunals," *Brigham Young University Law Review* 27, 5 (September 2007): 1370; John D. Dealy, "Subordination of Powers: *Hamsdan v. Rumsfeld*, 126 S. Ct. 2749 (2006)," *Harvard Journal of Law & Public Policy* 30, 3 (Summer 2007): 1071; Quimby, "*Hamdan v. Rumsfeld*," 326.

20. 66 Fed. Reg. 57833, 57834. See also 548 U.S. 557, 568–69. See also Christensen, "Extending *Hamdan v. Rumsfeld* to Combatant Status Review Tribunals," 1370; Ku and Yoo, "*Hamdan v. Rumsfeld*," 182; Quimby, "*Hamdan v. Rumsfeld*," 324.

21. 548 U.S. 557, 569. See also Christensen, "Extending *Hamdan v. Rumsfeld* to Combatant Status Review Tribunals," 1370; Quimby, "*Hamdan v. Rumsfeld*," 326.

22. 548 U.S. 557, 569–70. See also Christensen, "Extending *Hamdan v. Rumsfeld* to Combatant Status Review Tribunals," 1370; Dealy, "Subordination of Powers," 1072; Quimby, "*Hamdan v. Rumsfeld*," 326–27.

23. 548 U.S. 557, 570. See also Christensen, "Extending *Hamdan v. Rumsfeld* to Combatant Status Review Tribunals," 1370.

24. 548 U.S. 557, 571–72. See also Christensen, "Extending *Hamdan v. Rumsfeld* to Combatant Status Review Tribunals," 1372; Dealy, "Subordination of Powers," 1072; Quimby, "*Hamdan v. Rumsfeld*," 327–28.

25. 548 U.S. 557, 572.

26. 548 U.S. 557, 563. See also Estreicher and O'Scannlain, "*Hamdan*'s Limits and the Military Commissions Act," 407–9.

27. 548 U.S. 557, 567.

28. 548 U.S. 557, 567.

29. 548 U.S. 557, 590.

30. 548 U.S. 557, 590.

31. 548 U.S. 557, 593–94, 597–98. See also *Ex parte Quirin*, 317 U.S. 1 (1942).

32. 548 U.S. 557, 600–13.

33. 548 U.S. 557, 636.

34. 548 U.S. 557, 638.

35. 548 U.S. 557, 637–38.

36. 548 U.S. 557, 639.

37. 548 U.S. 557, 645.

38. 548 U.S. 557, 647.

39. 548 U.S. 557, 655.

40. 548 U.S. 557, 664–65.

41. 548 U.S. 557, 669.

42. 548 U.S. 557, 680.

43. 548 U.S. 557, 720.

44. 548 U.S. 557, 724.

45. 548 U.S. 557, 725.

46. 548 U.S. 557, 726.

47. 548 U.S. 557, 733.

48. Military Commissions Act of 2006 (MCA), Public Law 109–366, 120 Stat. 2600 (Oct. 17, 2006). A subsequent case, *Boumediene v. Bush*, 553 U.S. 723 (2008), held that the MCA unconstitutionally limited the rights of foreign nationals to challenge their detention through a habeas corpus appeal.

49. William Glaberson, "Defense Challenges Enemy Combatant Status of Detainee," *New York Times* (December 6, 2007): A32; Markon, "Goal of the Hamdan Trial," A2; Shephard, "Bin Laden's Driver Talks," A1; Williams, "Hamdan Helped Bin Laden Succeed, Agent Says," A10.

50. William Glaberson, "Detainee Challenges Guantánamo by Describing Life There," *New York Times* (July 16, 2008): A13; William Glaberson, "Military Judges Dismiss Charges for 2 Detainees," *New York Times* (June 5, 2007): A1; William Glaberson, "Prosecution Rests, Then Terror Trial Enters Secret Session to Hear Defense Testimony," *New York Times* (August 1, 2008): A13; William Glaberson, "Terror Trial Nears End as Defense Rests Case," *New York Times* (August 2, 2008): A9.

51. William Glaberson, "A Conviction, but a System Still on Trial," *New York Times* (August 10, 2008): 27; William Glaberson, "Panel Sentences Bin Laden Driver to a Short Term," *New York Times* (August 8, 2008): A1.

52. *Hamdan v. United States*, No. 11–1257 (16 October 2012), Available at http://www.cadc.uscourts.gov/internet/home.nsf. Accessed August 27, 2013. See also "U.S. Sending a Convict Back to Yemen," *New York Times* (November 25, 2008): A23; Del Quentin Wilber, "Court Overturns Conviction of Bin Laden's Driver," *The Washington Post* (October 17, 2012): A2.

53. An earlier case, *Hamdi v. Rumsfeld*, 542 U.S. 507 (2004), held that a U.S. citizen detained at Guantánamo Bay had the right to due process in challenging his detention. Because *Hamdan* involved a noncitizen, it raised a different set of legal issues.

54. 548 U.S. 557, 567.

Conclusion

We were arrested, my mother and I, on a hazy, humid Sunday afternoon in October when I was 14 years old. She was 37. Handcuffed, mom was forcibly dragged from her automobile and unceremoniously shoved into a police cruiser to be transported to the Florence, South Carolina, inmate detention center for processing and, presumably, eventual rehabilitation. She cried out to anyone who cared to listen about her constitutional rights and other esoteric irrelevancies as she was propelled into the backseat. Our fellow motorists in the license-check roadblock turned away in horror and disgust, stepping on their accelerators to escape the plaintive wails of a patently disturbed woman. I did not share my mother's penchant for exhortation. Thus, I was apprehended with much less brouhaha. Bowing to the inevitable, I offered no resistance as four burly police officers escorted me to the transport vehicle. I was not handcuffed.

Thanks to my unfamiliarity with the vagaries of the criminal justice system, our engagement with practitioners of the law enforcement arts that Sunday left me with a sense of anxiety about authoritarian power that persists to this day. I had never thought of my mother and me as criminals, but the local police insisted that we were, so our culpability seemed reasonably assured. We shared our neighbors' faith in the sanctity of law and order, and the maxim "where there's smoke, there's fire." It was only when the smoke engulfed us that we reevaluated our notions of guilt and innocence.

If I tell this tale from the beginning, the incident really started two months before we encountered Florence's Finest in the license check. Mom had driven her 1969 Chevy Nova to the Crown Theatre. While she was inside watching a movie with friends, vandals broke into the Nova and stole the car radio. The unknown Visigoths also cut the interior upholstery with a knife and broke off the turn signal lever. Mom alerted the police after she discovered tell-tale signs of forced entry, but the reprobates responsible for the heinous act had long since absconded with their booty.

As a single mother practicing secretarial science, mom possessed almost no discretionary income. She vowed to have the turn signal control fixed when she could afford to do so. In the meantime, the Nova could not pass the state-mandated safety inspection without properly operating equipment, which included a working turn-signal lever. The scene was set. On a warm Sunday afternoon two months after the hooligans had worked their magic on the automobile, we drove up to a roadblock on State Route 64 in front of the Wayside Baptist Church and encountered four police officers, one of whom noticed the expired inspection sticker. He decided to make an example of my mother.

"Lady, listen here." The officer leaned into the driver's window. His broad, freckled, sunburned face filled the space. Sweat dripped from his sandy-blonde crew-cut and carved a swath through the pimples and dirt adorning his cheeks. Mirrored sunshades masked his eyes, but a toothpick propped in the corner of his mouth was expressive enough. "Your inspection sticker has expired."

"What?" Mom was genuinely surprised. The cigarette almost fell from her lips. With a multitude of events crowding her life, she had forgotten about the inspection sticker.

Nodding, the policeman tapped his finger on the outside of the windshield. "Yep. Expired October 1." He displayed a single digit by way of illustration.

"Oh, my. Goodness gracious."

The toothpick danced across his lips in a kind of country ballet. "License and registration, please, ma'am."

"Where did I put that registration card?" Mom clawed through her purse. "Mike. Open the car pocket and see if I left the registration card in there." Mom's brow was wrinkled.

I did as I had been instructed. Except for credit card receipts and an owner's manual, the glove compartment was empty. "No, ma'am. I don't see it."

"Let's go, lady. I ain't got all day now. Daylight's a-burnin.'"

"Give me just a minute, please, officer. It's here somewhere."

The policeman's face reappeared in our window. "Look, either you have a license and registration or you don't." He heaved a deep sigh.

Mom held up her driver's license. "I know my registration card is here somewhere. I changed pocketbooks last week, but I remember putting it in the new one."

The officer snatched her driver's license and examined it carefully. "Okay, Miz Mar-tee-nez, while you look for the registration, I gotta ask you to pull over on the shoulder so other motorists can get by." He pointed to the lawn of the Wayside Baptist Church. "You can just pull up on the grass over there."

Mom steered her Nova onto the side of the road so that half the tires were parked on the grass and gravel shoulder and half were on the roadway. She turned the ignition switch; the engine sputtered and died. A second later, she turned on the hazard lights, which blinked on and off in a staccato rhythm, much like a metronome.

The policeman leaned into the window to address mom again. "I'll give you a couple of minutes and then, if you can't locate the registration card, we'll have to impound the vehicle." The toothpick slid back and forth across his lips with lightning rapidity.

Mom was incredulous. "Impound the vehicle? Don't you think that's a bit much?"

"Look, I don't make the rules, ma'am. We gotta make sure the car's not stolen."

"Stolen? Oh, for Pete's sake. If I was going to steal a car, do you think I would steal this one?"

His voice assumed an icy coldness that, in retrospect, was pregnant with hostility. At the time, we ignored this first warning sign. "Look—you're just lucky I don't take you in."

"Take me in? To the station? To *jail?* Isn't that a bit extreme?"

"Mama, are we goin' to jail?"

"Oh, hush up, Mike. Even these idiots aren't that stupid. Ah-ha!" Her face beamed in her moment of triumph. She had found the ticket to our salvation. "It was stuck to the back of a picture. Oh, thank God." She smiled. "Here you go."

Jerking the card from her hand, the officer stood, lifted up his sunglasses, and squinted while he read the insurance card. He kneeled and handed it back to her after a moment.

"Okay. You're clean. This is your lucky day, Miz Mar-tee-nez. You can go, but I gotta write up your expired inspection sticker. You'll have to pay a fine."

"Goodness gracious. A fine? How much?"

He shrugged. "Ain't up to me."

"It's not fair." Her voice sounded weary. Our household budget was already stretched to the breaking point.

He smiled. "Tell it to the magistrate."

Mom did not know when to leave well enough alone. Had she held her tongue, the incident would have ended right then and there—except for paying the fine. "Well, okay, but it's not fair," she muttered in a frustrated, stream-of-consciousness tirade. "Somebody breaks into my car and I gotta pay a fine. The damage was more than my insurance deductible. I tell you what. It's not fair. The least you police could have done is catch the people who did this instead of making me pay a fine."

The officer had slipped a ticket booklet from his belt and was kneeling by the car, hunched over his pen, when Mom offered her sotto voce opinion. He stopped writing in mid-word and raised his head. "What did you say to me?"

"When?"

He gestured at her. "Just now. You said something to me just now."

Sucking nicotine into her lungs, mom brandished her cigarette and feigned ignorance. "Hmm? Did I?" She blew smoke from her mouth in a long gray cloud. "If I did, I don't remember what it was."

He would have none of her chicanery. "Look here, Miz Mar-tee-nez, I've been very patient with you. You think I like standing out here in a hundred-and-five-degree heat stopping people like this?"

"No, I just . . ."

"You think I wanna sit here and have you blow smoke in my face?"

"I wasn't blowing smoke in your face, officer."

"Maybe a night in jail would teach you some manners."

"Now, hold on a minute." She turned to look at me, and then turned her attention back to the cop with nostrils flared. "You've got no call to be so nasty. I've done everything you told me to. I realize I've got to have the car inspected, but you certainly have nothing to arrest me for, so there's no call to get all high and mighty, Buster." She gestured with both hands, wielding her Salem Light 100 with the skill of an expert swordsman.

The young officer's voice squeaked. He sounded frightened and angry, a man-child who had reached the end of his tether. "Listen, Miz Mar-tee-nez, you had better watch your mouth, okay? I could take you to jail if I wanted to."

"Oh, yeah? On what charge?"

"Just watch yourself, lady."

"Okay, tough guy, if you can take me to jail, then do it."

The officer reached through the window and, in one quick, sure motion, yanked the keys from the ignition. Mom had thrown down the gauntlet and he was determined to pick it up.

Her mouth dropped open in surprise. "What are you doing?"

"Please step out of the car, ma'am."

"Now, look here . . . I wasn't serious. Let's not get carried away."

The policeman was adamant. "I said 'please step out of the car, ma'am.'"

"Why?"

"You are under arrest."

"Arrest? You can't be serious. On what charge?" Mom still sounded frightened, but she was curious as well.

The officer drummed his fingers on the roof of our car while he considered his options. "Resisting arrest."

"Resisting arrest?" My mother was incredulous. "How can you arrest me for resisting arrest when I haven't been arrested before you charge me with resisting arrest?" Mom raised an interesting point: The guardian of law and order had created a tautology, a carefully crafted bit of circular reasoning, but he did not wish to debate logical niceties by the side of the road.

"And disturbing the peace."

"Oh, please. How am I disturbing the peace?"

"You are undermining police authority. Every minute I deal with you is a minute I could be checking other motorists."

"You can't be serious."

He opened the driver's door and leaned into Mom's face. "Now don't make me ask you again, Miz Mar-tee-nez." The toothpick traveled around his mouth faster than ever. "Please step out of the car."

"Look, this has gone far enough. I get your point. I'm sorry I smarted off. It won't happen again."

The officer of the law wrapped his hand around mom's bicep and pulled her from the car. She was caught off balance and, as a result, tumbled into the weed-infested gravel. Watching the scene in horror, I gasped aloud.

Perhaps if the temperature had been mild that day, tempers would not have flared. Looking back on the incident from the comforting perspective of three-plus decades, I think that had October acted a little more like October and a little less like August, we might have escaped unscathed. Alas, the temperature was hot, and so were the tempers. Escape was not in the cards.

The arrest had taken on a life of its own, and its momentum would not be stalled. The word had gone forth from that time and place that a genuine public nuisance was in the clutches of the law enforcement community, and everyone wanted to get in on the act. In short order, it had evolved into the biggest case our town had seen since Manny Lee Law had escaped from the state hospital four years earlier and menaced an elderly couple in their mobile home before being apprehended by hound dogs as he hid in a pine tree. It was the kind of case that could be fashioned into a folk tale for policemen to share with their grandkids in the years to come: *Once I cornered a crazy woman who had no respect for law and order. I showed her a thing or two!*

The arresting officer obviously had acquired long experience in dealing with criminal offenders. In one swift motion, he pulled mom to her feet, swung her around, and grabbed her arms behind her back. He produced a pair of metal handcuffs seemingly from thin air and tightened them on her wrists. The graceful dance reminded me of a grotesque ballet.

"Ouch. That hurts," she squealed to no avail.

A bevy of additional patrolmen marched over to the scene to lend assistance. The mob of beefy law enforcement professionals, with the motto "to protect and to serve" foremost in its collective consciousness, hustled my only parent to a waiting patrol car.

Mom looked back at me. "Hold on. You can't just leave my son here. He's a minor child. He's only fourteen."

I hid my eyes behind my hand. Oh, the shame of being the minor child of a criminal suspect.

"Mike. C'mon, son. Come with your mama."

"He's not under arrest," the officer told her. "You are."

Mom launched into a tutorial on constitutional protections. "I have my rights. I have my rights. You can't do this to me without reading me my rights!"

"I'll show you what you can do with your rights." The officer waved his nightstick in her face.

"You can't do this. I have rights."

One of the other officers pushed her into the backseat of the patrol car and slammed the door.

Her face was still visible from the car window. "What about my son? What about my son? He's a minor child."

The patrolman trotted toward the Nova, where I still sat quietly. "I guess she's right," he muttered. "Listen here, kid. You'd better not cause trouble." The officer waved his nightstick at me. I looked at my mom sitting in the back of the patrol car. Her eyes were wide and edged with tears. Her mouth was opened in a perfect "o" shape. She looked horrified.

"No, sir." I opened the door and stepped from the Nova.

The four police officers descended on me like locusts swooping in to feast on an abundant harvest. Arms and elbows flailed all about me. The scene reminded me of the Iwo Jima Memorial where each soldier struggled to raise the American flag. They did not seem to be raising the American flag at that moment, though—far from it. The men held my arms in their iron grip, as though I might tear free and flee the jurisdiction at any moment.

When he realized that I would not protest the loss of my liberty and dignity with the vehemence of my mother, the lead officer slid the nightstick into his belt and relaxed his facial muscles slightly. His co-conspirators pushed me toward the patrol car with such speed and fervor that my legs barely supported my weight. No one slapped handcuffs on me, although I don't know if this was an oversight or if the fact that I was not actually under arrest was a factor in their decision.

In any case, they flung open the door, tucked my head down, and threw me into the vehicle with great force. I landed in my mother's lap. She cried out in pain as my face struck her in the chest. I barely had time to pull my legs inside the compartment before the door slammed behind me with a resounding thud.

I gazed around the car. We were separated from the front seat by a wire-mesh divider. The back doors did not have handles and the windows would not roll down. We were trapped.

And so at the ripe old age of 14, I learned firsthand the importance of constitutional criminal procedure.

The episode occurred long ago, and the world changed a great deal in the 36 years between my family's encounter with the police and the moment I sat down to write these words. I was a frightened child in 1977, and now I am a grown man. My mother died many years ago. It would be too much akin to psychobabble to suggest that my desire to be a lawyer was born at that instant, but certainly the encounter left an indelible mark. I appreciated Josef K.'s situation when I read Kafka's classic book, *The Trial*, years later. I doubt I would have understood it nearly as well had I not experienced firsthand the intricacies of seemingly inexplicable police procedures.[1]

The world has changed, but human nature has not. The incident vividly illustrated, at least for me, the fear a citizen feels when faced with the power of the police. Although most cases recounted in this book involve serious circumstances and allegations of felonious conduct far beyond my childhood experience, any police–citizen encounter pits the might of the state against the relatively meager resources of the individual. The participants in such encounters operate under stress and must respond to the challenges of the moment, often with little or no understanding of the potential outcome or legal consequences. To ensure that societal needs are balanced against individual rights, therefore, the courts have established an elaborate system of rules designed to "operationalize" the Bill of Rights.

At the same time that individual rights are upheld, police officers are tasked with protecting the public from criminal behavior before offenses happen and, afterward, investigating crimes that occurred despite their best efforts. Law enforcement personnel must possess sufficient authority and discretion to perform their tasks appropriately. Offenders who act with the foreknowledge that they probably will not be apprehended or, if apprehended, will be lightly punished no doubt will be encouraged to engage in all manner of mischief. To hamper effective police work by unnecessarily burdening law enforcement professionals with cumbersome requirements that do not enhance public safety or protect individual liberty is to err too far on the side of a permissive society. The goal, therefore, is to strike a proper balance between the freedom of the individual and the authority of the government.

The cases discussed in this book illustrate, sometimes in dramatic fashion, the challenges and difficulties in striking the proper balance. As society changes, the needs of individuals change. The legal system must respond accordingly.

The exclusionary rule provides a compelling example of evolving legal standards that affect citizen–police encounters. When the Court established the exclusionary rule in *Weeks v. United States* in 1914, the justices of the U.S. Supreme Court believed that the judiciary had to provide sanctions in instances where overly zealous police officials seized evidence in violation of the Fourth Amendment. By excluding evidence from trial, the Court ensured that law enforcement officers in most instances would exercise restraint and consider the strictures of the Bill of Rights when confronting criminal suspects.[2] Fourteen years later, in *Olmstead v. United States*, the Court backed away from rigorously applying—or perhaps expanding—the rule when the justices determined that wiretapping evidence acquired without a warrant could be admitted at trial because it did not involve the physical intrusion necessary to trigger Fourth and Fifth Amendment protections.[3] The

Court modified the exclusionary rule yet again in subsequent cases. *Katz v. United States* in 1967 overruled *Olmstead* by determining that an individual enjoys a reasonable expectation of privacy inside a telephone booth. Placing a wiretap on a telephone without securing a search warrant beforehand is unconstitutional, even though physical instruction has not occurred.[4] Following this apparent reinvigoration of the exclusionary rule, the U.S. Supreme Court again narrowed the concept by deciding in *United States v. Leon* that a good faith exception existed.[5]

Changes in the exclusionary rule reflect changes in the public's desire for robust law enforcement. Through it all, one thing is clear: Adjudicating criminal cases is an iterative, never-ending process. To make sense of the evolving process, students are well advised to explore classic cases as a means of understanding the Court's changing sensibilities. With that end in mind, the purpose of this book has been to recall the stories and drama that have shaped modern American criminal procedure.

NOTES

1. My mother's case never went to trial. Instead, she paid a monetary fine for the expired inspection sticker and all charges were dropped. Our visit to the Florence City-County Complex inmate detention center lasted only a few hours. Mom was placed behind bars while I waited in the drunk tank adjacent to the breathalyzer machine until she summoned a friend to pay the fine and transport us back to the car. Although she was denied the opportunity to break off the police encounter and leave the scene—necessary elements in determining whether a person has been taken into police custody—my mother was never advised of her *Miranda* rights, and our booking officer later insisted that she had never been "technically under arrest." Despite her questionable status within the legal system, my mother was fingerprinted and photographed at the police station in an apparently successful effort to "teach the big mouth a lesson," as one patrolman eloquently described the incident. Aside from the minor traffic violation, the police officers that day did not possess reasonable suspicion or probable cause that a crime had been, or likely would be, committed. Mom considered filing a civil lawsuit for wrongful arrest and false imprisonment against the Florence, South Carolina, Police Department in the wake of the affair, but ultimately she declined to take action when she realized the time and money it would require to pursue the case. Years later, she told me that the episode was so demeaning that she wanted to put it behind her and move on with her life. Never underestimate the value of humiliation in socializing the citizenry. Indeed,

humiliation apparently was a crucial weapon in the arsenal of the Florence, South Carolina, Police Department circa 1977.

2. 232 U.S. 383 (1914).
3. 277 U.S. 438 (1928).
4. 389 U.S. 347 (1967).
5. 468 U.S. 897 (1984).

Bibliography

INTRODUCTION AND ACKNOWLEDGMENTS

Kafka, Franz. *The Trial.* London, England: The Folio Society, 2011 [1925].

CHAPTER 1: *HURTADO v. CALIFORNIA* (1884) AND 19TH-CENTURY CRIMINAL PROCEDURE

"The Case of Hurtado." *Sacramento Daily Union* 18, 118 (January 9, 1884), 3.

Davies, Thomas Y. "The Supreme Court Giveth and the Supreme Court Taketh Away: The Century of Fourth Amendment 'Search and Seizure' Doctrine." *The Journal of Criminal Law and Criminology* 100, 3 (Summer 2010): 933–1041.

"The Death Sentence." *Sacramento Daily Union* 15, 90 (June 6, 1882).

Dripps, Donald A. *About Guilt and Innocence: The Origins, Development, and Future of Constitutional Criminal Procedure.* Westport, Conn.: Praeger, 2003.

Dripps, Donald A. "The Fourteenth Amendment, the Bill of Rights, and the (First) Criminal Procedure Revolution." *Journal of Contemporary Legal Issues* 18, 1 (2009): 469–500.

Hoffmeister, Thaddeus. "The Grand Jury Legal Advisor: Resurrecting the Grand Jury's Shield." *The Journal of Criminal Law and Criminology* 98, 4 (Summer 2008): 1171–1230.

"Hurtado." *Sacramento Daily Union* 54, 104 (December 21, 1885), 3.

Hurtado v. People of the State of California, 110 U.S. 516 (1884).

Latzer, Barry. "Toward the Decentralization of Criminal Procedure: State Constitutional Law and Selective Disincorporation." *The Journal of Criminal Law and Criminology* 87, 1 (Autumn 1996): 63–129.
McKanna, Clare V., Jr. *Race and Homicide in Nineteenth Century California.* Reno and Nevada: University of Nevada Press, 2002.
"Murder." *Sacramento Daily Union* 14, 144 (February 7, 1882).
Ramsey, Carolyn B. "Was the Bill of Rights Irrelevant to Nineteenth-Century State Criminal Procedure?" *Journal of Contemporary Legal Issues* 18, 1 (2009): 501–11.
Samaha, Joel. *Criminal Procedure.* 8th ed. Belmont, Calif.: Wadsworth, 2012.
"San Francisco Items." *Sacramento Daily Union* 15, 86 (June 1, 1882).
"Trial of Hurtado for Murder." *Sacramento Daily Union* 15, 63 (May 5, 1882).

CHAPTER 2: *WEEKS v. UNITED STATES* (1914) AND THE ORIGINS OF THE EXCLUSIONARY RULE

Adams v. New York, 192 U.S. 585 (1904).
Agnello v. United States, 269 U.S. 20 (1925).
Amar, Akhil Reed. "The Fourth Amendment, Boston, and the Writs of Assistance." *Suffolk University Law Review* 30, 1 (1996): 53–80.
Amar, Akhil Reed. "Fourth Amendment First Principles." *Harvard Law Review* 107, 4 (February 1994): 757–819.
Boyd v. United States, 116 U.S. 616 (1886).
Bram v. United States, 168 U.S. 532 (1897).
Dash, Samuel. *The Intruders: Unreasonable Searches and Seizures from King John to John Ashcroft*. New Brunswick, N.J.: Rutgers University Press, 2004.
Davies, Thomas Y. "Recovering the Original Fourth Amendment." *Michigan Law Review* 98, 3 (December 1999): 547–750.
"Exclusionary Rule." *The Journal of Criminal Law & Criminology* 65, 4 (December 1974): 460–65.
Frese, Joseph R. "James Otis and Writs of Assistance." *The New England Quarterly* 30, 4 (December 1957): 496–508.
Gouled v. United States, 255 U.S. 298 (1921).
Hirsch, Milton. "Big Bill Haywood's Revenge: The Original Intent of the Exclusionary Rule." *St. Thomas Law Review* 22, 1 (October 2009): 35–86.
Jaffe, Louis L. "The Judicial Universe of Mr. Justice Frankfurter." *Harvard Law Review* 62, 3 (January 1949): 357–412.
Kamisar, Yale. "Some Reflections on Criticizing the Courts and 'Policing the Police.'" *Criminology and Police Science* 53, 4 (December 1962): 453–62.
Maclin, Tracey. "The Central Meaning of the Fourth Amendment." *William and Mary Law Review* 35, 1 (1993): 197–249.
Nardone v. United States, 308 U.S. 338 (1939).
People v. Defore, 242 U.S. 13, 150 N.E. 585, (1926).

Shenfield, Mark Harold. "Fruit-of-the-Poisonous-Tree Doctrine." *California Law Review* 60, 3 (May 1972): 870–81.
Silverthorne Lumber Company v. United States, 251 U.S. 385 (1920).
Sklansky, David. "The Fourth Amendment and Common Law." *Columbia Law Review* 100, 7 (November 2000): 1739–1814.
"Tickets of Santo Domingo Lottery Sold in Kansas City." *The Omaha Daily Bee*, 41, 162 (December 23, 1911), 1.
United States v. Leon, 468 U.S. 897 (1984).
Weeks v. United States, 232 U.S. 383 (1914).
Weinreb, Lloyd L. "The Exclusionary Rule Redux—Again." *Fordham Urban Law Journal* 37, 3 (May 2010): 873–88.
Wolff, Aaron S., editor. "The Federal Search and Seizure Exclusionary Rule: Its Origin, Development, Present Status and Trend." *Journal of Criminal Law, Criminology & Police Science* 45, 1 (May/June 1954): 51–61.
Yeager, Daniel B. "Search, Seizure and the Positive Law: Expectations of Privacy Outside of the Fourth Amendment." *The Journal of Criminal Law & Criminology* 84, 2 (July 1993): 249–309.

CHAPTER 3: *OLMSTEAD v. UNITED STATES* (1928) AND WIRETAPPING THE "BABY LIEUTENANT"

Brennan, Christopher. "*Katz* Cradle: Holding on to Fourth Amendment Parity in an Age of Evolving Electronic Communication." *William & Mary Law Review* 53, 5 (April 2012): 1797–1823.
Brown, Dorothy Marie. *Mabel Walker Willebrandt: A Study of Power, Loyalty, and Law.* Knoxville: University of Tennessee Press, 1984.
Clark, Norman H. *The Dry Years: Prohibition and Social Change in Washington.* Seattle: University of Washington Press, 1965.
Clark, Norman H. "Roy Olmstead, a Rumrunning King on Puget Sound." *The Pacific Northwest Quarterly* 54, 3 (July 1963): 89–103.
Dash, Samuel. *The Eavesdroppers.* New Brunswick, N.J.: Rutgers University Press, 1959.
Federal Judicial Center Website. "*Olmstead v. United States:* The Constitutional Challenges of Prohibition Enforcement—Historical Background and Documents: A Short Narrative." <http://www.fjc.gov/history/home.nsf/page/tu_olmstead_narrative.html.> Accessed February 12, 2013.
Hamm, Richard F. *Shaking the Eighteenth Amendment: Temperance Reform, Legal Culture, and the Polity, 1880–1920.* Chapel Hill: University of North Carolina Press, 1995.
Katz v. United States, 389 U.S. 347 (1967).
Kitch, Edmund W. "*Katz v. United States:* The Limits of the Fourth Amendment." *The Supreme Court Review* 1968, 1 (1968): 133–52.

McInnis, Tom. "The Changing Definition of Search or Seizure." *Insights on Law and Society* 11, 2 (May 2011): 10–13, 28.

Metcalfe, Philip. *Whispering Wires: The Tragic Tale of an American Bootlegger.* Portland, Ore.: Inkwater Press, 2007.

Murchison, Kenneth M. "Prohibition and the Fourth Amendment: A New Look at Some Old Cases." *The Journal of Law & Criminology* 73, 2 (Summer 1982): 471–532.

Murphy, Walter F. *Wiretapping on Trial: A Case Study in the Judicial Process.* New York: Random House, 1965.

Olmstead v. United States, 19 F.2d 842 (9th Cir. 1927), *aff'd*, 277 U.S. 438 (1928).

Pesciotta, Daniel T. "I'm Not Dead Yet: *Katz*, *Jones*, and the Fourth Amendment in the 21st Century." *Case Western Reserve Law Review* 63, 1 (Fall 2012): 187–255.

Richards, Neil M. "The Puzzle of Brandeis, Privacy, and Speech." *Vanderbilt Law Review* 63, 5 (October 2010): 1295–1352.

Steiker, Carol S. "Brandeis in *Olmstead:* 'Our Government Is the Potent, the Omnipresent Teacher.'" *Mississippi Law Journal* 79, 1 (Fall 2009): 149–78.

Willebrandt, Mabel Walker. *The Inside of Prohibition.* Indianapolis, Ind.: Bobbs-Merrill, 1929.

CHAPTER 4: *POWELL v. ALABAMA* (1932) AND THE SCOTTSBORO BOYS

Baker, Debra. "Trials of the Century." *ABA Journal* 85, 1 (January 1999): 42–49.

Carter, Dan T. *Scottsboro: A Tragedy of the American South.* Revised Edition. Baton Rouge: Louisiana State University Press, 2007.

Curriden, Mark. "The Saga of the Scottsboro Boys Begins—March 25, 1931." *ABA Journal* 99, 3 (March 2013): 72.

Gildersleeve, Shanna. "The Struggle for Justice: How the Media Convicted and Freed the 'Scottsboro Boys,' 1931–1937." *The Atlanta Review of Journalism History* 8, 1 (September 2009): 90–113.

Goodman, James. *Stories of Scottsboro.* New York: Doubleday, 1995.

Klarman, Michael J. "Scottsboro." *Marquette Law Review* 93, 2 (Winter 2009): 379–432.

Miller, James A. *Remembering Scottsboro: The Legacy of an Infamous Trial.* Princeton, N.J.: Princeton University Press, 2009.

Miller, James A., Susan D. Pennybacker, and Eve Rosenhaft. "Mother Ada Wright and the International Campaign to Free the Scottsboro Boys, 1931–1934." *The American Historical Review* 106, 2 (April 2001): 387–430.

Neal v. Delaware, 103 U.S. 370 (1881).

Norris, Clarence, and Sybil D. Washington. *The Last of the Scottsboro Boys.* New York: Putnam, 1979.

Norris v. Alabama, 294 U.S. 587 (1935).
Patterson v. Alabama, 294 U.S. 600 (1935).
Powell v. Alabama, 287 U.S. 45, 71 (1932).
"Scottsboro Hero." *Time* 30, 5 (August 2, 1937): 45–47.
Simkins, Francis Butler, and Charles Pierce Roland. *A History of the South*. 4th ed. New York: Knopf, 1972.

CHAPTER 5: *BROWN v. MISSISSIPPI* (1936) AND FUNDAMENTAL FAIRNESS

Blackmon, Douglas A. *Slavery by Another Name: The Re-Enslavement of Black Americans from the Civil War to World War II*. New York: Doubleday, 2008.
Brown v. Mississippi, 297 U.S. 278 (1936).
Cortner, Richard C. *A "Scottsboro" Case in Mississippi: The Supreme Court and Brown v. Mississippi*. Jackson: University of Mississippi Press, 1986.
Darmer, M. Katherine B. "Reliability, Waterboarded Confessions and Reclaiming the Lessons of *Brown v. Mississippi* in the Terrorism Cases." *Guild Practitioner* 66, 1 (Spring 2009): 18–34.
Dray, Philip. *At the Hands of Persons Unknown: The Lynching of Black America*. New York: New American Library, 2002.
Foner, Eric. *Forever Free: The Story of Emancipation and Reconstruction*. Illustrations edited with a commentary by Joshua Brown. New York: Knopf, 2005.
Foner, Eric. *Reconstruction: America's Unfinished Revolution: 1863–1877*. New York: Francis Parkman Prize Edition, History Book Club, 2005 [1988].
Klarman, Michael J. *From Jim Crow to Civil Rights: The Supreme Court and the Struggle for Equality*. New York and Oxford: Oxford University Press, 2004.
Klarman, Michael J. "The Racial Origins of Modern Criminal Procedure." *Michigan Law Review* 99, 1 (October 2000): 48–97.
Lears, Jackson. *Rebirth of a Nation: The Making of Modern America, 1877–1920*. New York: HarperCollins, 2009.
Lemann, Nicholas. *The Promised Land: The Great Migration and How It Changed America*. New York: Vintage, 1992.
Link, Anne Elizabeth. "Fifth Amendment—The Constitutionality of Custodial Confessions." *The Journal of Criminal Law & Criminology* 82, 4 (Winter 1992): 878–903.
Litwack, Leon F. *Trouble in Mind: Black Southerners in the Age of Jim Crow*. New York: Vintage, 1998.
Logan, Rayford W. *The Betrayal of the Negro: From Rutherford B. Hayes to Woodrow Wilson*. Cambridge, Mass.: Da Capo Press, 1997 [1965].
McMillen, Neil R. *Dark Journey: Black Mississippians in the Age of Jim Crow*. Champaign: University of Illinois Press, 1990.

Moore v. Dempsey, et al., 261 U.S. 86 (1923).

Valelly, Richard M. *The Two Reconstructions: The Struggle for Black Enfranchisement*. Chicago and London: The University of Chicago Press, 2004.

Wilkerson, Isabel. *The Warmth of Other Suns: The Epic Story of America's Great Migration*. New York: Random House, 2010.

Woodward, C. Vann. *Origins of the New South, 1877–1913*. Baton Rouge: Louisiana State University Press, 1951.

Woodward, C. Vann. *The Strange Career of Jim Crow*. 2nd. ed. New York and Oxford: Oxford University Press, 1966.

CHAPTER 6: *MAPP v. OHIO* (1961) AND THE EXCLUSIONARY RULE REDUX

Beth, Loren P. "Mr. Justice Black and the First Amendment: Comments on the Dilemma of Constitutional Interpretation." *Journal of Politics* 41, 4 (November 1979): 1105–1124.

Blauner, Peter. "King on the Ropes: Boxing's Gabby Promoter Fights for His Professional Life." *New York Magazine* 24, 11 (March 18, 1991): 40–46.

Boyd v. United States, 116 U.S. 616 (1886).

Dempsey, John S., and Linda S. Forst. *An Introduction to Policing*. 6th ed. Clifton Park, N.Y.: Delmar Cengage Learning, 2011.

Dorin, Dennis D. "Marshalling *Mapp:* Justice Tom Clark's Role in *Mapp v. Ohio*'s Extension of the Exclusionary Rule to State Searches and Seizures." *Case Western Reserve Law Review* 52, 2 (Winter 2001): 401–40.

Driver, Justin. "The Constitutional Conservatism of the Warren Court." *California Law Review* 100, 5 (October 2012): 1101–67.

Graham, Fred P. *The Due Process Revolution: The Warren Court's Impact on Criminal Law*. New York: Hayden Book Company, 1970.

Kantrowitz, R. Marc. "Good Golly, Miss Dolly." *Rhode Island Lawyers Weekly* (April 28, 2011). Available at http://rilawyersweekly.com/blog/2011/04/28/good-golly-miss-dolly/. Accessed April 14, 2013.

Katz, Lewis R. "*Mapp* after Forty Years: Its Impact on Race in America." *Case Western Reserve Law Review* 52, 2 (Winter 2001): 471–87.

Long, Carolyn N. *Mapp v. Ohio: Guarding against Unreasonable Searches and Seizures*. Lawrence: University Press of Kansas, 2006.

Mapp v. Ohio, 367 U.S. 643 (1961).

McInnis, Thomas. *The Evolution of the Fourth Amendment*. Lanham, Md.: Lexington Books, 2009.

Miller, Eric J. "The Warren Court's Regulatory Revolution in Criminal Procedure." *Connecticut Law Review* 43, 1 (November 2010): 1–82.

Newfield, Jack. *The Life and Crimes of Don King: The Shame of Boxing in America.* Sag Harbor, N.Y.: Harbor Electronic Publishing, 2003.
Palko v. Connecticut, 302 U.S. 319 (1937).
Price, Polly J. "*Mapp v. Ohio* Revisited: A law Clerk's Diary." *Journal of Supreme Court History* 35, 1 (2010): 54–70.
Rochin v. California, 342 U.S. 165 (1952).
Scully, Leon. "Civil Wrongs." *National Review* 44, 10 (May 25, 1992): 22–28.
Scully, Leon F. Jr. *Bombers, Bolsheviks and Bootleggers: A Study in Constitutional Subversion.* Charlottesville, Va.: Publius Press, 2001.
State v. Lindway, 131 Ohio St. 166 (1936).
Stewart, Potter. "The Road to *Mapp v. Ohio* and Beyond: The Origins, Development and Future of the Exclusionary Rule in Search-and-Seizure Cases." *Columbia Law Review* 83, 6 (October 1983): 1365–1404.
Traynor, Roger J. "*Mapp v. Ohio* at Large in the Fifty States." *Duke Law Journal* 1962, 3 (Summer 1962): 319–43.
United States v. Leon, 468 U.S. 897 (1984).
Wolf v. Colorado, 338 U.S. 25 (1949).
Zotti, Priscilla H. Machado. *Injustice for All: Mapp v. Ohio and the Fourth Amendment.* New York: Peter Lang, 2005.

CHAPTER 7: *GIDEON v. WAINWRIGHT* (1963) AND THE RIGHT TO COUNSEL

Baum, Laurence. *The Supreme Court.* 3rd ed. Washington, DC: CQ Press, 1989.
Betts v. Brady, 316 U.S. 455 (1942).
Colbert, Douglas L. "Connecting Theory and Reality: Teaching *Gideon* and Indigent Defendants' Non-Right to Counsel at Bail." *Ohio State Journal of Criminal Law* 4, 1 (Fall 2006): 167–82.
Evans, Colin. "Clarence Earl Gideon Trials: 1961 & 1963." Pp. 494–97. In *Great American Trials: From Salem Witchcraft to Rodney King.* Edward W. Knappman, Editor. Detroit, Mich.: Visible Ink Press, a Division of Gale Research, Inc., 1994.
Gideon v. Wainwright, 372 U.S. 335 (1963).
Jacob, Bruce R. "50 Years Later: Memories of *Gideon v. Wainwright.*" *Florida Bar Journal* 87, 3 (March 2013): 10–17.
Jacob, Bruce R. "Memories of and Reflections about *Gideon v. Wainwright.*" *Stetson Law Review* 33, 1 (Fall 2003): 181–298.
Johnson v. Zerbst, 304 U.S. 458 (1938).
Kamisar, Yale. "*Gideon v. Wainwright:* A Quarter-Century Later." *Pace Law Review* 10, 2 (Spring 2010): 343–78.

Kuhns, Allison D. "If You Cannot Afford an Attorney, Will One Be Appointed for You? How (Some) States Force Criminal Defendants to Choose between Posting Bond and Getting a Court-Appointed Attorney." *Iowa Law Review* 97, 5 (July 2012): 1787–1810.

Lain, Corinna Barrett. "Countermajoritarian Hero or Zero? Rethinking the Warren Court's Role in the Criminal Procedure Revolution." *University of Pennsylvania Law Review* 152, 4 (April 2004): 1361–1452.

Lewis, Anthony. *Gideon's Trumpet.* Birmingham, Ala.: The Notable Trials Library, 1991 [1964].

Meares, Tracey L. "What's Wrong with *Gideon?*" *The University of Chicago Law Review* 70, 1 (Winter 2003): 215–31.

O'Brien, David M. *Storm Center: The Supreme Court in American Politics.* New York: Norton, 1986.

Podgor, Ellen S. "*Gideon* at 40: Facing the Crisis, Fulfilling the Promise." *The American Criminal Law Review* 41, 1 (Winter 2004): 135–56.

"Rethinking the Boundaries of the Sixth Amendment Right to Choice of Counsel." *Harvard Law Review* 124, 6 (April 2011): 1550–71.

Simon, David A. "Equal before the Law: Toward a Restoration of *Gideon*'s Promise." *Harvard Civil Rights-Civil Liberties Law Review* 43, 2 (Summer 2008): 581–94.

Sobel, Allan D. "Fulfilling the Promise of *Gideon.*" *Judicature* 88, 1 (July/August 2004): 5, 37.

Walsh, Mark. "Living Up to the *Gideon* Ideal." *ABA Journal* 99, 3 (March 2013): 45–49.

Wright, Ronald F. "Anatomy of a Public Defender System: Public Defender Elections and Popular Control over Criminal Justice." *Missouri Law Review* 75, 3 (Summer 2010): 803–29.

Yakey, Randal. "Panama City Case Changed Legal History 50 Years Ago." *New Herald* (Panama City, Florida, 17 March 2013).

CHAPTER 8: *MIRANDA v. ARIZONA* (1966) AND THE RIGHT TO REMAIN SILENT

Allen, Ronald J. "*Miranda*'s Hollow Core." *Northwestern University Law Review* 100, 1 (Special Issue 2006): 71–85.

Baker, Liva. *Miranda: Crime, Law and Politics.* New York: Atheneum, 1983.

Berghuis v. Thompkins, 130 S.Ct. 2250 (2010).

Cassell, Paul G. "*Miranda*'s 'Negligible' Effect on Law Enforcement: Some Skeptical Observations." *Harvard Journal of Law & Public Policy* 20, 2 (Winter 1997): 327–46.

Cassell, Paul G. "Protecting the Innocent from False Confessions and Lost Confessions—And from *Miranda.*" *The Journal of Criminal Law & Criminology* 88, 2 (Winter 1998): 497–556.

Dickerson v. United States, 530 U.S. 428 (2000).

Einesman, Floralynn. "Confessions and Culture: The Interaction of *Miranda* and Diversity." *The Journal of Criminal Law & Criminology* 90, 1 (Fall 1999): 1–47.

Escobedo v. Illinois, 378 U.S. 478 (1964).

Evans, Colin. "Ernesto Miranda Trials: 1963 & 1967." Pp. 505–08. In *Great American Trials: From Salem Witchcraft to Rodney King*. Edward W. Knappman, Editor. Detroit, Mich.: Visible Ink Press, a Division of Gale Research, Inc., 1994.

Graham, Fred P. "Curb on Police Questions Is Ruled Not Retroactive; Supreme Court Says Limits Placed on Interrogation Last Monday Apply Only to Trials after That Date." *New York Times* (June 21, 1966): A1.

Graham, Fred P. "High Court Puts New Curb on Powers of the Police to Interrogate Suspects." *New York Times* (June 14, 1966): A1.

Harris v. New York, 401 U.S. 222 (1971).

Haynes v. Washington, 373 U.S. 503 (1963).

Inbau, Fred E. "Overreaction—The Mischief of *Miranda v. Arizona*." *The Journal of Criminal Law & Criminology* 89, 4 (Summer 1999): 1449–64.

Jackson, Liane J. "Turning *Miranda* 'Upside Down'?" *ABA Journal* 96, 9 (September 2010): 20–21.

Kinports, Kit. "The Supreme Court's Love-Hate Relationship with *Miranda*." *The Journal of Criminal Law & Criminology* 101, 2 (Spring 2011): 375–440.

Krock, Arthur. "In the Nation: The Wall between Crime and Punishment." *New York Times* (June 14, 1966): A46.

Leo, Richard A. "The Impact of *Miranda* Revisited." *Journal of Law & Criminology* 86, 3 (Spring 1996): 621–92.

Leo, Richard A., and Richard J. Ofshe. "Using the Innocent to Scapegoat *Miranda:* Another Reply to Paul Cassell." *The Journal of Criminal Law & Criminology* 88, 2 (Winter 1998): 557–77.

Lief, Michael S., and H. Mitchell Caldwell. "You Have the Right to Remain Silent." *American Heritage* 57, 4 (August/September 2006): 48–59.

Malone, Patrick A. "'You Have the Right to Remain Silent': *Miranda* after Twenty Years." *American Scholar* 55, 3 (Spring 1986): 367–80.

"*Miranda* Needs No Improvement." *New York Times* (January 10, 1986): A26.

Miranda v. Arizona, 384 U.S. 436 (1966).

Missouri v. Seibert, 542 U.S. 600 (2004).

New York v. Quarles, 467 U.S. 649 (1984).

The Omnibus Crime Control and Safe Streets Act of 1968. Pub. L. 90–351, 82 Stat. 197. Enacted June 19, 1968. Codified at 42 U.S.C. § 3711, *et seq*.

Payne, Brian K., and Victoria M. Time. "Support for *Miranda* among Police Chiefs: A Qualitative Examination." *American Journal of Criminal Justice* 25, 1 (Fall 2000): 65–76.

Rogers, Richard. "A Little Knowledge Is a Dangerous Thing . . . Emerging *Miranda* Research and Professional Roles for Psychologists." *American Psychologist* 63, 8 (November 2008): 776–87.
State v. Arizona, 401 P.2d 721 (1965).
Stuart, Gary L. *Miranda: The Story of America's Right to Remain Silent.* Tucson: University of Arizona Press, 2004.
Vander Giessen, Michael L. "*Berghuis v. Thompkins:* The Continued Erosion of *Miranda*'s Protections." *Gonzaga Law Review* 46, 1 (2011): 189–214.
Walsh, Edward. "High Court Upholds *Miranda* Rights; Rehnquist Calls Warnings Part of 'National Culture.'" *The Washington Post* (June 27, 2000): A1.

CHAPTER 9: *KATZ v. UNITED STATES* (1967) AND THE RIGHT TO PRIVACY

Brennan, Christopher R. "*Katz* Cradle: Holding on to Fourth Amendment Parity in an Age of Evolving Electronic Communication." *William & Mary Law Review* 53, 5 (April 2012): 1797–1823.
Collins, Sue Carter. "The Case of *Katz v. United States* (1967)." Pp. 9–25. In *Criminal Procedure and the Supreme Court: A Guide to the Major Decisions on Search and Seizure, Privacy, and Individual Rights.* Rolando V. Del Carmen and Craig Hemmens, Editors. Lanham, Md.: Rowman & Littlefield, 2010.
The Communications Assistance for Law Enforcement Act of 1994 (CALEA). Pub. L. No. 103–414, 108 Stat. 4279. Enacted October 25, 1994. Codified at 47 USC §1001 *et seq.*
The Electronic Communications and Privacy Act of 1986 (ECPA). Pub L. 99–508, 100 Stat. 1848. Enacted October 21, 1986. Codified at 18 U.S.C. §§ 2510, *et seq.*
Emas, Judge Kevin. and Tamara Pallas. "*United States v. Jones:* Does *Katz* Still Have Nine Lives?" *St. Thomas Law Review* 24, 2 (2012): 116–217.
Fradella, Henry R., Weston J. Morrow, Ryan G. Fischer, and Connie Ireland. "Quantifying *Katz:* Empirically Measuring 'Reasonable Expectations of Privacy' in the Fourth Amendment Context." *American Journal of Criminal Law* 38, 3 (Summer 2011): 289–373.
Goldman v. United States, 316 U.S. 129 (1942).
Katz v. United States, 389 U.S. 347 (1967).
McInnis, Tom. "The Changing Definition of Search or Seizure." *Insights on Law & Society* 11, 2 (May 2011): 10–13, 28.
The Omnibus Crime Control and Safe Streets Act of 1968. Pub. L. 90–351, 82 Stat. 197. Enacted June 19, 1968. Codified at 42 U.S.C. § 3711, *et seq.*
Reid, Melanie. "*United States v. Jones:* Big Brother and the 'Common Good' versus the Fourth Amendment and Your Right to Privacy." *Tennessee Journal of Law and Policy* 9, 1 (Spring 2013): 7–43.

Schneider, Harvey A. "*Katz v. United States:* The Untold Story." *McGeorge Law Review* 40, 1 (2009): 13–23.
Silverman v. United States, 365 U.S. 505 (1961).
United States v. Jones, 132 S.Ct. 945 (2012).
Uniting and Strengthening America by Providing Appropriate Tools Required to Intercept and Obstruct Terrorism Act of 2001 (USA PATRIOT). Pub. L. 107–56, 115 Stat. 272. Enacted October 26, 2001. Codified at 18 USC §2712, 31 USC §5318A, 15 USC §1681v, 8 USC §1226A, 18 USC §1993, 18 USC §2339, 18 USC §175b, 50 USC §403–5b, 51 USC §5103a.
Winn, Peter. "*Katz* and the Origins of the 'Reasonable Expectation of Privacy' Test." *McGeorge Law Review* 40, 1 (2009): 1–12.

CHAPTER 10: *TERRY v. OHIO* (1968) AND THE STOP-AND-FRISK SEARCH

Alioto, Nicholas R. "Unreasonable Differences: The Dispute Regarding the Application of *Terry* Stops to Completed Misdemeanor Crimes." *St. John's Law Review* 83, 3 (Summer 2009): 945–76.
Bandes, Susan. "*Terry v. Ohio* in Hindsight: The Perils of Predicting the Past." *Constitutional Commentary* 16, 3 (Winter 1999): 491–97.
Butterfoss, Edwin J. "Bright Line Seizures: The Need for Clarity in Determining When Fourth Amendment Activity Begins." *The Journal of Criminal Law & Criminology* 79, 2 (Summer 1988): 437–82.
Cole, David. "The Usual Suspects." *The Nation* 294, 27/28 (July 2/9, 2012): 4–6.
Corona, Tiffany D. "A Public Safety Approach: Reconciling *Terry* with Individual Rights." *McGeorge Law Review* 41, 4 (October 2010): 905–28.
Grano, Aidan Taft. "Casual or Coercive? Retention of Identification in Police-Citizen Encounters." *Columbia Law Review* 113, 5 (June 2013): 1283–1321.
Hiibel v. Sixth Judicial District Court of Nevada, et al., 542 U.S. 177 (2004).
Illinois v. Wardlow, 528 U.S. 119 (2000).
Juviler, Hon. Michael R. "A Prosecutor's Perspective." *St. John's Law Review* 72, 3–4 (Summer-Fall 1998): 741–47.
Katz, Lewis R. "*Terry v. Ohio* at Thirty-Five: A Revisionist View." *Mississippi Law Journal* 74, 2 (2004): 423–86.
Minnesota v. Dickerson, 508 U.S. 366 (1993).
Richardson, L. Song. "Police Efficiency and the Fourth Amendment." *Indiana Law Journal* 87, 3 (Summer 2012): 1143–82.
Saltzburg, Stephen A. "*Terry v. Ohio:* A Practically Perfect Doctrine." *St. John's Law Review* 72, 3–4 (Summer-Fall 1998): 911–74.

Starkey, Brando Simeo. "A Failure of the Fourth Amendment & Equal Protection's Promise: How the Equal Protection Clause Can Change Discriminatory Stop and Frisk Policies." *Michigan Journal of Race & Law* 18, 1 (Fall 2012): 131–87.

Terry v. Ohio, 392 U.S. 1 (1968).

CHAPTER 11: *CHIMEL v. CALIFORNIA* (1969) AND SEARCHES INCIDENT TO ARREST

Agnello v. United States, 269 U.S. 20 (1925).

Arizona v. Gant, 556 U.S. 332 (2009).

Blasi, Vincent. *The Burger Court: The Counter-Revolution That Wasn't*. New Haven, Conn.: Yale University Press, 1983.

Carroll v. United States, 267 U.S. 132 (1925).

Chimel v. California, 395 U.S. 752 (1969).

Corradi, Sara M. "Be Reasonable! Limit Warrantless Searches Smart Phone Searches to *Gant*'s Justification for Searches incident to Arrest." *Case Western Reserve Law Review* 63, 3 (Spring 2013): 943–63.

Cray, Ed. *Chief Justice: A Biography of Earl Warren*. New York: Simon & Schuster, 1997.

Deters, Kelly A. "The 'Evaporation Point': *State v. Sykes* and the Erosion of the Fourth Amendment through the Search-Incident-to-Arrest Exception." *Iowa Law Review* 92, 5 (July 2007): 1901–27.

Diamond, Martin. "Democracy and *The Federalist:* A Reconsideration of the Framers' Intent." *American Political Science Review* 53, 1 (March 1959): 52–68.

Dorn, James A. "The Scope of Government in a Free Society." *Cato Journal* 32, 3 (Fall 2012): 629–42.

Go-Bart Importing Company v. United States, 282 U.S. 344 (1931).

Harris v. United States, 331 U.S. 145 (1947).

Johnson, Charles A. "Personnel Change and Policy Change on the U.S. Supreme Court." *Social Science Quarterly* 62, 4 (December 1981): 751–57.

Lane, Roger. "Urban Police and Crime in Nineteenth-Century America." *Crime & Justice* 2, 1 (1980): 1–43.

"The Legacy of the Warren Court," *Time* 94, 1 (July 4, 1969): 64–67.

Logan, Wayne A. "An Exception Swallows a Rule: Police Authority to Search Incident to Arrest." *Yale Law & Policy Review* 19, 2 (2002): 381–441.

Long, Carolyn N. "The Origins of the Fourth Amendment." *Insights on Law & Society* 11, 2 (May 2011): 4–29.

Marron v. United States, 275 U.S. 192 (1927).

Moskovitz, Myron. "A Rule in Search of a Reason: An Empirical Examination of *Chimel* and *Belton*." *Wisconsin Law Review* 2002, 3 (2002): 657–97.

New York v. Belton, 453 U.S. 454 (1981).
Ostrom, Vincent. *The Political Theory of a Compound Republic: Designing the American Experiment*. 8th ed. Lanham, Md.: Lexington Books, 2008.
Oxton, Chelsea. "The Search Incident to Arrest Exception Plays Catch Up: Why Police May No Longer Search Cell Phones Incident to Arrest Without a Warrant." *Creighton Law Review* 43, 4 (June 2010): 1157–1220.
Schulhofer, Stephen J. *More Essential Than Ever: The Fourth Amendment in the Twenty-First Century*. New York and Oxford: Oxford University Press, 2012.
Stoughton, Seth W. "Modern Police Practices: *Arizona v. Gant*'s Illusory Restriction of Vehicle Searches Incident to Arrest." *Virginia Law Review* 97, 7 (November 2011): 1727–73.
Taggart, William A., and Matthew R. DeZee. "A Note on Substantive Access Doctrines in the U.S. Supreme Court: A Comparative Analysis of the Warren and Burger Courts." *Western Political Quarterly* 38, 1 (March 1985): 84–93.
Trupiano v. United States, 334 U.S. 699 (1948).
United States v. Lefkowitz, 285 U.S. 452 (1932).
United States v. Rabinowitz, 339 U.S. 56 (1950).
Weeks v. United States, 232 U.S. 383 (1914).

CHAPTER 12: *UNITED STATES v. LEON* (1984) AND A GOOD FAITH EXCEPTION TO THE EXCLUSIONARY RULE

Alschuler, Albert W. "'Close Enough for Government Work': The Exclusionary Rule after *Leon*." *The Supreme Court Review* 1984, 1 (1984): 309–58.
Arizona v. Evans, 514 U.S. 1 (1995).
Bloom, Robert M. "*United States v. Leon* and Its Ramifications." *University of Colorado Law Review* 56, 1 (Winter 1985): 247–63.
Bradley, Craig M. "The 'Good Faith Exception' Cases: Reasonable Exercises in Futility." *Indiana Law Journal* 60, 2 (Spring 1984): 287–304.
Crocker, Lawrence. "Can the Exclusionary Rule Be Saved?" *The Journal of Criminal Law & Criminology* 84, 2 (Summer 1993): 310–51.
Davis, Rebecca. "The Good Faith Exception in a Computerized Society: State Court Reactions to *U.S. v. Leon* and *Arizona v. Evans*." *The Justice Professional* 12, 1 (June 1998): 45–63.
Duke, Steven B. "Making *Leon* Worse," *The Yale Law Journal* 95, 7 (June 1986): 1405–23.
Fettig, Derik T. "When 'Good Faith' Makes Good Sense: Applying *Leon*'s Exception to the Exclusionary Rule to the Government's Reasonable

Reliance on Title III Wiretap Orders." *Harvard Journal on Legislation* 49, 2 (Summer 2012): 373–410.

Herring v. United States, 555 U.S. 135 (2009).

Illinois v. Krull, 480 U.S. 340 (1987).

Josephson, Matthew Allan. "To Exclude or Not to Exclude: The Future of the Exclusionary Rule after *Herring v. United States*." *Creighton Law Review* 43, 1 (December 2009): 175–203.

Kamisar, Yale. "In Defense of the Search and Seizure Exclusionary Rule." *Harvard Journal of Law & Public Policy* 26, 1 (Winter 2003): 119–40.

LaFave, Wayne R. "The Smell of *Herring:* A Critique of the Supreme Court's Latest Assault on the Exclusionary Rule." *The Journal of Criminal Law & Criminology* 99, 3 (Spring 2009): 757–87.

Mapp v. Ohio, 367 U.S. 643 (1961).

Massachusetts v. Sheppard, 468 U.S. 981 (1984).

Melilli, Kenneth J. "What Nearly a Quarter Century of Experience Has Taught Us about *Leon* and 'Good Faith.'" *Utah Law Review* 2008, 2 (2008): 519–62.

Misner, Robert L. "Limiting *Leon:* A Mistake of Law Analogy." *Journal of Law & Criminology* 77, 3 (Fall 1986): 507–45.

Taslitz, Andrew W. "The Expressive Fourth Amendment: Rethinking the Good Faith Exception to the Exclusionary Rule." *Mississippi Law Journal* 76, 2 (2006): 483–593.

United States v. Leon, 468 U.S. 897 (1984).

Weeks v. United States, 232 U.S. 383 (1914).

Wolf v. Colorado, 338 U.S. 25 (1949).

CHAPTER 13: *CALIFORNIA v. HODARI D.* (1991) AND DETERMINING WHEN A "SEIZURE" OCCURS

Bronner, Ethan. "Justices Enhance Police Power to Give Chase." *Boston Globe* (April 24, 1991).

Brooks, Michael E. "Flight as Justification for Seizure: Supreme Court Rulings." *FBI Law Enforcement Bulletin* 69, 6 (June 2000): 28–32.

Brown v. Texas, 443 U.S. 47 (1979).

California v. Hodari D., 499 U.S. 621 (1991).

Clancy, Thomas K. "The Future of Fourth Amendment Seizure Analysis after *Hodari D.* and *Bostick*." *American Criminal Law Review* 28, 4 (1990–1991): 799–842.

Devetski, Timothy J. "Fourth Amendment—Protection against Unreasonable Seizure of the Person: The New (?) Common Law Arrest Test for Seizure." *The Journal of Criminal Law & Criminology* 82, 4 (Winter 1992): 747–72.

Florida v. Bostick, 501 U.S. 429 (1991).
Florida v. Royer, 460 U.S. 491 (1983).
Grano, Aidan Taft. "Casual or Coercive? Retention of Identification in Police-Citizen Encounters." *Columbia Law Review* 113, 5 (June 2013): 1283–1321.
Greenhouse, Linda. "Evidence a Fleeing Suspect Drops Is Ruled Legal." *New York Times* (April 24, 1991): A20.
Holcomb, Jayme W. "Abandonment of Items Associated with the Person." *FBI Law Enforcement Bulletin* 76, 8 (August 2007): 23–32.
Immigration and Naturalization Service v. Delgado, 466 U.S. 210, 219 (1984).
Katz v. United States, 389 U.S. 347 (1967).
Kessler, David K. "Free to Leave—An Empirical Look at the Fourth Amendment's Seizure Standard." *The Journal of Criminal Law & Criminology* 99, 1 (Fall 2008): 51–88.
Marcus, Ruth. "Rights Discarded with Evidence, Court Says." *The Washington Post* (April 24, 1991): A4.
Michigan v. Chesternut, 486 U.S. 567 (1988).
Piedrahita, Randolph Alexander. "A Conservative Court Says 'Goodbye to All That' and Forges a New Order in the Law of Seizure—*California v. Hodari D.*" *Louisiana Law Review* 52, 5 (May 1992): 1321–55.
Sklansky, David. "The Fourth Amendment and Common Law." *Columbia Law Review* 100, 7 (November 2000): 1739–1814.
Terry v. Ohio, 392 U.S. 1 (1968).
United States v. Mendenhall, 446 U.S. 544 (1980).
Urbonya, Kathryn R. "Justice on the Run." *ABA Journal* 85, 10 (October 1999): 38.

CHAPTER 14: *HAMDAN v. RUMSFELD* (2006) AND TRIAL BY JURY

Abuza, Zachary. "Tentacles of Terror: Al Qaeda's Southeast Asian Network." *Contemporary Southeast Asia* 24, no. 3 (December 2002): 427–65.
Boumediene v. Bush, 553 U.S. 723 (2008).
Christensen, Brian M. "Extending *Hamdan v. Rumsfeld* to Combatant Status Review Tribunals." *Brigham Young University Law Review* 27, 5 (September 2007): 1365–1412.
Clinton, Bill. *My Life*. New York: Knopf, 2004.
Dealy, John D. "Subordination of Powers: *Hamdan v. Rumsfeld*, 126 S. Ct. 2749 (2006)." *Harvard Journal of Law & Public Policy* 30, 3 (Summer 2007): 1071–84.
"Detention, Treatment, and Trial of Certain Non-Citizens in the War against Terrorism." 66 Fed. Reg. 57833 (November 13, 2001).
Doran, Michael. "The Pragmatic Fanaticism of al Qaeda: An Anatomy of Extremism in Middle Eastern Politics." *Political Science Quarterly* 117, 2 (Summer 2002): 177–90.

The Editors of Life. *Brought to Justice: Osama Bin Laden's War on America and the Mission That Stopped Him.* New York, Boston, and London: Little, Brown and Company, 2011.

Estreicher, Samuel, and Diarmuid O'Scannlain. "*Hamdan*'s Limits and the Military Commissions Act." *Constitutional Commentary* 23, 3 (Winter 2006): 403–21.

Ex parte Quirin, 317 U.S. 1 (1942).

Gerges, Fawaz A. *The Rise and Fall of Al-Qaeda.* New York and Oxford: Oxford University Press, 2011.

Glaberson, William. "A Conviction, but a System Still on Trial." *New York Times* (August 10, 2008): 27.

Glaberson, William. "Defense Challenges Enemy Combatant Status of Detainee." *New York Times* (December 6, 2007): A32.

Glaberson, William. "Detainee Challenges Guantánamo by Describing Life There." *New York Times* (July 16, 2008): A13.

Glaberson, William. "Military Judges Dismiss Charges for 2 Detainees." *New York Times* (June 5, 2007): A1.

Glaberson, William. "Panel Sentences Bin Laden Driver to a Short Term." *New York Times* (August 8, 2008): A1.

Glaberson, William. "Prosecution Rests, Then Terror Trial Enters Secret Session to Hear Defense Testimony." *New York Times* (August 1, 2008): A13.

Glaberson, William. "Terror Trial Nears End as Defense Rests Case." *New York Times* (August 2, 2008): A9.

Gunaratna, Rohan. *Inside Al Qaeda: Global Network of Terror.* New York and London: Columbia University Press, 2002.

Hamdan v. Rumsfeld, 548 U.S. 557 (2006).

Hamdan v. United States. No. 11–1257. 16 October 2012. Available at http://www.cadc.uscourts.gov/internet/home.nsf. Accessed August 27, 2013.

Hamdi v. Rumsfeld, 542 U.S. 507 (2004).

Hoodbhoy, Pervez. "Afghanistan and the Genesis of Global Jihad." *Peace Research* 37, 1 (May 2005): 15–30.

Jansen, G. H. *Militant Islam.* New York: Harper & Row, 1979.

Katyal, Neal K., Giorgio Bongiovanni, and Chiara Valentini. "Terrorism, Emergency Powers, and the Role of the U.S. Supreme Court: An Interview with Neal K. Katyal." *Ratio Juris* 20, 4 (December 2007): 443–55.

Kohn, Margaret. "Due Process and Empire's Law: *Hamdan v. Rumsfeld.*" *Dissent* 54, 1 (Winter 2007): 5–8.

Ku, Julian, and John Yoo. "*Hamdan v. Rumsfeld:* The Functional Case for Foreign Affairs Deference to the Executive Branch." *Constitutional Commentary* 23, 2 (Summer 2006): 179–225.

Lesch, Ann M. "Osama Bin Laden: Embedded in the Middle East Crises." *Middle East Policy* 9, 2 (June 2002): 82–91.

Mahler, Jonathan. "The Bush Administration vs. Salim Hamdan." *New York Times Magazine* (January 8, 2006): 44–51, 81, 86–88.

Mahler, Jonathan. *The Challenge: Hamdan v. Rumsfeld and the Fight over Presidential Power.* New York: Farrar, Strauss and Giroux, 2008.

Markon, Jerry. "Goal of the Hamdan Trial: Credibility; Prosecutors Seek Decisive Conviction of Former Driver." *The Washington Post* (July 27, 2008): A2.

McCann, Joseph T. *Terrorism on American Soil: A Concise History of Plots and Perpetrators from the Famous to the Forgotten.* Boulder, Colo.: Sentient Publications, 2006.

Military Commissions Act of 2006 (MCA). Public Law 109–366, 120 Stat. 2600 (Oct. 17, 2006).

Nasir, Sohail Abdul. "Al Qaeda, Two Years On." *Bulletin of the Atomic Scientists* 59, 5 (September/October 2003): 32–41.

National Commission on Terrorist Attacks upon the United States. *The 9/11 Commission Report.* New York and London: Norton, 2004.

Quimby, Amy. "*Hamdan v. Rumsfeld:* Reviewing the Geneva Convention Rights of the Unlawful Enemy Combatants Detained at Gitmo." *Widener Law Journal* 17, 1 (Spring 2010): 317–53.

Runkle, Benjamin. *Wanted Dead or Alive: Manhunts from Geronimo to Bin Laden.* New York: Palgrave-MacMillan, 2011.

Sale, Richard. *Clinton's Secret Wars: The Evolution of a Commander in Chief.* New York: Thomas Dunne Books, St. Martin's Press, 2009.

Shamir-Borer, Eran. "Revisiting *Hamdan v. Rumsfeld*'s Analysis of the Laws of Armed Conflict." *Emory International Law Review* 21, 2 (2007): 601–19.

Shephard, Michelle. "Bin Laden's Driver Talks." *Toronto Star* (August 17, 2009): A1.

"U.S. Sending a Convict Back to Yemen." *New York Times* (November 25, 2008): A23.

Wilber, Del Quentin. "Court Overturns Conviction of Bin Laden's Driver." *The Washington Post* (October 17, 2012): A2.

Williams, Carol J. "Hamdan Helped Bin Laden Succeed, Agent Says." *Los Angeles Times* (July 26, 2008): A10.

Wright, Lawrence. *The Looming Tower: Al-Qaeda and the Road to 9/11.* New York: Knopf, 2006.

Wright, Robin. *Rock the Casbah: Rage and Rebellion across the Islamic World.* New York: Simon & Schuster, 2011.

CONCLUSION

Katz v. United States, 389 U.S. 347 (1967).

Olmstead v. United States, 19 F.2d 842 (9th Cir. 1927), *aff'd,* 277 U.S. 438 (1928).

United States v. Leon, 468 U.S. 897 (1984).

Weeks v. United States, 232 U.S. 383 (1914).

Index

About the Author

J. MICHAEL MARTINEZ began his career in the private practice of law. Today, he works in Monroe, Georgia, as corporate counsel with a manufacturing company. He also teaches political science, criminal justice, and public administration courses as a part-time faculty member at Kennesaw State University, the University of South Dakota (online), and the University of Georgia, respectively. He is the author of seven previous books, including *Terrorist Attacks on American Soil: From the Civil War Era to the Present* (Rowman & Littlefield, 2012) and *American Environmentalism: Philosophy, History, and Public Policy* (CRC Press, 2014). Visit him on the Internet at www.jmichaelmartinez.com.

www.ingramcontent.com/pod-product-compliance
Lightning Source LLC
Chambersburg PA
CBHW071301180926
51613CB00001B/93
* 9 7 8 1 4 4 0 8 2 8 6 8 3 *